TEACHING FROM AN ETHICAL CENTER

TEACHING FROM AN ETHICAL CENTER

Practical Wisdom for Daily Instruction

CARA E. FURMAN

Harvard Education Press
Cambridge, Massachusetts

Paperback ISBN 9781682538982

Library of Congress Cataloging-in-Publication Data

Names: Furman, Cara E., author.
Title: Teaching from an ethical center : practical wisdom for daily
    instruction / Cara E. Furman.
Description: Cambridge, Massachusetts : Harvard Education Press, [2024] |
    Includes bibliographical references and index.
Identifiers: LCCN 2023054996 | ISBN 9781682538982 (paperback)
Subjects: LCSH: Teaching—Moral and ethical aspects. | Analysis
    (Philosophy) | Teachers—Training of. | Teaching—Methodology. |
    Hermeneutics. | Value affirmations. | Applied ethics.
Classification: LCC LB1027 .F925 2024 | DDC 174/.937—dc23/eng/20240324
LC record available at https://lccn.loc.gov/2023054996

Published by Harvard Education Press,
an imprint of the Harvard Education Publishing Group

Harvard Education Press
8 Story Street
Cambridge, MA 02138

Cover Design: Endpaper Studio
Cover Image: Endpaper Studio

The typefaces in this book are Adobe Garamond Pro, Helvetica Neue, and ITC Legacy Sans.

*To Ethan and Max and to the teachers
I've taught and taught with. May classrooms
be worthy of you.*

Contents

Foreword   ix
By David T. Hansen

INTRODUCTION: CULTIVATING A VISION   1

PART 1: THE NEED FOR A COMPASS

1   IDENTIFYING AN ETHICAL COMPASS   27

PART 2: STUDYING PHILOSOPHY AND EDUCATION

2   ROOT TO RISE: HOW I CAME TO BE   55

3   NO, DAVID! HERMENEUTICS   81

4   LANGUAGE GAMES: READING THE WORLD,
      READING THE WORD   103

5   TO BE A RESPECTFUL NEIGHBOR: WHAT LISTENING
      AND READING PHILOSOPHY CAN BE   131

6   COLLABORATIVE GRAPPLING IN CULTURE CIRCLES   156

PART 3: TEACHING FROM ONE'S MORAL CENTER

7   WHOM DO YOU WALK WITH?   181

8   PRACTICAL WISDOM: AN ETHICAL COMPASS
      TO NAVIGATE ALL TERRAIN   205

Appendix: Reference List of Children's Books   231
Notes   241
Acknowledgments   273
About the Author   275
Index   277

Foreword

Which came first in human culture: philosophy or teaching? One famous, influential response was given 2,500 years ago by Plato. His dialogue *The Meno* begins with a well-known orator by that name asking Socrates: "Can you tell me, Socrates, is virtue something that can be taught?" In one and the same breath, this question asks about teaching—"can you tell [teach] me?"—and raises a profound philosophical issue—what is virtue, or goodness, such that it might be something that could be taught. Thus, Plato's response is that philosophy and teaching *emerged together*. He had seen in Socrates's conduct that philosophy constitutes a distinctive mode of inquiry into the meaning and consequences for practical affairs of people's core assumptions about life. He had also learned from Socrates why teaching can be distinguished from socialization. Everyone a child encounters contributes to the latter's socialization. But for Plato, a *teacher* plays a unique, dual role, not just as a socializer but as an educator who helps the student take a step outside their socialization and learn to think reflectively and imaginatively about the world around them.

Cara Furman enacts this outlook on seemingly every page of her new book. Her direct focus is on teaching, teachers, and learning how to teach. The structure of the book is built around a single teacher education methods course that she has taught and refined for a decade. The structure also includes numerous vignettes and references to elementary school classrooms where she has taught or observed or that she has read about. Every chapter includes highly specific practical recommendations and advice for teachers and fellow teacher educators. There are countless illuminating quotes from teacher candidates about their experience learning how to teach in and through Furman's course. Furman juxtaposes this testimony with equally enlightening quotes from thinkers as diverse as Patricia Carini, John Dewey, Paulo Freire, bell hooks, John Locke, and María Lugones.

All this has the sound of a useful textbook on pedagogy. But *Teaching from an Ethical Center* is not a textbook. It is a full-blown philosophical engagement with what teaching is, what it means to become a teacher, what grounds the practice of teaching as the vital ethical endeavor it is, and more. By "engagement," I do not mean the book morphs into a philosophy rather than practitioner textbook. I mean that this author has somehow succeeded in infusing virtually every sentence in the book with philosophical depth. Put another way, every sentence seems to have emerged from systematic philosophical reflection, even as every sentence has the concrete quality of a stone one could hold in hand.

At first glance, I did not see all this as a reader. I had the feeling I was reading a serious-minded, well-crafted discussion of teaching and teacher education, something I had previously encountered in Furman's recent excellent book with her colleague Cecelia Traugh, *Descriptive Inquiry in Teacher Practice: Cultivating Practical Wisdom to Create Democratic Schools.* (In the present volume, Furman touches on Descriptive Inquiry again, once more demonstrating how highly empowering is this approach to teacher development.)

It was only on second glance, so to speak, that I began to see what Furman means in characterizing herself as a philosopher-teacher. I saw that, for her, we could reverse the terms and speak of a teacher-philosopher. Furman privileges neither term over the other, any more than she privileges thinking over caring for students or being patient with students over thinking critically about guiding educational values or studying texts by philosophers over studying thoughtful how-to materials for classroom activity. There is no ideational or experiential hierarchy here, for Furman, just as there is no hierarchy between the elementary school classroom and the university teacher education classroom. There is only *accompaniment*, a term Furman and I have talked about ever since we first met several years before she joined our doctoral program in Philosophy and Education at Teachers College in 2008. I was struck then, when I first met her, and I remain impressed now at how fluidly Furman fuses deep philosophical thinking with a steady focus on the educational well-being of both students and teachers. She was in no rush to undertake doctoral study. She was immersed in teaching children in a wonderful elementary school that she later invited me to visit and where I could witness her practice in person. But she *felt* the press and the lure of philosophy. She *felt* the deep questions of meaning and purpose that every dedicated teacher learns are the very core of the work. She wanted to study: to learn better how to accompany the practical with the philosophical, the hands-on with the minds-on, the most abstract questions such as "What is education?" with the most flesh-and-blood questions such as "How do I do right by this child in this challenging moment, right now at 10:19 a.m. on a Tuesday morning?"

Years later, the reader can accompany Furman as she takes us through, in a fine-grained manner, an array of closely related aspects of teaching. These range from the physical setting of the classroom to the elements of a curriculum to modes of assessment to forms of pedagogy, all saturated by questions of value, purpose, meaning, and abiding ethical commitment. The latter aspects are never absent in the account, even if not always named as such, nor are they ever cast adrift from the concrete realities of the teacher's world. Instead, they permeate the numerous practical exercises Furman describes, each infused with fundamental philosophical questions for the teacher, such as *What is this you are doing or propose doing? Why are you doing this or wanting to do this? What outcomes are you imagining? What outcomes would worry you?*

Furman cultivates across her chapters a dynamic philosophical concept she has written and spoken about previously: practical wisdom. She roots her conception of this term in her study of Aristotle's influential work on ethics, wherein he posits practical wisdom as one of the very highest and most significant human capacities—"high" because teachers with practical wisdom know how to climb a reflective ladder so they can see the lay of land in their classroom well and "significant" because the wisdom *in* practice, the wisdom *of* practice, *practical wisdom*, constitutes the teacher's ethical and pedagogical compass. It guides them in the day-by-day, moment-by-moment human interactions that are the very substance of classroom teaching. Furman shows teacher educators how to tap into candidates' insight and nascent wisdom about teaching, of which they themselves are often quite unaware. Through carefully planned activities, which this book includes in abundance, the teacher educator can help candidates engage their own minds and imaginations rather than presuming they have little agency, autonomy, or leadership potential in organizing a good classroom learning environment. Along the way, candidates slowly develop their own practical wisdom and, simultaneously, their *insight* into the meaning and value of practical wisdom in teaching.

All that I have said in these brief remarks indicates why this book should not be hastily placed on the same shelf as educational textbooks. At the same time, it should not be hastily placed on the shelf marked "Philosophy," for it constitutes something other than a traditional philosophical argument. There is argument aplenty here, but as importantly the book *shows*, *portrays*, and *illustrates*—a splendid mirror in its own way to the very best children's books Furman used herself for years and now puts in the hands of her teacher candidates. So where should this book be placed?

This question reflects a challenging aspect about the culture of education in the United States that confronts every teacher at every level of the system. That aspect is the rupture of the organic connection—one that Plato first saw millennia ago—between philosophy and education. A frustrating anti-intellectualism in society continues to work against celebrating the life of the mind, including the mind of the child and the mind of the teacher. A belligerent rejection of reflection, philosophizing, thinking, and questioning continues to undermine the holistic, caring pedagogical practice Furman exemplifies in this book. A focus on narrow quantitative metrics, itself a sign of an impoverished educational imagination, crowds out more meaningful modes of assessment not just *of* learning but *for* learning. Like numerous colleagues in schools and in teacher education programs, Furman appreciates how the current zeitgeist can "de-magnetize" the teacher's ethical compass by making it hard to bring to life their guiding educational commitments and principles. Teachers can lose their way.

But while there are no certification programs in schools and colleges of education for "philosopher-teachers" or "teacher-philosophers," Furman shows how every teacher can infuse philosophical thinking into their practice as well as practice into their philosophical thinking. Through constant communications with one another and through ongoing exercises of self-examination and self-cultivation, teachers can build a strong, sustainable compass to guide them when face-to-face with their students. From this perspective, I see another response to the question of which bookshelf is the right one for Furman's accomplishment. Let's place it on the shelves of education and of philosophy but post a sign on both that says: "See also the section titled 'Practical Wisdom in Thought and Action.'" I hope every educator goes to that shelf because they will find a unique book for teachers, parents, and everyone who cares about the educational well-being of our children.

David T. Hansen
Teachers College, Columbia University
October 1, 2023

INTRODUCTION: CULTIVATING A VISION

I really just think, if I wasn't staying true to my values, I wouldn't want to be teaching. I feel like if I'm following the crowd or doing what everyone else is doing, I just wouldn't be happy in my space. And I wouldn't enjoy working with children to the extent that I do when I'm staying true to myself. And I would feel more stress at the end of the day. And I would feel more anxiety going into my day. And I just think [it is very helpful] if you are able to communicate your values, and really give support for them to the people that maybe are questioning them, or aren't allowing you to necessarily, like go all the way with your values, because you're not in the lead [teacher role] or you're not in control of that space.

—Liz,[1] early childhood educator

Teacher educators, like myself, can help novice teachers develop a vision for good work. This usually takes the form of an articulated "philosophy of teaching." Our role is to enable new teachers to sustain and enact their normative commitments when they are inducted into the profession.

—Doris Santoro[2]

I am an experienced elementary school teacher sitting in a diner chatting with a mentor, experienced teacher and former principal Jane Andrias. I am telling Jane about Devon, a child in my first-and-second-grade class who does well in meetings when he sits on a chair.[1] "But then," I say with worry, "as soon as I move him to the floor [where most children sit], he struggles." Jane looks at me with puzzlement. "So why would you have him sit on the floor?" This simple question throws me. Yes, why sit Devon on the floor if he can sit comfortably in a chair? Why hadn't it occurred to me to simply let Devon sit as he preferred? More importantly, are there any reasons why I shouldn't make this change?

I share this story as a window into the daily challenges that teachers grapple with and the ethics that undergird these challenges. One approach to resolving this dilemma is through the lens of "evidence-based" techniques.[3] Some resources tell me that all children should be seated in a particular manner to learn while others privilege choice.[4] Another entry point into this quandary is scientific. Data shows children learn better when they are physically comfortable, and different bodies feel comfortable in different chairs and positions.[5]

Yet this book is based on the contention that more is at stake. Namely, what philosophers of education like Doris Santoro in the epigraph refer to as normative questions, concerns around *What is right?* or *How do we achieve the good?* and *According to whom?* Considering Devon and the meeting area, such questions might include, Why do we make children sit the same way? Is equality equity? When does one child's need impinge on another's?

These are ethical questions with ethics defined as acting in correspondence with an understanding of what is right.[6] Some see what is right as based on "morals," externally derived norms and customs. Where one's ethos does have cultural derivation and is externally influenced, it is also to a degree personally derived and maintained. With methods such as those presented in this book, an ethos is identified, interrogated, and recommitted to in a constant iterative process. Referring to the undergirding philosophies of ethos, throughout this book I will also use the words *values* and *commitments*. In relying on these familiar words with colloquial associations, I seek accessibility and to highlight that even without the language of ethics, an ethical stance undergirds teachers' work.

Back to Devon. When I consider my values, I find that I want my students to be comfortable and able to focus on the work. When I read picture books, I want them to see the images. When we practice sounding out words on the whiteboard, I want them to follow along—noticing each letter. I want to ensure no child is distracting another. Upon reflection, I am committed to honoring physical needs, an engaging learning environment, and equity. I want all children to have access to the curriculum, and equitable access is not the *same* access.

With these values in mind, I consider whether Devon can sit on a chair. I determine that if this is his preference, it certainly won't hurt *him* to sit on a chair. Unless the chair is in front of his classmates, it won't interfere with their view of the board. It won't hurt Devon's classmates if I give them the option of sitting on chairs too or communicate that they can have other physical needs met. I already let kids stand behind their seated classmates when they get restless so they can wiggle and pace.

In weighing my values, I also determine that my goal is that Devon participates and that is more important than regulating the minutiae of how he participates. Returning to school the next day, I offer Devon a chair and explain to him and his classmates that everyone should be comfortable in school. Devon is happier. Most of his classmates don't want chairs. They like the floor. A few do ask for a chair, and I invite them to pull one up. Most lose interest in this option soon after it is made available. Everyone sits more comfortably.

Teaching is a profoundly ethical endeavor.[7] In its attention to quotidian demands, Devon's story represents the daily dilemmas. They are typically not glamorous or particularly dramatic but, as I argue throughout this book, the stakes are high.[8] What is it like sitting all day in a manner that constricts the body? What is the effect of being told that one's preferred way of sitting is not appropriate? What happens when a child is told they are only paying attention in a particular physical position and this doesn't ring true to their experience? What does it mean to watch a classmate be forced to uncomfortably contort or face discipline? Alternatively, what is the effect of seeing a classmate encouraged to be at ease? How does it influence children when an authority offers choices and allows space to make requests?

In each of these examples, the challenge is for the teacher to see, as Liz articulates in the epigraph, the bigger purpose behind the details of daily practice: to ask not *what works* but, what I argue next is a philosophical line of questioning, *what works for what purpose, how something works,* and *for whom.*[9] These ethical questions demand that the actor figure out first what is right and second whether an action fits with those values. As a discipline committed to the examination of what it means to live well, philosophy provides both tools of inquiry and concepts that help teachers grapple with these questions.[10]

WHO IS A PHILOSOPHER-TEACHER?

Thinking with and as a philosopher supports being an ethical practitioner.[11] Avoiding gatekeeping, labels, and a focus on official titles,

I define a philosopher broadly based on the kinds of questions one asks, the tools one uses to ask those questions, how one approaches situations and challenges, and whom one chooses as interlocutors. Conscious of gatekeeping and hierarchies around who is and isn't labeled a philosopher, in this book I ambivalently introduce people with their titles to highlight that those from a broad range of fields—teachers, philosophers, geographers, botanists—do philosophy.

Putting forth a philosophical way of being as necessary for justice, novelist and essayist James Baldwin calls us to "ask questions of the universe, and then learn to live with those questions."[12] Similarly, philosopher Socrates identified questioning as the keystone of living well in his repeated commitment to inquiry and contention that he knows only that which he does not know. As he famously stated, "I am wiser than this man; it is likely that neither of us know anything worthwhile, but he thinks he knows something when he does not, whereas when I do not know, neither do I think I know."[13] Building on this foundation, thinking philosophically demands a dwelling in inquiry and a commitment to regularly unsettle that which appears settled.

Relatedly, philosophy often works in schemas and frames.[14] This can be a descriptive project. What are the schemas that define us, where did they come from, and how have they evolved?[15] It can be aspirational—what kind of orientation would help us live more justly?[16] Philosophy also supports deconstruction—after naming the abiding frames that orient us and where they came from, a question becomes, How can unjust frames be taken apart and shifted so we can live better?[17]

To reiterate, philosophy is not simply a particular system of ideas to pass down but also a way to approach the world, ask questions, and, especially important, think about daily situations. Philosopher Pierre Hadot refers to this orientation as philosophy as a way of life, an approach in which one pursues questions and grapples with weighty issues to live better day-to-day.[18] Hadot traces a narrow lineage of Western thinkers for whom philosophy was a way of life that includes Socrates, Friedrich Nietzsche, and Michel Foucault. I add to Hadot's list contemporary teacher-philosophers like Paulo Freire, bell hooks, and Vivian Gussin Paley and the many practicing teachers like Liz quoted throughout this book who go to work every day quietly practicing philosophy as a way of life for the benefit of their students.[19]

What does this philosophical orientation look like more precisely? In a call for thinking philosophically with teachers, philosopher of education Megan Laverty describes three key interrelated roles for the philosopher of education as they work with practitioners:

> First, we need to be able to identify what we believe and what we mean by our concepts, in order to determine whether or not they accord with the conceptual and normative commitments of our actions. Second, we need to be able to evaluate what we are compelled by, as well as our beliefs and commitments to ensure that both are as truthful as possible. Third, we need to determine the practical implications of our beliefs and commitments, both as a means of evaluating them and as a means of developing practices properly reflective of them.[20]

To be a philosopher-teacher, within this frame, is to be someone who constantly seeks to interrogate and live out one's ethics.[21] To do so, a philosophical teacher education helps a teacher:

- form and ask normative questions that center around purpose and meaning;
- dwell in these questions—embracing paradox and unknowing;
- employ tools drawn from the study of philosophy that guide inquiry; and
- include philosophers and philosophically informed teachers as interlocutors.

A PEDAGOGICAL APPROACH TO CULTIVATING
A PHILOSOPHICAL TEACHER

I take on the call for philosophy with teachers as a conjointly philosophical and pedagogical inquiry. Much of the literature on teacher ethics has focused on calling for and defining the parameters of philosophy with teachers or describing how teachers engage philosophically in the field.[22] This book serves as a prequel to those texts. While, for example, Santoro heard in teachers' frustrations ethical dilemmas, she notes that the teachers in her study did not, prior to her prodding, frame their concerns in the language of ethics and most reported that, until reading Santoro's depictions of their teaching, they had never deeply considered their teaching along ethical lines.[23] In response to these findings, as alluded to in the epigraph, Santoro queries, What would it look like were we to frame preservice and in-service instruction along ethical lines? This text responds with pedagogy. Namely, I offer a philosophically oriented approach to teacher education by showcasing what this looks like primarily within methods courses for preservice and in-service teachers and in-service professional development.

In a research study on teachers' ethical centers, I found that teachers and teacher educators see values as deriving from pivotal experiences (including in childhood and coursework and while teaching) and interactions with others (including books, mentors, and peers). Where a philosophy is certainly picked up in these contexts, it tends to not be named or coherently revised. In this book, I support adding layers of intentionality to how teachers grow and live their philosophy.

In evaluations of an elective course on the theoretical foundations of early childhood education (referred to herein as Theories), multiple students said the course was one of the most valuable they had taken during their coursework and suggested this elective should be required. Though I loved teaching this course and the students, based on evaluations and informal feedback, loved taking it, the course itself moved out of my rotation. With course schedules dominated almost entirely by meeting state-required methods courses, it wasn't a course many students took.[24]

Taking to heart student feedback that the course on philosophy was needed, I adapted the original Theories course into my literacy methods courses going forward. As a former practicing teacher and teacher educator with nearly twenty years of classroom experience from infants to higher education, I have done activities from this book with children, preservice undergraduates, in-service teachers with associate's degrees completing their bachelor's degrees, in-service teachers working toward a master's in education, and experienced teachers with whom I've engaged as colleagues providing and participating in professional development (see the accompanying website for teacher adaptations to many of the activities shared). Though I draw primarily from the literacy courses, I include activities from a broad range of courses including math methods, families and communities, social studies, and introduction to teaching to describe throughout how activities can be adapted to different course topics, populations, and teachers with a range of experiences.

Most of my examples and research are drawn from a mixed-income ethnically diverse group of children and their teachers in public schools in a large city and students and graduates at a rural public liberal arts college with, at the time of this project, a 97 percent acceptance rate. At this college, the premier teacher education school in the state, I worked with teachers and future teachers who were extremely academically motivated as well as students who struggled with skills associated with success in philosophy such as reading and writing. In sharing work done with academically and ethnically diverse populations, I showcase how philosophical work can live in teacher education with populations often dismissed as not particularly philosophical.

When not specifically designated, I use the word *teacher* to refer to both in-service and preservice teachers as both engage in teaching relationships with students. *Student* refers to anyone in a course or class. Where a few of my examples come from foundations courses and electives like a families and communities course, I have drawn the majority of my examples from literacy methods courses primarily because methods courses in which some content is determined externally by state and national requirements make up the bulk of most teachers' educational experiences.

Teacher educators Django Paris and Samy Alim developed the phrase "culturally sustaining pedagogy" to describe teaching practices that build from, affirm, and support the sustenance of a student's culture.[25] Though widely applicable, Paris and Alim's focus is on sustaining the cultures of communities of color and those who are part of communities subjected to systemic oppression. Further, while their focus is on affirmation and sustenance, Paris and Alim build in room for criticality and revision around oppressive cultural practices. In a commitment to awareness of local culture, an important part of this book is that each activity responded to a particular context. Specifically, working with primarily white-identifying students, many of whom came from rural and mostly white communities, I catered many activities to name and sustain elements of the students' culture while also working to challenge white supremacy. Conversation around racism in urban interracial classrooms looked different. As relevant, I share both how an activity worked with a given population and how it was modified to support other communities.

SPEAKING AS A PHILOSOPHER-TEACHER

Much has been offered by way of providing teachers with other people's philosophies of education. For example, textbooks for foundations courses tend to give an overview of the thinking of famous philosophers.[26] Sometimes these philosophers are presented in excerpted form with a primary source so edited that the scope of the philosopher's thinking is limited by the editor.[27] Other texts offer a biographical overview of the life and thoughts of particular thinkers.[28] A few texts draw lines between a philosopher's theory and how it might play out in practice.[29] All of these texts are helpful in giving an overview of an idea or introducing a thinker, but, as Laverty highlights, honing morally rooted wishes for education into a coherent philosophy requires systematic reflection on one's own values, the ability to articulate and name what these values are, and the capacity to link these values to practices.[30]

When dwelling in an environment that asks philosophical questions, considers philosophical ideas, and slowly reads philosophical texts (broadly defined), teachers will readily voice their concerns and describe their teaching along philosophical lines. Teacher colleagues, teacher educators, and professional developers concerned with ethics should create such an environment. In fact, despite stereotypes to the contrary, I argue with examples throughout this text that a philosophical approach is a natural orientation for teachers.[31]

That said, though natural companions, philosophers and teachers, philosophy and teaching, are not always associates. The last course I took for my master's in elementary education was a philosophy of education course to fulfill the one foundations requirement. In papers I wrote for that class, I lamented that, fixated on method, my teacher education classmates were often dismissive of more philosophical questions, courses, and readings. In other words, while there is much potential and need for teachers and philosophers to engage, interactions are minimal and sometimes perceived as being resisted when teachers call for direct connections with practice.[32]

This book bridges this gap by addressing one issue. Namely, when philosophers reach out to teachers, the teacher is often positioned as the outsider, invited into the world of philosophy and, upon joining this world, asked to speak in the discourse of academic philosophy.[33]

Philosopher and literary critic Mikhail Bakhtin uses the word "hybridization" to describe "a mixture of two social languages [in this case many more] within the limits of a single utterance, an encounter, within the arena of an utterance, between two different linguistic consciousnesses, separated from one another by an epoch, by social differentiation or by some other factor."[34] Hybridization well describes the language that develops as philosophy and teaching discourses are bridged. I offer an invitation that does not ask the teacher to assimilate but instead, through the encounter between teacher and philosopher, new ways of speaking are developed.[35]

Positioned to support this bridge, I have an undergraduate degree in history with a focus on the history of ideas, a doctoral degree in philosophy and education, and a master's in elementary education. I have taught many classes in philosophy as well as methods. I have also worked as a classroom teacher and then support teacher in a progressive public elementary school. As a teacher, I plodded through philosophers like Hannah Arendt, John Dewey, and Michel Foucault on the twenty-minute train ride between home and work. My editions of these texts are full of shaky-from-the-train notes and underlining that made connections back to my day in the classroom. Children's names and comments are written in the margins as their insights spoke with the philosophers. I was later the philosophy student who woke up at 6:00 a.m. to teach in an elementary school and ended my days in a doctoral seminar reading thinkers like Jean-Jacques Rousseau.[36] Therefore, I write this book and teach my courses as one with a hybrid identity: a mixture of philosopher and educator who finds myself speaking fluently in both discourses and dually at home in both communities.

I also rest this book on years of studying and practicing Descriptive Inquiry.[37] A philosophy and a set of practices, Descriptive Inquiry developed as practitioners spearheaded by educator Patricia Carini studied teaching practices and philosophical texts together. Adding to the majority of publications from this community that highlight how Descriptive Inquiry is used to study children's work, children, and teaching practices, this book will highlight how the Descriptive Processes can and do support the study of text and philosophy.

Having worked with a broad range of populations, I write for preservice and in-service teachers who want to think philosophically and coaches, administrators, and teacher educators who want to support teachers in this work. I write for philosophers of education seeking methods to engage meaningfully with teachers and school-based professionals. Though I zoom in on my specialization, early childhood and elementary education, this book is for anyone interested in engaging in philosophy with teachers, and all methods can be tweaked and applied broadly.

My goals are multifold:

- In hearing how I and other teachers grappled with philosophy, a reader will see how powerful philosophy can be for teachers and what excellent philosophers teachers make.
- Readers will be inspired to read and do philosophy.
- Readers will get specific and practical ideas for teaching and doing philosophy with and as teachers.

- Finally, I hope the book will serve as a "provocation" (to borrow a term from the early childhood educators in Reggio Emilia) and provoke readers to consider and reconsider how philosophy and education live in teaching.

PHILOSOPHICAL FRAMEWORK

My teaching of philosophy and this book draw on a few key pedagogical tenants defined here and applied to activities throughout the book: practical wisdom as an integration between philosophy and practice, attending with care, building from the learner, experiential learning, and the value of interruption and disruption. While rooted in philosophy that acknowledges the personal and cultural relativity of core values, I do not take a values-neutral stance. I write from a commitment to human dignity that I see as demanding diversity, equity, inclusion, and belonging in schools. Classroom anecdotes have been chosen to address concerns for the dignity of the person and the child in classrooms and the ways in which these commitments can be hard to realize in daily conundrums. From a host of examples from experience and interviews, I have chosen stories to focus on those where the resolution promotes human dignity.

Practical Wisdom

The philosopher Aristotle uses the ancient Greek word *phronesis*, the concept of practical wisdom, to describe knowing how to act in accordance with one's values in context.[38] Within this schema, values and actions are symbiotically dependent on each other.[39] I take from this an understanding that all educational acts are value laden though these values, when not reflected on, are often not recognized.[40] Couched in the language of best practice, discussions in education often focus on what works and leave out questions concerning *what works for what.*[41] Challenging this, to teach ethically one must know one's values, and this, as I argue throughout the text, is a task aided by studying philosophy. Likewise, philosophy practiced apart from the world can be an empty, and even dangerous, exercise.[42] An idea may seem appealing and then prove very harmful.[43] Teachers and philosophers benefit from looking at philosophy in context and cultivating and practicing practical wisdom.

Attend with Care

Former elementary school teacher and teacher educator Carla Shalaby calls teachers to "*be love*" by which she means that "what you model is the belief—through the everyday things you do—that no human being deserves to suffer any threat to or assault on her personhood."[44] For many people ethical decisions are made by considering what it means to offer care within a relationship.[45] Applying this idea to teaching, philosopher Nel Noddings argued that an ethic of care requires that we see someone as the end—not a means to an end.[46] Within this schema, the child's goals become pressing as we determine how to care. For example, Noddings urges us to follow a student's interests as opposed to our own and emphasizes that using a student's interest to realize one's own goals (such as teaching mathematics) is a manipulation.

Using the phrase "attending with care," Carini puts forth Descriptive Inquiry as a particular way of paying attention to students that puts their needs and humanity at the forefront of instruction.[47] Returning to Shalaby, this ethic is both necessary and challenging, as we must "be love" "even in the face of a young person constantly calling out, cursing you out, or throwing a chair."[48] To do so demands practical wisdom because, as Shalaby demonstrates, being love is difficult and nuanced, requiring significant energy and constant calibration.

Build from the Learner

Care ethics demands that we, in Shalaby's words, "be love" by considering who the learners are and what they need.[49] Culturally sustaining pedagogy adds an additional layer. The starting point and the route followed are not simply derived from observing the individual learners but considering who they are and what they need within a cultural context.[50]

In a learning theory that honors the capacity of each learner, psychologist Jerome Bruner claimed that you could teach any concept to any child as long as it was introduced step-by-step, often referred to as scaffolding.[51] Physician and educator Maria Montessori beautifully illustrates how scaffolds can support students with her meticulously developed and intentionally sequenced materials and lessons.[52] Though individual differences affect interests and aptitudes, I take from both thinkers that if instruction begins with the student and proceeds with incremental steps, people can make extraordinary leaps in their understanding and work with a broad range of concepts and materials.[53] There is no formula for these steps, but instead success requires that the teacher pay careful attention to the individual learner, be cognizant of a range of pedagogical supports, and create a supportive environment.[54] Coupling building from the learner with care ethics, I diverge from developmental theorists who emphasize predetermined and externally derived goals.[55]

Experiential Learning

Philosopher John Dewey argued that we often learn by engaging in experiences and then reflecting on them.[56] In this way, one moves between experience and generalization, from the tangible to the abstract. The toddler learns the word *hat* by wearing a hat. That said, Dewey emphasized that not everything needed to be accessed firsthand or physically to be experienced. One can learn about a helmet by reading a book alongside one's firsthand experience of hats. Further, meaningful experiences look different at different stages in one's learning. Writing of math education, James Alexander McLellan and Dewey explain that we must return to the concrete whenever something is new or particularly unclear.[57] Thus, as learners, we ideally move between more concrete and more abstract engagements throughout our development. Teacher educator Eleanor Duckworth showcased how through experiences people can build understanding of extremely abstract concepts such as density and the cycles of the moon.[58] She argues that even adults need this tangible experience because a deeper understanding of these concepts has been neglected.

Importantly, an overreliance on one's own firsthand experiences can lead to the dismissal of others and a very narrow perception of the world. Experience and reflection must be shared in diverse contexts if we are to construct robust accounts of reality.[59] As argued by theorist and educator bell hooks and philosopher María Lugones, we must seek out accounts of women and people of color. Accounts of experience that ignore or disregard these populations are not only limited but also unjust.

Interruption and Disruption

Baldwin argues that living well and pursuing a just society demand that we constantly question.[60] Describing the effect of his questions, Socrates's interlocutor, Meno, introduces the metaphor of the "torpedo fish," translated as a stingray, to describe Socrates's relentless questioning as zapping someone into befuddlement.[61]

Socrates refines this characterization to note that, unlike the sting-ray, he himself is paralyzed by questions and, in asking them, also paralyzes his interlocutors. The frozen experience Socrates and Meno both describe is referred to in the ancient Greek as *aporia*—a state of befuddlement where one does not know what one knows or how to act.

For Socrates, as with Baldwin, aporia is first needed if one is to pursue wisdom. Dewey connects this state of unknowing spe-cifically with growth and new understanding. He argues that we learn when we are disrupted.[62] Using the metaphor of a rock rolling down a hill and meeting a boulder, Dewey argues that the rock might hit the boulder and not move or, with enough force, smash through the boulder. A being capable of learning and growth can face the boulder and adapt. It might step over it or around it or find a way through it. At the core of Baldwin's, Socrates's, and Dewey's learning philosophies is that learning includes being paused in one's previous tracks and that this pausing can be disarming and uncomfortable.

Yet calling for a society of questioners, Baldwin acknowledges that those who challenge and unsettle are rarely popular and, in fact, tend to be seen as threatening.[63] Not all of Socrates's interlocu-tors grow upon being thrown into aporia. Some walk away from Socrates unchanged. Some respond to the disconcerting state of unknowing by ultimately silencing Socrates, famously putting him on trial and executing him. A question for me in orienting around not knowing becomes, *How do we help students face the inevitable unease and dwell with it productively?*

In recent years, the notion of grit has come to dominate dis-course in many schools.[64] Those who have a "growth mindset," which includes the ability to work through discomfort, will perse-vere in the face of challenge. Understanding that the act of learning is inherently uncomfortable and that this discomfort, and even fear, can lead the learner to shut down, I showcase how through attending with care I work to create environments in which students take risks with me and each other.[65]

STUDENTS AND TEACHERS AS AUTHORS

In the democratically oriented and philosophically intentional Italian preschools in Reggio Emilia, the young students, teachers, and families are all referred to as protagonists.[66] This has always struck me as important and exciting. I am troubled that teachers, children, and families are often positioned as objects and researchers as subjects. My dissertation on books authored by teachers challenged the rarity of teachers as authors of their own curriculum or classroom environments, let alone of books.[67] Students are even more rarely the authors.[68] Where students do speak back, it tends to be anonymous (in course evaluations) or in research studies heavily mediated by the professors' or researchers' perspective.

In an oft-quoted phrase, Dewey argues that there is a profound "waste and loss" in the teaching profession because teachers tend to operate without witness and their work is rarely documented or passed on beyond their individual schools, let alone classrooms.[69] One of my favorite philosophical texts is Jean-Jacques Rousseau's *The Solitaries*. It follows *the Emile*, a fictionalized account of a child's educational journey with his tutor. *The Solitaries* consists of letters from the fictional student, Emile, back to his tutor. The tutor whose actions were the focus of the original book and who never leaves Emile's side is now ominously absent and nowhere to be found. *The Solitaries* is striking in many ways, but here I reference it as an intriguing example of a student speaking back on his education. In my book, neither teachers nor teacher education students are absent. Instead I include teachers' and future teachers' voices not as objects of study but as participants in the experience of authoring.

In doing so, a bit about voice. First names indicate pseudonyms. Many of these comments are drawn from a research study where teachers spoke under the protective shade of anonymity. Quotes, edited slightly for readability, and my analysis have been shared whenever logistically possible with the teachers to maintain their authority and ensure quotes were correctly understood. Full names indicate that those quoted have given permission and edited as they see fit. I quote at length including from my own teaching journals and documents to preserve voice and the speakers' meaning. Again, slight edits with permission have been made for readability.

This decision to include teachers as authors is philosophical and political. Teachers are sophisticated meaning makers—philosophers, in fact. Yet this view of teachers now, and perhaps always, is under siege. The phrase "teacher proof" abounds, carrying with it the notion that teachers are either so foolish or so corrupt that they would ruin everything if they had any control. At the time of publication, many teachers are required to follow scripts and assessed on following a curriculum to what is referred to as fidelity. School boards often determine curriculum and in some cases the individual books teachers are allowed to read to their students. My former students and teacher colleagues quoted throughout clearly attest to a teacher's practical wisdom and care. Further, as teachers address throughout the book, the opportunity to think philosophically was empowering and transformative.

STRUCTURE OF THE BOOK

I have organized the book around the arc of a course, guiding the reader through a sequence and practices I draw on each term. The book can be read alongside a methods course such as literacy or in foundations courses.

A popular teaching structure that scaffolds learning in the company and support of others is *I Do, We Do, You Do*. The teacher first models something, a group then works through it together, and then the student, graduating to more independence, tries it. Each chapter begins with an *I Do*, first-person account of a teaching dilemma in which I zoom in on daily, often banal, thorny issues that teachers face. In drawing them from practice (as opposed to composites), I include and showcase the nuance and messiness of the classroom and have chosen stories where finding a way forward demands attention to this nuance.[70] Details have been changed to ensure anonymity with some superficial elements fictionalized. After sharing the teaching story, I introduce a philosophical approach, arguing how particular tools from philosophy can help the teacher think through the shared dilemma.

Moving to *We Do*, each chapter features what I often refer to in class as "What We Did," methods that can be adapted and tweaked. Activities are accompanied in many cases with student samples.[71] After putting forth methods, I offer reflection: a "Practical Wisdom: Why We Did It?/Values in Action" section. Practical wisdom occurs when an effective use of methods in context connects back to core values. Connecting "What We Did" with "Why We Did It" is an activity my students do all semester. Practicing this movement between theory and practice helps teachers solidify these links. The chapters close with *You Do*. First, I offer another anecdote from practice where the philosophical approach is drawn. I then conclude guiding the reader through activities from the chapter to try.

Mirroring Laverty's schema in which she focuses first on naming, defining, and redefining and then enacting, in chapter 1 of part 1, "The Need for a Compass," I articulate why teachers' naming and ongoing development of their values matter. This articulation is dually rooted in narratives from the classroom as well as framing from philosophers and philosophy of education.

In part 2, "Studying Philosophy and Education," each chapter introduces a different philosophical approach or way of unpacking ideas as a philosopher. Chapters build on each other, with later chapters in the section integrating a range of philosophical approaches. Chapter 2 grounds readers in their own experiences. Chapter 3 turns outward to close reading of mostly familiar texts to unpack messages. Chapter 4 then focuses on word choice and metaphor to consider more closely the ethical nature of the language of classrooms. Chapter 5 draws on a range of approaches modeled in earlier chapters to go deeper into the meaning of less familiar texts, specifically offering methods for taking on philosophical texts. Chapter 6 then offers a nuanced way of engaging with different ideas in which conversations are scaffolded to support expanded perspective. Pivoting to part 3, "Teaching from One's Moral Center," chapter 7 introduces readers to a range of approaches including genealogy to help them consider the perspective they bring to the classroom and how it is informed by cultural context and lineage.

Just as Laverty highlights the need to directly integrate philosophy with practice, the last chapter of the book, chapter 8, describes how teachers attend to dilemmas in the field with ethics in mind. I zoom in on narratives of common teacher quandaries to describe how thinking philosophically helps the teacher navigate difficult terrain. I also offer summative activities for drawing together and articulating a coherent philosophy of education.

I have culled sample syllabi, resources that I share with students, and handouts that teachers have created for children based on the activities in the book. Visit https://www.carafurman.com/ to access these resources along with videos and a podcast that are linked to extend the book.

SETTING UP TEACHERS FOR SUCCESS

What does it look like when teachers consistently wed philosophy and teaching, theory and practice, weaving them into philosophy as a way of teaching life? As she finished up coursework and prepared mentally for student teaching, Erin Silver, one of the teachers featured in this book, asked to meet. She had fallen in love with progressive education during Theories and she wondered if she could be happy teaching in schools that fell so far short of her ideals.

We strategized that day about finding a job and community where Erin would feel supported. I left the meeting anxious for this young, ethically driven person and the hard path ahead, and I worried that in a few years she would become one of Santoro's demoralized teachers—full of ideals and talent and wanting to leave.

This did not happen. That spring, Erin began student teaching in a placement that she loved. When we spoke for the first time after graduation and following a year of pandemic teaching, Erin presented as a confident, resilient, creative teacher who was very clear about her values and how to enact them. Though she spoke wistfully of someday finding a progressive placement, Erin seemed happy in what she described as more conservative schools.

Erin could clearly state the values she would not compromise on—brave enough to directly stand up to supervisors and carve out space for relationship building and children's physical needs.

Erin described the course she took with me where she learned about progressive education as transformative in helping her determine the kind of teacher she wanted to be. Her only lament was that she had taken it so late in her undergraduate career. She would have liked more time to study progressive education after she identified it as her calling and before going into the field. In Erin's words, the course had helped her figure out who she wanted to be in the classroom. Asked what helps her stay committed, she said that she sometimes reads resources introduced in the course, Dewey and *Loving Learning*, a contemporary book about progressive education.[72]

Erin's values and pedagogical ideals were keeping her steady in the midst of incredibly difficult teaching times. It is my hope that developing a similar ethical compass and clarity will inform and empower the readers of this book. And so, turning now in chapter 1 to a teacher's ethical center, we begin.

PART 1

THE NEED FOR A COMPASS

CHAPTER ONE

IDENTIFYING AN
ETHICAL COMPASS

*I would say everything I do in my classroom is for the children's best
interest even if it goes against policy. I like to think that if you're doing
an activity or changing something in your classroom, if you have the
children's best interest in mind, you can never be wrong . . . I like to
think about why I am doing it. Like am I doing it because this is going
to make my classroom look cute, or am I doing it because there's actually an academic purpose? So, a lot of my stuff doesn't look particularly cookie cutter. It's more about the process in their learning.*

—Juliet, early childhood educator

I t is my third week of school, and I am a first-year teacher. The
month has been hard. After describing my improved support of
some children, I write in my teaching journal:

> I sing with them and feel on my way to creating that world of
> song and art and writing and math and minds at work that is
> my Platonic ideal for learning. I contact Amy Vorenberg, my

third grade teacher and now the head of a school, for the first time since I was eight, and tell her of the universe she and her co-teacher, Christine Vulopas created for us and how it resonated so deeply and how I have eternally searched for that world of social and intellectual smoothness where everything was integrated and everything worked and we had constant meetings like "why should we keep our hands out of the fish tank" and "let's all talk about the fact that someone stole John's shoe as a joke" and "give me a math sentence to leave the meeting area" and trips. They brought the ocean, life, the world, into the classroom and . . . taught us that our dreams were worthwhile, and that playing with sand and water could be science and that everything in the world is connected. A memory to aspire to and when my students on Friday beg for "journaling time" and then four create stages and puppets for the plays that I let them work on together in writing workshop and when I see dragons in their stories and pictures everywhere after we've been reading *My Father's Dragon*, I start to believe that I'm not there yet certainly but I'm working towards that world, and this isn't all a waste of time and dreams and love.[1] They are finally lighting up with me and with my lessons and so my two weeks of acting like I love them and love learning when all I love is my bed and miss my summer of late nights and friends and all that begins to pay off and I am back to where I was when I began this quest to teach, dreaming of recreating Amy and Christine's class for me and the students. Dreaming of a place where fantasy and reality were integrated.

After the staff meeting on Thursday, I leave the school smiling and tell my principal Michelle Harring, "I'm in much better shape than last week" and she grins and says, "and so is your class!"

In sharing this passage, I seek to highlight a few key components:

- I was and am a teacher with a vision for my classroom that involves both actions (such as singing and creative play) and feelings (such as "love[ing]" students and helping children "love learning").

- My vision, what I describe as a "Platonic ideal for learning," motivated my "quest to teach." While elements have been refined and evolved over time, much remains the same since those first days.
- This vision comes from a variety of places, and one strong influence is my third-grade teachers.
- My vision in those first weeks is not consistently realized, and I am still "dreaming of a place where fantasy and reality [are] integrated." Turns out, this is a lifelong process.
- As my final paragraph suggests, both my own and the children's success is integrated with working toward this vision.

Asked why they want to be teachers, my undergraduate students in a rural public college often respond that they find children "cute," have "always loved children," or have fond memories of playing a teacher with younger children and dolls. When I taught master's students in an urban setting, they often described wanting to "make the world better" or spoke in broad terms of righting racial injustice. Teacher educators often dismiss the former statements as sugary, superficial, and ill-informed about the nature of teaching. The latter comments are dismissed as overly idealistic or clueless about the realities of schools. Later, in the field, teacher expressions of frustration or refusal to follow curriculum or rules are often trivialized as griping.[2] I feel differently. Having spent my adult life working with and listening to teachers, I hear these comments as often stemming from a deep-seated and complex ethos.[3]

Teachers don't necessarily connect their language with ethics either.[4] In a reading group on philosopher of education Doris Santoro's book *Demoralized: Why Teachers Leave the Profession They*

Love and How They Can Stay with faculty in education, some of my teacher educator colleagues felt talking about ethics was important and needed, but they weren't entirely sure how to discuss the ethics of practice with teachers.

As described in the Introduction, philosopher Pierre Hadot puts forth philosophy as a way of life that helps one live out an ethos in daily action.[5] Socrates is famous for quoting the inscription at the Oracle of Delphi to "know thyself," which according to Socrates's interpretation means that one must articulate what one does not know.[6] What is less widely known is that Socrates tells this story in a dialogue with Alcibiades, a young, vain, charismatic statesman whom Socrates hopes to help better know himself so he can lead well. Socrates maintains that "if we know ourselves, then we might be able to know how to cultivate ourselves, but if we don't know ourselves, we'll never know."[7] Knowing thyself is always necessary to first learn and then act better among others. Knowing oneself ethically then must be the work of the teacher.

According to philosopher Michel Foucault, we cultivate an ethos through practice, building the muscles and flexibility of ethical thought slowly and consistently over time.[8] Just as a wrestler practices certain moves for battle, ethical exercises such as reflecting on our values help us strengthen awareness so we are better prepared for daily challenges. Getting in the habit of naming and noticing values that guide our teaching makes us more aware. By having teachers name their guiding ethos from the start of a class, my goal is not to reify those commitments or spend the semester simply determining the practices that match an ethos. Instead, naming values can help us both solidify and identify what we might want to reconsider.

With an eye toward slowly exercising philosophical muscles, I begin this book as I begin my courses: first by highlighting teaching situations in which a subtle understanding of values matter and then by showing how I help teachers begin to note and articulate the values they bring to teaching. Following the arc of a course, we begin with week 1, day 1.

WHAT WE DID

As illustrated in the teaching stories I've shared so far, teachers enact their values in small, daily pedagogical acts.[9] Philosopher of education David Hansen describes:

> The mundane, all-too-familiar act of setting up the classroom in advance is part of teaching indirectly, even though it takes place before students have arrived on the scene. When students walk through the classroom door, they will encounter a setting organized in a deliberate way. I envision two benefits for learning. The first is the sheer fact that the setting displays an intention rather than none. It is not a random setting, and thus, hopefully, does not promote random thought. The second benefit resides in the message emitted by the classroom layout. My hope is that the physical setting expresses the idea of valuing what is about to take place: namely, shared inquiry into the practice of teaching rather than, say, the distribution of information about teaching over a transom. I hope that as students enter the room and settle in their seats, they will orient themselves, however subtly or unselfconsciously, toward our reasons for being there in the first place.[10]

As students begin the semester, they "orient" themselves—physically and intellectually taking in the surroundings. For Hansen, orienting students requires that he prepare for literal placements of bodies in the room as this placement influences how students will think together.

Veteran kindergarten teacher Julie Diamond describes moves between minutia and meaning, writing of room setup:

> I think about how children will move around the room. There's more than one pathway to the rug, so it can be approached from different directions. Papers and writing materials are accessible in several places: there are paper trays, markers, and pencils in the art area and also on a set of shelves near the low table; there's a basket with clipboards and writing pads in the pretend area; and later in the year, I'll add index cards and markers to the block area. The organization of the room is simple and uncluttered; it is easily comprehended. I want the children to be able to read the environment, to find what they want, to know where to put things away.[11]

In this short passage, Diamond showcases an ethos: with attention to the flow of the room, she attends to inclusion with an eye toward children's ease of mobility and accessibility. Describing the range of materials, she showcases respect for children as makers. She encourages creativity and learning through play, mixing writing materials into the pretend play and block areas. Finally, wanting children to "read the environment" so they can gradually take on more autonomy, Diamond gives repeated attention to the coherency of item placement.

How do I orient my students toward our ways of being together? Like Hansen and Diamond, I want my first class to communicate intentionality. I invite you along:

> It is early September, and the days are still hot. From the classroom window, students can see a bright blue sky and mostly green trees with a few red leaves. Like Hansen and Diamond, I like to get to class very early, but I have rushed in from dropping off my children at school with only a few minutes to spare. I find my students sitting in table groups in the dark. The room is full,

and most briefly glance at me and then their eyes return to their phones. A few chat with each other. As I enter, I turn on the light and mumble an apology as their eyes adjust.

I unpack a large binder with a printed-out plan and then stand still for a moment behind the large desk, letting my body and mind have quiet as a transition. "Okay, guys," I say at exactly the moment that class time begins, "I'm going to have to ask a favor. I know you are all comfortable, but we are going to rearrange things. Can you please move the desks so they make a circle around the edge of the room?"[12] I write on the board, support the movement of a table or two, and then place a tub of unit blocks in the now-open space at the center of the room.[13]

The board reads "Prof. Furman," the name of the course (undergraduates often end up in the wrong room), and a schedule on the far left:

- Welcome
- Introductions: Gifts and Offerings
- Read Aloud: *The Year We Learned to Fly*[14]
- Syllabus Review and First Assignment
- Reading Workshop: Read with a partner from a carefully curated collection of high-quality picture books that include a diversity of authors and characters. Books are chosen around a welcoming theme like home or families.[15]

On the far right, I've written the following core values that will orient the course:

- Freedom is important and comes with responsibility.
- We support the needs of the individual alongside the needs of a community. Special attention is paid to the needs of the most vulnerable.
- Students need time to dwell in experiences (do less but go deeper).
- We learn through and with our bodies and not despite them.
- Literacy demands work habits as well as skills.

- There are a lot of ways to teach literacy, and they complement what you believe. The goal is not only what's most effective but what's most effective for you and your class.
- Place the child at the center of your curriculum (the child's personality and culture must be affirmed and sustained).
- Literacy is a way of making sense of the world; instruction should be meaningful to the learner.

Then I tell students, "Nearly everything you do in this class I've done or seen done with young children. We will begin with an activity that helped my first and second graders settle after an excitement like recess."

- Let's spend a minute locating ourselves in space. You may keep your eyes open or closed, however you feel more comfortable.
- Note your thoughts. Perhaps consider how you got here. Did anything happen right before you came to class? Is there something you are especially worried or excited about?
- Notice your body within your seat. Your temperature. What parts touch surfaces? Notice where your bottom touches the chair, your feet the floor. Make adjustments to be more comfortable.
- Now notice how your head sits on your shoulders. Your shoulders on your back. Where do your hands and arms rest? Make adjustments to be more comfortable.
- Notice your location in the room. Who is around you? Where are you? Are you near sources of natural or artificial light? How do you feel about this spot? Perhaps you'd like to move later.
- Now take a moment to rescan your whole body. Now scan your thoughts. What thoughts would you like to carry into class? What might be better to put aside for later?
- Now we begin.[16]

After reading the schedule, it is time for introductions. These should be brief but orient students to each other and the course. For example, I always build an inclusive community around gifts and offerings. Ecologist Robin Wall Kimmerer writes, "The [Haudenosaunee Confederacy] Thanksgiving Address reminds us that duties and gifts are two sides of the same coin. Eagles were given the gift of far sight, so it is their duty to watch over us. Rain fulfills its duty as it falls, because it was given the gift of sustaining life. What is the duty of humans? If gifts and responsibilities are one, then asking 'What is our responsibility?' is the same as asking 'What is our gift?'"[17] We each bring a unique gift. This gift is needed, and because we uniquely offer it, it is our responsibility to share. Put differently, what everyone has to offer is necessary. To emphasize this, our next move is a go-round in which each person shares their name and pronouns if they want and responds to a prompt. Before we begin, I pass out blank paper and ask students to take notes as each classmate speaks to start to learn names and keep track of each other's offerings.

To stress the individual need for each person and the responsibility that each person has to bring themself to the community, here is one prompt:

> A focus of this class is the special knowing teachers have and develop! Practical wisdom is an ancient Greek concept that comes from Aristotle and is the best way I've found to describe teacher-knowing. You probably haven't heard the phrase, but you'll recognize what I'm talking about immediately. Basically, this is knowing how to act according to your values in a specific situation, and it comes from experience and maybe some natural proclivity too. I have practical wisdom as a teacher; I can adapt quickly and smoothly. If you put me in a new context, I can pay attention to my students and still, usually, do well. When I moved from the city to the country and had to drive, it was clear

to me I did not have practical wisdom with cars. If anything goes wrong with my car, I need help from others. Share your name, your pronouns if you want, and an area where you have practical wisdom.

We have begun to build a community by sharing names and offerings. Now we must build something tangible together.

- Everyone rise and stand around the blocks.
- Choose a block that speaks to something you are offering the class.
- We will each place a block on a shared structure. The blocks do not need to touch, but they should "interact" with each other to create a structure or scene.
- When you are ready, raise your hand.
- The person who has just gone will call on the next person with a gesture.

The philosopher John Dewey characterizes an experience as a time when a person has done or undergone something and then reflected.[18] I want education students to reflect on activities so they can consider the purpose and whether they will incorporate them into their teaching repertoire. Throughout the semester, students analyze activities using a What We Did chart that asks them to do the following:

- Describe the activity.
- Consider the values and/or purposes of doing it.
- Share how they might adapt it.
- Add the relevant learning standards (at the end of the semester so predetermined and external learning standards don't completely drive our work).

Table 1.1 is an excerpt from then preservice elementary educator Hailey Hall's completed chart from a K–3 literacy class.

TABLE 1.1 What we did/Why we did it

What we did	Why we did it	How I might use it	Learning standards
Phonics dance	We did this activity as a way to practice breaking/chunking words but also bring an interactive and creative element into it.	I would use this during my phonics time in my classroom and have students work in groups to allow them to practice working collaboratively. I would also have students do this activity to help with the memorization of different sets of vocabulary words.	Reading 2: Demonstrate understanding of words, syllables, and sounds (phonemes). Reading 3: Know and apply grade-level phonics and word analysis skills in decoding words.
Book character portrait	We did this as a way to think of a connection between traits in ourselves that are similar to a character in a children's book. This allows the practice of describing and illustrating characters and identifying character traits.	I would either have students pick a book character that they like or relate to or have them choose a character in a book we are reading in class. I would then have students draw this character and allow them to share their drawing and why they drew it with the class.	Reading 6: Analyze how and why individuals, events, and ideas develop and interact over the course of a text.
Writing workshop	Encourages students to become confident and capable writers and allows them to understand the process of producing a finished piece of work.	I would do this during the writing period in my class schedule to allow students to freely write about any topic of their choice while providing guidance and mini-lessons on writing mechanics and the parts of a story.	Writing 2: Develop, strengthen, and produce polished writing by using a collaborative process that includes the age-appropriate use of technology.

Philosophy subtly undergirds. For example, in Hailey's focus on helping students be "confident," she attends to social-emotional components of learning. Her emphasis on process suggests a shared commitment to experiential learning. In choosing to highlight the "phonics dance," she foregrounds an approach to phonics that recognizes the body as teacher.

To plant the philosophical seeds, at this juncture I focus on the values, asking students to share what a teacher might be conveying by introducing this block activity on the first day of class, and as they share, I direct their attention to the list of values I've written up. They note:

- The value of community that honors both the group and the individual. One of the first things we did was make something together. Each person had an individual part as we created a whole together.
- The value of different modes of thinking: building with blocks, communicating with body language and in silence, and then reflecting orally. In a literacy class, I highlight that I want them to think outside the box of reading and writing. In math methods, blocks are a keystone of instruction.
- The value of aesthetics. I typically share that I've purchased an expensive set of blocks because the wood is smooth and perfect. It matters that one of the first items they touch in the class is beautiful, and I hope with this beauty I convey respect for them and for learning.
- The value of doing and reflecting. They have tried the activity, and then they consider the implications for learning.

When we turn to "how they might adapt it," I share that when I taught first and second grade, I had a block corner. In our school, we introduced materials one at a time and taught children how to use each material and put it away before using the materials for learning.[19] To open up the block area, I would gather the whole class. Noiselessly, one by one, we would build a structure together by each person adding one block and then selecting the next person. Then we would let the structure stand—protecting it—and, after a week, we would one by one put the blocks away. After this, children could come during an open work period and build.[20]

After we finish reflecting, we leave the structure in the center of the room for the remainder of class—dodging it carefully as students move around the room for activities. Class ends with us silently putting away the blocks in reverse order. Though they are encouraged to assist each other if someone can't remember their turn, no student has ever forgotten their place in the order or their block.

Directly following the block activity, we turn to the syllabus. I used to dread reading it, but I now enjoy having students read it in the following way. In the margins, put the following:

"?" where you have a question

"*" on at least one thing you are excited about

"V" on indication of my values and the agenda I bring to this class

After reviewing questions and providing more information on areas that I anticipate students will find unusual or confusing, students share some things they are excited about. We then have a longer discussion about the core values I wrote on the board at the start. For example, for me a democratic classroom involves significant freedom and significant responsibility. I highlight the absence of a cell phone policy and instead say they will have the freedom to check their phones if they need to but we as a class will assume that if their phone is out, something very important is going on.

Just like they responded to the block activity, students identify what they can learn about me from the syllabus by sharing the values they noted.

WHO ARE YOU: VALUES INTERVIEW
IN WEEKLY LETTERS

Language and literacy professor Gholdy Muhammad instructs to "ask students to tell you in their own words how they see their various identities. And when they tell you who they are, listen and trust them . . . our students are the best people to speak about their own lives. Our young people of color have a history of others speaking for them or telling their stories without their permission."[21] Students need spaces to be heard. To provide an ongoing space for personal reflection and sharing, I assign ungraded weekly "letters" in which students respond to prompts. I call these letters to emphasize that they are informal places for written conversation. These are dialogic spaces in which I offer extensive comments in the margins: asking questions, highlighting places of personal resonance, sharing resources, and, once I have a sense of what the student seems to be trying to accomplish, offering suggestions. To showcase this, in the letter samples throughout this book, I've included my margin notes to give you the full scope of the conversation.

To create a portfolio that can be easily referenced, students use one document so that it's searchable and new entries start at the top of the document, making it easier to find the newest work.

In one of the first letter prompts, students reflect on their values. Often this is done in an interview with a classmate. Here are my assigned interview questions with the answers of then preservice early childhood teacher Katelyn Beedy, as conducted and transcribed by her friend and classmate Sasha Hampton.

Journal 1: Interview with Katelyn

1. *What are your core values?*
Healthy relationships, communication, empathy, respect, perseverance

2. *What are your core values about teaching?*
Healthy relationships with children and parents, communication with colleagues and parents, inclusion because I am the type of teacher who believes that if everyone can't do an activity then I won't do it, and collaboration (cooperation and individuality).
[MY NOTE IN MARGIN: Agreed. We can talk some about managing the class in small groups too if that's helpful. I've found small groups are needed for skill work.]

3. *How do these values influence your teaching?*
My value of relationships influences my teaching because the children's learning won't be at its best if the children don't feel safe and comfortable in their environment and with their teacher. That's why I will do my best to create positive relationships with my students.

4. *What would you like your future teaching environment to look like?*
I want it to be inviting, not too bright, and have children's work on the walls for display because it gives the children a sense of pride. I will have a special area in the room for the children to relax and collect themselves if they're having a difficult time, and there will be a basket full of calming activities

for the children to do on their own. I picture my room as one big group instead of children split up, which will show a sense of inclusion.

5. *Describe a lesson you've seen or experienced that you thought was awesome.*

My mentor teacher in one of my practicums would collect pieces of work the students were proud of and she'd put it in a binder with a picture of them and their name on it. Then, if the children were having a bad day or difficult time, she'd let the children look at it. At the end of the year, she gave it to the children to bring home and show to their parents. I think this was good to see because it was good momentum for the children and a reminder of what they're capable of.
[MY NOTE IN MARGIN: How lovely! This reminds me of the way they collect work in Reggio Emilia. This book might interest you; I have it in my office. *The Diary of Laura* by Caroline Edwards and Carlina Rinaldi]

6. *Identify a teacher whom you admire. What do you admire about them?*

I admire my literature teacher from last semester, Kathryn Will, because she was incredibly energetic about what she was teaching and I could tell she enjoyed teaching it to us. She was also very easy to talk to in the sense that she made you feel like you were her equal. At the end of the year, she read us a passage and showed how much she believed in us. I admire her genuine compassion for her students and their success.
[MY NOTE IN MARGIN: That's lovely. Please tell Dr. Will; it will mean so much to her to know that. What a lovely way to end the semester. A nice thing to do with children as well.]

7. *Are there areas where you're not sure how to implement a value in your teaching?*

I may have difficulty figuring out a way to implement my value of empathy in my students because it can be hard to understand how others are feeling and why they're feeling that way. It's definitely something that comes with age. Empathy is probably something that I would teach to my students in a spur of the moment situation and it's something I would model and not necessarily plan a lesson around.

8. *Is there a time you've experienced a disconnect between your values and your teaching practice?*

I remember seeing a teacher who had her students doing quite a few worksheets, and there was one day they were working on a literacy activity that involved some coloring and the children went up to her when they finished to get her approval to move on and the teacher was a little harsh to the first graders. . . . I am a firm believer in children being imaginative and allowing them to show their creativity.

[MY NOTE IN MARGIN: Someone else shared this as well. Check out this book. I have it in my office and love it. I read it in the intro class. *The Artist Who Painted a Blue Horse* by Eric Carle]

Note the interplay between Katelyn's sense of values and the particular details of practice. Katelyn wants every child to feel welcome and determines that she shouldn't do an activity if not everyone can do it. She treasures healthy relationships and gives an example of a professor who treated her like an equal and was easy to talk with. In contrast, she describes a disconnect when a teacher only gave approval of pictures done in a very particular way. This both seemed "harsh" and went against Katelyn's value of imagination.

PRACTICAL WISDOM: WHY WE DID IT?/VALUES IN ACTION

Integration Between Philosophy and Practice

As teachers begin to identify their ethical core, I showcase a fluid movement between theory and practice—the lines constantly blurred between the two in what philosopher Mikhail Bakhtin refers to as "hybridization."[22] I always begin with an icebreaker like the collaborative block building that carries both practical and symbolic value. By practical, I mean that the activity relates to the content of the course—albeit sometimes in unusual ways—and can be done with children. By symbolic, I mean that the activity when reflected on and remembered can serve as a touchstone to connect back to the ethos of the course.

By orienting ourselves in space as the first way into the classroom, I commit to the students' bodies and the here and now. Locating ourselves as we do first with the meditation helps students be aware of where they are and what they bring and helps them transition from whatever came before. As they notice their physical center, they are primed to consider an ethical center.

The block activity is easy to implement with children, and many teachers enthusiastically report that they try this immediately in their own placements. It also (re)familiarizes them to one of the most important tools in early childhood: unit blocks.[23] It gives us a memory of working together and adding our part, of drawing on different modes of thinking, of experiencing beauty together, and of doing and reflecting. We carry that memory onward and reference it throughout.

As the students move between the block-building activity and their reflection and then my syllabus and core values, I model the movement I hope they will make throughout the term between action and values. In Katelyn's journal, she is asked to move between her values and practices—joining the two and noting places of disconnect. Hearing her do so gives me an entry point to offer feedback when Katelyn says that she values inclusion and therefore will ensure every activity is accessible to all children. I know from experience that in any given class, some children will not have the skills to do activities that others would benefit from. This can make differentiating challenging and frustrating. I therefore suggest utilizing small group work to help Katelyn meet this desire to include.

Attend with Care

This welcome is designed to build caring and collaborative relationships among the students and with me. With block building, I have chosen an activity where students have few preconceived notions of what excellence looks like. They can focus more on paying attention to what their peers have done and worry less about whether they did well. Noticing each other's work and then adding their own block helps them pay close attention and build on their peers' work from the very beginning.

The interview also builds connections. Students choose their partners so they can work with someone they feel comfortable with. Students report that interviews help them feel more connected with the person they speak with. Again, with oral interviews transcribed into journals, performance pressure is low. As one student writes out their peer's comments in the journal, there is no right answer. The activity is simply done.

Build from the Learner

A semester is a short amount of time, with each week packed with readings and activities. Ethics is rarely part of the official curriculum—neither what I must cover for accreditation nor what the students feel they've signed up for. In schools, there is even less time for professional development. Ethics is rarely the focus, with meetings typically about logistics such as a new dismissal policy or learning a new curriculum.[24]

As an elementary school teacher, I learned that if I wanted to follow a thematic curriculum outside the bounds of reading, writing, and math, it helped to start immediately and plant small seeds every day. This is how I approach teaching ethics. In fact, from the first activity in our class to the final assignment in which I ask students what they will take away from our time together, ethics is interwoven.

From the moment students arrange the circular seating together to their first assignment (the values journal), students are building the capacity to inquire collaboratively. As they discuss values in an activity together and hear me explain my own thinking, they are introduced to a way of thinking. Some will already have fluency with this kind of talk. Many describe it as brand-new. In placing blocks on the structure, one student will scaffold for another what can be done with this material. In the interviews, ideas are also built and grown. For some, reflecting on values, even this early in the semester, will be intuitive; others will need to draw heavily on their peers' thinking to articulate their own thinking.

An important part of Lev Vygotsky's schema about scaffolding is that it is relational.[25] It is important to consider not only when a student is ready for a particular piece of information but also when they are ready to hear it from the teacher. As Katelyn was a student I had taught before and Sasha was one of my advisees, I dove right in with suggestions of strategies and resources. In doing so, I focused on both items that were complementary to what Katelyn was saying, such as suggesting the picture book, and ideas that might push her thinking further along a path I saw her traveling, such as my comments about group work. Finally, by listing suggestions as offerings and not requirements, teachers get to choose their own adventure, so to speak. They decide when they are ready for something and what they are hoping to pursue.

Experiential Learning

Building community by doing something proves powerful and memorable for the students. As they place the blocks and call on each other, students report feeling connected with each other. In fact, one student commented at the end of the semester that they entered class as strangers and, as they placed the blocks, they came to know each other as peers. The interview process helps them feel the power of thinking together—not just being told it's a value.

Interruption and Disruption

The beginning of a class tends to be jarring. Students must locate literally in space—finding their seats and those with whom they will sit. I've been surprised that students will sit together every day in one class and sit with an entirely different group in another. In one class, they will sit right up close to me; in another, at the back. Students must locate themselves within a teacher's approach. They must locate themselves within the social dynamics of a class. Personalities sometimes change from one group to the other.

As defined in the Introduction, aporia is the stunned or disoriented feeling that occurs when one's way of thinking or knowing is disrupted. It is important for growth, but it can also turn learners away. I avoid significant challenges and moments of intense aporia in the first weeks. We work with blocks and collaborative stories and interviews because this is work that everyone can do. I choose activities where there is no obvious measure of success and therefore little performance anxiety. Just as I wait with students before giving critical feedback, I start the semester by building a sense of trust and comfort before any attempts at significant interruption and disruption. That said, the constant pausing in class to reflect can be felt as an interruption and disruption. The movement is literally stopped as we step back to look at what we've done.

Further, by working with blocks on the first day of a literacy class, I seek a gentle interruption. In a literacy class, students are surprised by this material because it doesn't fit with most preconceived notions of what literacy is. This helps us build a more expansive view of literacy as involving multiple modalities.[26] It also encourages students to think outside the box of phonics to consider literacy skills such as fine motor control and habits of mind such as the capacity to revise that can be developed with materials such as blocks.[27]

EQUITY AND BAND-AIDS

The semester following the Theories course, Sasha did an independent study alongside student teaching in which we wrote letters back and forth. Many of our letters were about her growing capacity to listen and be responsive to individual students in the moment. For example, in one of our last letters, she described a child acting up in a meeting and ignoring her gentle redirection. Speaking to him after the meeting, she learned that he was upset about something, and she was relieved that she had not punished him but listened. Continuing a theme addressed in Katelyn's interview, Sasha also grappled with equity as she developed confidence that what was right for one child wasn't always right for another. After sharing her difficulty finding time to work with everyone, I commented:

> Not everyone needs us always and in the same ways. [Sasha had highlighted this phrase.] It might help to think about equity here: what does everyone actually need to make sure they can do their best. One kid might need 15 minutes of your time. Another might simply need, "I notice you were counting by moving the pieces along. This is a great strategy." Just keep note of whom you spent a long time with and make sure on another day or another period you spend a long time with others.
> [SASHA'S NOTE TO ME IN MARGIN: This is very true. I don't think about it like this, but I am glad you brought it to my attention.]

A few years after graduation, Sasha participated in an inquiry group that my colleague, Kathryn Will, and I hosted for alumni. Participants were asked to share a community-building activity they liked using in their classroom. Before sharing her story, Sasha explained that the activity had come from someone else. She said that while she worked to give each student what they seemed to need, at the start of the year, her fourth-grade students were bickering regularly—jealous when one student got something different from another. Sasha described sitting them all down in a circle and telling a story about getting a scrape and needing a Band-Aid. She then asked each student to share a time when they had been hurt. After each story, she commented, "I'm sorry that happened. Here is a Band-Aid." The students quickly protested; none needed a Band-Aid for their particular hurt. Sasha then explained the value of giving people what they need as opposed to giving everyone the same thing. She and the students connected this back to the bickering and jealousies in class. Smiling, Sasha told the inquiry group that for the rest of the year, students were far more tolerant of each other's needs and constantly referencing the Band-Aid story. She then closed her story by saying, "Hmm, we haven't done this yet with my new class, and it might be time."

It is often said that new teachers let go of values they accumulate in teacher education classes as soon as they face resistance in the field.[28] Sasha and the other teachers featured in this book offer a very different story. Equity was important for Sasha—something she worked through first in class and later in student teaching. This commitment was challenged in the field as a new teacher when her students behaved jealously. Sasha, though, did not give up on equity but looked for a way to help her students understand why it mattered. Drawing from her ethical center, when she heard her colleague share this activity, she knew it was just right for what she wanted to accomplish. When Sasha told her Band-Aid story, it resonated with other teachers who similarly were committed to equity, and Sasha likely inspired some to return to their own placements and adapt the activity.

I close by drawing attention to the word *equity* and how it proved useful. In the Introduction, I define this word and explain how an understanding of it helped me redefine where and how my students sat. I drew on this understanding of equity when suggesting to Katelyn (and indirectly Sasha) that Katelyn can be inclusive by offering different entry points with small group work. In my feedback to Sasha during student teaching, I defined equity to think through what fairness could be in her classroom. She then drew on this commitment to equity as a classroom teacher. How might teachers develop this capacity to interrogate values and words with the attention of a philosopher?

Additionally, in this chapter, I have argued that teachers bring specific and core values to their teaching. Many of these values are right at the surface, emerging with a little reflection. Having a chance to reflect can help the teacher better determine their purpose. Other times, the underlying ethos is less transparent. In the chapters that follow, we will interrogate further, building on what is apparent at the surface and interrogating that which is hidden or more subtle.

Finally, and before moving on, in beginning with a direct articulation of my own commitments, I model and encourage teachers to be up-front with their ethos.[29] Teacher beliefs guide their work and live in their actions regardless of acknowledgment.[30] When unnamed and unacknowledged, a teacher's values tend to pervade and dominate as a norm—felt but hard to reinforce or challenge. Committing to human dignity and honoring the gifts and responsibilities one brings to a community are at the core of my teaching.

YOU DO

What does it look like to create with others? How does it feel to introduce yourself through materials?

- Get a collection of blocks, Legos, or recycled materials, or go outside and gather natural items like sticks, rocks, and leaves.
- Have each person select an item to introduce themselves.
- One by one have people place their item in a shared structure and share why they chose what they chose.
- How did the item influence your thinking? What did you learn about yourself and others? About community?

Who are you as a teacher? What do you value?

- Interview another educator using the values interview.
- What did you learn about yourself? Your peer?
- How might this inform your teaching tomorrow?

PART 2

STUDYING PHILOSOPHY
AND EDUCATION

CHAPTER TWO

ROOT TO RISE: HOW I CAME TO BE

*I would say that my biggest two [values] were welcoming and safe en-
vironment as well as respect and kindness. I grew up . . . I don't know
if the term bullied is exactly right because I know that has a very strict
definition. But I grew up being made fun of myself due to my weight.
And I remember thinking when I did finally decide . . . finally, I mean,
I was in second grade, when I decided I wanted to be a teacher myself,
I knew that I wanted all students to feel welcome and safe. I'm not
saying that all students have to be best friends. But we definitely need
to treat others with kindness.*

—Jessie, fourth-grade teacher

The fall that I taught Theories, I was returning after having
my first baby. Each Saturday, I pulled myself from my baby,
my work, and my domestic chores to go to yoga class. Prior to
pregnancy, yoga had been a steady part of my life. I had begun
my pregnancy with a prenatal class and then continued with a
postnatal class that was set up to support women with pregnancy,

delivery, and then postdelivery healing. I then graduated (in my mind) to regular yoga classes.

One repeated practice and phrase particularly struck me: "root to rise."[1] Every class included balance poses in which one started with two feet firmly engaging with the ground. Guided to attend to how my feet felt on the mat, the sturdiness of my legs, and a focus point in the room, I would then slowly raise a leg and then my arms. When I paid attention and felt firmly rooted, I could balance quite well. If I rushed and pulled up my leg without awareness of my body in its surroundings, I would tip. Further, the more I did these poses, the quicker I could balance, and eventually, I could even balance with less conscious attention.

I also found myself slowly reawakening parts of my body that had been inaccessible during pregnancy, such as my stomach muscles. Grounding in what my body previously knew helped me access wider movement. I was pleased to find that post-pregnancy, much of what I could do before having a child remained accessible after a few classes and that the experience of having a child opened new vistas. Most powerfully, I often found myself momentarily restricted by what my son could do at that juncture. I'd think, for example, how could I roll given how he might roll? Then I'd remember I wasn't limited to his developmental capacity. I was now interconnected with another's body in ways I had never been, and that changed me.

Much of yoga focuses around one's core muscles in the abdomen from which strength and movement stem. Core exercises and routines are key. If you study with the same teacher, then typically each week you follow the same routines with small changes that pose new and interesting physical and mental challenges. From that core, you see areas to grow and find the strength to do so.

Returning to the classroom to teach the Theories course, the refrain "root to rise" followed me as I found myself relying on old fluencies, rooting, discovering shifts, and finding areas where I now had to let go. Again, much of my core remained intact and helped me grow. Yet so much was different. Drawing on where I came from and who I was, I grew in the midst of new disequilibrium. As the class and I studied ideas together, the phrase "root to rise" echoed in my head. I thought constantly about how we root in our sense of self, and from that place we can handle disequilibrium and then rise to new challenges and ways of knowing.[2]

Another story about the core and roots. The summer after I started coursework for my master's degree in elementary education and before student teaching, I took a guided tour to Germany and Poland to Holocaust-related sites such as concentration camps and cities like Krakow and Berlin. Our interfaith and intercultural group of young adults and guides hailed from the United States, Germany, and Poland and consisted of people who had a personal connection with the Holocaust. We spent the week engaging in exercises where we shared our connections together, participating in facilitated discussions, visiting sites in order to reflect on our own family history as it intersected with the Second World War, and considering the most peaceable and just ways forward.[3]

Poet and essayist Richard Hugo helped me work through my experience and student teaching.[4] In a response paper written at the time, I wrote:

> Now back in New York, every road I turn down leads me to the Holocaust. My student, Tanisha, insists on showing me, again and again, a picture of Martin Luther King Jr., saying, "See that, that Martin Luther King Jr. He dead,"[5] and I write about this in my student teaching journal and find it's a poem about the Holocaust. In class, I'm asked to make a clay figure to represent why I teach.

Describing my figure, I explain, "It's all about agency. I teach so my student will be the kind of person who hears, looks, listens, speaks up, acts." I teach to prevent genocide and cruelty. I'm obsessed, and it's embarrassing. And yet it feels organic.

As Hugo says, a good poem is not started to be about something but "what the poem is saying, just begins to show at the end but is nonetheless evident" (Hugo, 9). At the end of a thought, I find myself at the Holocaust, and because it was not forced, it seems to be the only conclusion.

And yet I didn't fully and accurately represent the situation with Tanisha. I started to write about her and found it was about the Holocaust, and then, in finding it was about the Holocaust, as I indicated at the end of the poem, I found, hours later, that suddenly I better understood what she, Tanisha, was actually saying and the final poem became about her. Owning my obsession seemed to allow me to somewhat, at least momentarily, see past it.

All of this has informed my teaching. Immersion can be useful but also stifling. Therefore, while all ideas and acts may, for me, be linked to one idea, I don't need to constantly tell this to my students. This may overload them and prevent them from finding their own compulsions. I also need to be careful not to read my obsessions onto my students. Tanisha was not speaking about the Holocaust when she mentioned Martin Luther King Jr., and she might not view her dead as I view mine. It's important that I respect this. On the other hand, letting students fixate, as I eventually let Tanisha, may help them as well. Tanisha will see death until she stops seeing it, not when I tell her to change the subject. Therefore, allowing her to obsess in different mediums may help her to see something differently (as I did) and is healthier than repression.

Asked where their values came from, teachers in my interviews referenced a range of influences including field experiences, courses and professors, and thinkers and approaches to learning. In this chapter, I begin with one of the most salient origins of ethics in the interviews—teachers like Jessie quoted in the epigraph, and like me in my response paper, attributed values to personal experiences.[6]

Social justice activist and professor of education Denise Taliaferro Baszile writes, "Self-love blossoms out of a willful self-knowing or a journey that always underscores the fact that we teach–in a classroom or a community center or a book–who we are and who we are always becoming."[7] I build on Baszile's insights to argue that identifying who we are and how we want to be is a "journey" and an "always becoming." Self is fluid and constructed in relation with our surroundings.[8] For example, who I was and how I ethically oriented on my trip was an engagement with, to name just a few interlocutors, the grassy spaces of Berlin where Jewish residences used to be, fellow travelers, ancestors, and the trees of Auschwitz.[9] Similarly active in the conversation with Tanisha were the four walls of the classroom that pressured me to stay on task, my ancestors, my projections of Tanisha's history, the book in front of us, and of course everyone Tanisha was talking with.[10]

Brain researchers argue that we teach the way we have learned.[11] Somatic and antiracist counselor Resmaa Menakem extends this beyond firsthand experiences. Who we are and how we perceive and function ethically are rooted in experiences from our own lifetimes and our ancestors.[12] Menakem emphasizes that many communities, particularly communities of color or those whose experiences are not represented as part of a society's norm, are in touch with the ways in which their commitments are framed by their experiences. People whose lived experience closest corresponds with what a culture presents as normal are often oblivious to the effect of that experience on their commitments.[13] As philosopher Mary Midgley wrote, nearly all Western male philosophers were single men, and according to Midgely, this factor is generally not acknowledged as relevant. That said, Midgley assures the reader that the single male positionality influenced the kind of philosophy they wrote and the kind of philosophy many of us in the West are influenced by.[14]

Baszile writes specifically "toward a pedagogy of Black self-love." Grounding in self and asserting that philosophy stems from experience is political work in a context where normative conceptions of the person dominate and the experiences of those who are not white or male tend to be excluded as philosophical fodder.[15] Attention to the person who teaches and one's orientation toward the world pushes away assumptions about normative perspectives that are oppressive and, as Baszile stresses, silence and harm Black women.[16] The long-term collective of Black women, the Combahee River Collective, delineated the contours of contemporary Black feminism and emphasized that Black women in the United States are dually the target of racism and sexism, making them as a class especially vulnerable to injustice. The Collective writes, "We might use our position at the bottom, however, to make a clear leap into revolutionary action. If Black women were free, it would mean everyone else would have to be free since our freedom would necessitate the destruction of all the systems of oppression."[17] In drawing heavily from an ethics developed by Black women, as a white woman, I join first as an attentive listener (as discussed in chapter 5) in order to think with Black women without appropriating. In doing so, I support pedagogy in ethics rooted in experience to call for ways of knowing and acting that root out oppression.

According to Hugo, "most poets write the same poem over and over," and you write from what is "always in your hometown."[18] A keystone is a rock in an arch formation that helps two sides balance on each other. When Tanisha redirects an optimistic picture book focused on interracial comradery to talk about King's death, I hear her redirection through my own family trauma. The Holocaust and my commitment to teach for a better world were at the core of my desire to teach and permeated countless daily interactions.

So central and abiding, Jessie notes that she "finally" decided in second grade to ensure that other children didn't experience the pain she did. Other teachers are motivated by experiences such as a close encounter with a school shooting (rare), traumatic safety drills or preventive lockdowns related to school shootings (common), childhood illness, loss of a parent, an early encounter with racism, divorce, and community loss like the closing of a factory in a town that is dependent on it.[19]

These are all painful experiences, and often but not always hardships prove transformative. In contrast, philosopher, educator, and activist Paulo Freire describes watching a teacher grading:

> When my turn came, I noticed he was looking over my text with great attention, nodding his head in an attitude of respect and consideration. His respectful and appreciative attitude had a much greater effect on me than the high classification that he gave me for my work. The gesture of the teacher affirmed in me a self-confidence that obviously still had room to grow. But it inspired in me a belief that I too had value and could work and produce results—results that clearly had their limits but that were a demonstration of my capacity, which up until that moment I would have been inclined to hide or not fully believe in. And the greatest proof of the importance of that gesture is that I can speak of it now as if it had happened only today.[20]

A positive experience can also be a transformative keystone. Further, the transformative memory need not be by external standards a major event. It can be a simple, one-time interaction.[21] Again, as with my experience and Jessie's, Freire emphasizes that his teacher's attention was so powerful that he replays the moment and feels "as if it had happened only today."

Of note, and discussed more in this chapter and chapter 7, the purpose of exploring keystone experiences is to help the teacher reflect on what has shaped them and welcome their experiences.[22]

It is not to exploit particular life events or require sharing they may find uncomfortable. It is also not my role as teacher to name the experiences that shape.

Further, having an experience is not the same as developing an ethos. How does experience move to ethics? bell hooks explains, "To me, this theory emerges from the concrete, from my efforts to make sense of everyday life experiences, from my efforts to intervene critically in my life and the lives of others. This is to me what makes feminist transformation possible. Personal testimony, personal experience, is such fertile ground for the production of liberatory feminist theory because it usually forms the base of our theory making."[23] When I reflected about my interaction with Tanisha that night in my journal and over the course of the year in papers, I interwove her comments with my narrative and heard an important and pressing story about racial cruelty and Black lives being cut short.[24] Whether Tanisha intended this message, I cannot say. What I do know is that Tanisha's comments pushed away the picture book's account of racial solidarity and focused the other students gathered around Tanisha and me on King's death. The conversation with Tanisha pushed me going forward to be increasingly alert to systemic cruelty and attacks on Black bodies and to listen better and more proactively to address this cruelty.[25] This experience with Tanisha reconfirmed a commitment to listening to children even when, especially when, their actions surprised and baffled me.[26] I also recommitted to interrupting my own agenda to listen to children in the moment and have conversations that felt "hard" because they are seen as taboo or emotionally heavy.[27] Finally, this experience reinforced my commitment to teacher education and ethical development that recognize that experience is foundational.[28] As hooks emphasizes, grounded in experience, my philosophy grew.

A wise yoga instructor knows that particular moves support grounding such as being aware of where one's body touches surfaces, balance, and a still spot on which to rest one's eyes. Recognizing where we move from is important as we work to keep our values in alignment with our actions. It also helps us consider the strengths and limitations of our orientations as we trouble what might be taken for granted. Naming where my orientation came from and how I read Tanisha's situation helped me see where her own story and orientation might be different from mine. Naming and orienting helped me grow forward and destabilize in important ways.

The hometowns in Hugo's phrasing that orient us are not always apparent, even to ourselves. In fact, they tend to be obscured for others and even ourselves when not identified and reflected on. With this in mind, I have named these pivotal experiences as a "secret curriculum" that tends to drive students regardless of whether they are reflected on.[29] The exercises in this chapter center on locating oneself and, in doing so, finding one's secret curriculum to move in intentional and sometimes new ways.

WHAT WE DID

Root to Rise

Let's begin with a meditation offered by my friend and colleague, teacher educator and yoga instructor Kathryn Will:

- Stand, if you are able, with both bare feet placed firmly on the ground, allowing your arms to rest by your sides.
- Bring your attention to your feet. Feel the ground. Notice where you feel the connections between your feet and the ground.
- Shift your weight forward toward your toes, perhaps barely lifting your heels off the ground. Shift your weight backward, lifting your toes and the front of the ball of your foot

off the ground. Come back to center. Gently shift your weight to the outer blades of your feet. Gently shift your weight to the inner arches of your feet. Come back to center. Starting with your right foot, lift your toes up and spread them wide as you place them back to the ground. Then repeat with your left foot, lifting up your toes and spreading them wide as you place them on the ground.

- Notice your surroundings. What sensations do you experience? How does the air feel on your skin? Take a breath in and out.

- Find a place to fix your gaze. It is helpful to look at something that will remain still. Take a breath in and out.

- Press down into your feet, lifting your arms out and up over your head as you take a breath in. As you exhale, return your arms to your side, allowing them to relax.

- Engage your core, pulling your belly button back to your spine. Holding this engagement, press down into your feet, lifting your arms out and up over your head as you take a breath in. As you exhale, return your arms to your side, allowing them to relax.

- Shift your weight into your right foot, engage all the muscles in your right leg, and inhale as you bend and lift your left leg. Exhale and return your leg to the ground. Repeat on your left side.

- Engage your core, pulling your belly button back to your spine. Holding this engagement, press down into your feet, lifting your arms out and up over your head as you take a breath in. As you exhale, return your arms to your side, allowing them to relax.

- Refocus your gaze.

- Shift your weight into your right foot, engage all the muscles in your right leg, and inhale as you bend and lift your left leg, lifting your arms out and up over your head. Exhale and return your leg to the ground and your arms to your side. Repeat on your left side.

- Take a moment to press both feet into the ground, shifting your weight forward and back, lifting the toes of both feet and setting them down as wide as possible. Come to a place of stillness with your arms by your side, and take a deep breath in, raising your arms out and up over your head and exhaling them down by your side.
- Take a moment and notice the sensations and your surroundings.

ORIGINS AND OFFERINGS

In *Jumping Mouse: A Native American Legend of Friendship and Sacrifice*, Misty Schroe retells the Nipmuc origin story of the powerful soaring eagle.[30] A mouse has "a dream to go to the High Places" and is helped and helps along the way. Her name, Jumping Mouse, comes from the first gift she receives from Grandfather Frog, the capacity to jump. When Jumping Mouse helps a buffalo by giving sight, she finds that "the world had gone dark all around her, as if twilight had fallen on a moonless night." The buffalo then helps Jumping Mouse on her journey. Jumping Mouse gives up her sight unknowingly, but going forward, she offers her gifts repeatedly with awareness that loss will accompany care and gain. Sacrifice and balance are woven into this vision of reciprocity.

As described in chapter 1, I prime students for thinking about origin and identity with picture books. To consider oneself always in relation to others, after grounding in one's own body, students turn to the accounts of others. "How the world came to be" is a phrase I use to describe folktales like *Jumping Mouse* and contemporary tales written like folktales that give an account of how something in nature came to be the way it is (see appendix and https://www.carafurman.com/ for a collection).

Literacy professors Stephanie Jones and Lane W. Clarke argue that students should identify both connections and disconnections as they read.[31] Literacy professor Elizabeth Dutro emphasizes that the themes and emotions of a story can resonate even when the precise experiences are different.[32] To encourage students to think about their relationship to a text and its message, I provide sticky notes alongside the books and ask students to leave their reflections in the books themselves—helping build community as students read each other's responses. Readers can sign their comments or leave them unsigned as the goal is to consider perspective, not reveal biographical details.

Offering a similar orientation, my colleague and educator Virginia Dearani recently laid out a collection of texts she described as books about home for a workshop with in-service teachers. She asked teachers to read the texts they were drawn to and then choose one that resonated with their sense of home and to speak to that experience. In doing so with prompts from Dearani, teachers were stretched to think about the key factors that made something feel like home.

Wanting students to feel their way into community immediately, on the second day of class, I typically read *The Seven Chinese Sisters* because it offers a more familiar and straightforward message on gifts where one offers without losing anything.[33] *The Seven Chinese Sisters* mimics the arc of a folktale, in this case offering the origin story of Seventh Sister. The premise is that there are "seven Chinese sisters who lived together and took care of each other" and had much in common with "shining black hair and sparkling eyes. Each stood straight and tall except for Seventh Sister, who was just a baby." The sisters each have a special talent ranging from being able to "count—to five hundred and beyond" to being able to "catch any ball, no matter how fast and high it was thrown." No one though knows the talents of Seventh Sister as "she was so little she had never spoken even one word."

The plot centers around a dragon kidnapping Seventh Sister. Each sister uses her special talents in sometimes surprising and comical ways to work together so the baby can escape. In the process, the sisters learn the dragon is not so mean but simply hungry. The story hinges on Seventh Sister establishing her voice, first shouting "help" so her sisters can find her and then "no" when the dragon threatens to eat her, and satisfyingly, the book ends with a grown Seventh sister reading to children and the lines "And what did Seventh Sister do when she grew tall? / She became the best storyteller in the world, and she always told this story first."

Analyzing the text with methods offered in chapter 3, students quickly name messages they resonate with—collaboration, caring, personal empowerment, everyone deserves a chance. I then introduce the following exercise:

- Remember those special offerings you shared last class. Please pull those out.
- Okay, I want you to work with new people. Count off by four.
- So here's the task . . . You are the sisters from the story (or siblings or friends). The dragon has just stolen the baby! [Turn to the page in the book.]
- It is your job to finish the book with your own story.
- But here's the catch . . . You must use the talent you identified last class to work together.
- You can illustrate. You can write it as a story or play (and act it out). You can all write each part together or take on

different roles. You can work anywhere you are comfortable in this room, in the building, or outside as long as you return on time.

- Here are the boundaries. You must:
  - use the preidentified talents
  - work together
  - share the story with the class
- You have thirty minutes to work! As a teacher, you will need to sometimes create things for kids fast. Now go!

The writing is joyful. Full of giggles and often some sass. At the end, the readings are joyful too as students take pleasure in the creative way classmates integrated talents ranging from singing to listening to mediating to lacrosse and the similarities and differences in how the stories resolve.

WHERE I'M FROM

The next move is to reflect more directly on origins in relation to the present. On the first day of my graduate course on literacy, professor Stephanie Jones shared George Ella Lyon's "Where I'm From" poem and asked us to write our own in class.[34] Later, I was given the same assignment as professional development at the school where I taught. We then put up our written and illustrated poems in the hallway toward the front of the school. Since then, this activity has had a place in most of my courses. In an introduction to education course, students create the poem and illustrate it to introduce themselves to the class and to consider their origins for becoming teachers. In a families and communities class, they reflect more specifically on family and origin community. In literacy and math methods courses, I tweak the prompt (see later) to highlight who the person is within the discipline.

Stories go beyond the facts. They are framed, and in framing, an ethical orientation is revealed. Teacher inquirer Julie Fournier writes:

> Last year a study group in Phoenix read together the book, *The Truth about Stories* by Thomas King (2005). King, a Native American writer and storyteller asserts that we not only are defined by the stories we tell, but we in actuality *are* the stories we tell. I have come to believe this is true. With this in mind, I do not want to tell the story of loss and the outrage I feel for the politicians who have envisioned the profession of teaching and stolen away from children the kind of learning that fosters independent thought and decision making.
>
> This is not who I want to be.
> This is not who I want teachers to be.[35]

When I wrote my poem in my literacy class, I knew it would not be shared. When I wrote for the school, it was public, a way of communicating with children and families. The facts of my life stayed the same, and both poems were factually accurate, but I wrote very different poems.

Prior to asking teachers to write their poems, I directly instruct them to be aware of their audience and intentional about what *they* want to communicate. *You are introducing yourself to all of us. This is public. Whom do you want to be with us? You don't necessarily know us, so what do you feel secure sharing? Are there things you want only me, your professor, to know? Are there things your classmates should know but you'd rather not share with me?* A benefit of the medium of poetry is that through it one can be opaque.

The picture book *Windows* offers a useful way in.[36] A child strolls his city at dusk, peeking into windows. One full-page illustration offers an apartment building with different activities visible beyond each window frame. A window gives you a narrowed glimpse into a world. It is just a tiny frame, and you get some choice over what you present outward.

hooks writes, "It is often productive if professors take the first risk, linking confessional narratives to academic discourse so as to show how an experience can illuminate and enhance our understanding of academic material. But most professors must practice being vulnerable in the classroom, being wholly present in mind, body, and spirit."[37] Dutro argues that testimony begets testimony.[38] When we ask students to share, we do not demand their stories; instead, we offer our own. I move from the phrase "confessional narratives," a shift in keeping with hooks's contention that in sharing the goal is not absolution nor should a teacher be an authority demanding private stories. The purpose is also not to trick or entice students into revelation—in fact, I discourage this directly. Instead, we offer and in offering create a space in which, as hooks says, we can be "present in mind, body, and spirit." This, in turn, gives experiences that can be analyzed to "illuminate and enhance" our ethos.

In chapter 1, I argued that one must introduce oneself to students, to welcome them into the particular universe that they will be living in in one's class, and I did so largely by directly articulating the values I brought to the space. Here, I add another layer of introduction in which narratives and academic discourse go alongside each other—enhancing one's capacity to know and communicate what one brings.

My Offering (excerpted [See website for full samples])

Where I'm From as a Literacy Learner

I'm from memorizing Shakespeare sonnets at seven
for a penny from Grandpa.

bedtime books every night
dictating the play with Karen
scripting novellas with my dollhouse and barbies
crafting stories with my pencil and worlds with old boxes.
I'm from my mom's home daycare.
My house was a school
and schools always feel like home.

My account is personal and specific. I reference my family, but I don't share anything particularly intimate, and nothing deeply upsetting is apparent from this account. I keep it light and give my students space to keep it light. Some do. Many don't.

The Prompt

Letter 2

Where I'm From as a Literacy Learner

This week you have a two-part assignment! First you will write a poem in the same document you started in response to the following prompt. Then you will answer a few "process questions."

Modeled after the poems here[39] and also here,[40] create a written description of where you are from in terms of literacy.

❑ Include elements of personal history (could include experiences in school and at home)
❑ Include traits about yourself as a literacy learner
❑ You may use symbols and opaque references. I do not need to understand everything you have come up with.
❑ You may use images.
❑ Be prepared to share with your classmates. Bring a hard copy.

Process Questions

A. Tell us about your response to writing a poem. What was your initial reaction? Did this change?
B. What was your response to being told that you had to write in response to a particular poem?
C. How did you feel about sharing your work?
D. You were given a few "models." How did these influence you?

Student Sample: Preservice early childhood educator in a B–5 literacy class, Mattilda Rice (excerpted):

Where I'm From as a Literacy Learner

I am from the myths that lie under the stars of Flagstaff lake
Stories that read about a moon and a cow and mittens and kittens
I am from the land of my pop—who taught me faith in every way
Rock walls and gardens bound with fairytales my sister and I raised
I am from the narrative of my parents' stories
They always start with "back in the day . . ."
I am from the sound of my grampy's tender hands on a keyboard
Little black duck and a black bear in the front lawn watch me
    twirl about

Philosopher María Lugones uses the metaphor of the pilgrimage to argue that we listen carefully to other people's stories and ways of telling and in doing so travel to their worlds. With the language of pilgrims, this is hard, holy, and necessary work. To share their poems, students bring a paper copy to class for "a museum walk." Each poem is placed on the table, and students take about ten minutes to wander and read. Again, the focus is not on autobiography—there is too much information to take in, and the names are not always on the paper or easy to find. Instead, we first attend to the window offered and later will draw themes.

After reviewing the class set, students sit with a partner and trade poems to attend to one other person. They make a list of ten positive noticings about that person's work, one piece of warm praise, and a question they have about the person or their writing based on what they noticed. I circulate and chime in support when generating lists is slow going. After reading and noticing, students read what their partner saw and discuss.

hooks stresses that personal stories alone are not theory making.[41] After reading the collection and then closely attending to one person's story, students identify themes and outliers. For example, classes notice the frequency of reading with grandparents and older siblings and the embarrassment of being pulled out for extra help or because someone was identified as gifted. They speak of pressure to perform. They share authors who drew them in and some who repelled. They share where they read from in terms of both place and culture. For example, they mention hailing from farming, fishing, and urban communities. They note languages they grew up with. They speak to whether they felt safe and secure. This, though, isn't yet ethics either. But it moves us closer.

Ethics happens when we then reflect again—what might these experiences tell us about how we named our values in the first class? Might a commitment to inclusion stem from the felt sense that being separated is hurtful? Do we prioritize welcoming the whole body to class because we ourselves were uncomfortable when reading? *What*, I ask, *does this collection of poems have to tell us about who we might be as a group? What do your experiences have to do with what you value now and what commitments you want to bring to the classroom?* A common theme reflected in Mattilda's piece is the importance of relationships with particular trusted adults. The embarrassment of being separated from one's class as either gifted or needing extra help often leads to a commitment to more inclusive classrooms.

Prompted to name her core values in her portfolio at the end of the semester (an assignment I share in chapter 8), undergraduate elementary education major Abby Lash writes:

> I feel as though one of my values about teaching literacy consists of thinking about yourself as a writer/reader and how you have grown to be where you are today. The "Where I'm From" poem we read in class really made me think about how literacy is not just about the general reading and writing, it is about noticing yourself as well. I think seeing yourself as both a writer and reader is very beneficial in creating content that is not as scripted, but it has meaning because you are thinking about yourself while completing the task at hand.

PRACTICAL WISDOM:
WHY WE DID IT?/VALUES IN ACTION

Integration Between Philosophy and Practice

Our stories shape our values, and, likewise, our values shape our stories. hooks writes, "When our lived experience of theorizing is fundamentally linked to the process of self-recovery, of collective liberation, no gap exists between theory and practice. Indeed, what such experience makes evident is the bond between the two—that ultimately reciprocal process wherein one enables the other."[42] As students introduce themselves and enter the conversation of the course by way of their experiences and then use those experiences to reflect on the values they bring, they wed philosophy and practice.

Attend with Care

In chapter 1, I commit to creating a community where students feel seen and heard by each other and by me. Describing an assignment where students write and read aloud a paragraph, hooks writes, "Just the physical experience of hearing, of listening intently, to each particular voice strengthens our capacity to learn together. Even though a student may not speak again after this moment, that student's participation has been acknowledged."[43] The "Where I'm From" poem helps students name and recognize what they want to bring to a class in a public and affirming way. Having students go around the room and read each other's work and then provide warm feedback to one person makes the process affirming.

Another layer of care is being direct with students that they shape their stories and choose what is framed in the window. Students are often pressured to reveal personal details about themselves, a topic I take up more in chapter 7.[44] Revelation when trust is present and the person wants to share can be meaningful. Without trust and will, this vulnerability can be a violation.[45]

Build from the Learner

The structure of the "Where I'm From" poem helps students share before trust is built. The repeated refrain of "I'm from" yields work that students are proud of. As such, the assignment serves as a powerful start to a literacy semester—proving from day one that everyone can write.[46] Because they are proud of the writing, they feel more comfortable sharing their ideas.

We benefit from locating where our feet touch the ground when seeking balance. Planting ourselves in a new situation, we benefit from reflection on origins. "How the world came to be" books facilitate a soft entry as teachers consider origins from the fictional distance of myth. Placing the myths in class alongside texts that focus on racism such as *Born on the Water* links the general commitment to attending to origins to antiracist work.[47] The myths and mythical sounding language offer some distance that initiate conversations with less judgment and less self- and peer silencing (see chapter 6). That said, it must be stated directly that tracing racism in the United States covers factually accurate terrain.

Experiential Learning

As in chapter 1, we begin in our body and feel our way into awareness of where we are from and how we might shift and rise with balance. According to John Dewey, an experience is something that one has undergone or done and then reflected on.[48] To be intentional and, in that intentionality, to sometimes grow and change, we must dually do/undergo and reflect. Simply doing is not enough just as, according to hooks, telling one's story is not the same as theory making.[49] Applied to ethics, our conduct is a product of this doing and undergoing with shifts occurring primarily when we reflect.[50]

Moving from experience to ethics demands pulling themes and connections from the experiences that lead to one's philosophy. In chapter 1, I stated that an inclusive community where everyone brings their offerings is a core value. Through the "save the baby" activity, students get to feel being in community in a low-stakes way as they work together on a silly and fun project.

Crafting a narrative about their experiences with the "Where I'm From" poems and then analyzing the poems as a class, students are taking something that has happened and adding a layer of reflection. Reflecting upon what they notice after they share these experiences with others, they also learn more about themselves through similarities and contrast.

Interruption and Disruption

In reflecting on the balance meditation, awareness of oneself in space (practiced also in chapter 1) supports one's capacity to move to new and even uncertain ground. Many teachers have spent a lot of time thinking about themselves and their personal histories in relation to ethics. For others, this form of thinking may feel deeply unnatural and hard to access, and some teachers may even be skeptical.[51]

Attending to origins to grow can lead to disequilibrium. It is often very disorienting for white students to locate themselves in relation to racism and work to grow, sometimes away from their origins.[52] hooks writes:

> As I saw for the first time that there can be, and usually is, some degree of pain involved in giving up old ways of thinking and knowing and learning new approaches. I respect that pain. And I include recognition of it now when I teach, that is to say, I teach about shifting paradigms and talk about the discomfort it can cause. White students learning to think more critically about questions of race and racism may go home for the holidays and suddenly see their parents in a different light. They may recognize nonprogressive thinking, racism, and so on, and it may hurt them that new ways of knowing may create estrangement where there was none. Often when students return from breaks I ask them to share with us how ideas that they have learned or worked on in the classroom impacted on their experience outside. This gives them both the opportunity to know that difficult experiences may be common and practice at integrating theory and practice: ways of knowing with habits of being. We practice interrogating habits of being as well as ideas. Through this process we build community.[53]

I WANT THIS MORE THAN ALL
THE OTHER THINGS

In closing, I turn to third-grade social science and science teacher Anne's account in her interview:

> I think I've always been a person who wants to reflect, and that when I was younger, if I was frustrated with my parents or my

teachers, I held a grudge. I remember distinctly wanting a doll when I was little and my parents just didn't really mind that I wanted it and they were ready to move on. I remember the frustration of being like *I can't express to them that I want this more than all the other things that I've wanted in recent times, and they are brushing it off as the same, but they're not hearing me and they're not seeing this, and I really do want it and I have no power to get it.* And I really stuck that in my head. And then much later, I still think about that. When have I made that same mistake with my students? What am I not seeing that they're trying to indicate that something's important? How can I respond to that in the spaces that I have? So, a lot of it came from my own sense that I had had some injustice against me as a child, and you know, small ones like that, but as I got older, I became interested generally in social justice. And then specifically in college, I felt that I was least informed when it came to racial injustice, compared to what I knew about other categories, not necessarily compared to my peers, but then I put the effort in to really learn about that and see what I could do because I've always valued logic and research and the concept of scientific consensus means something to me. I think that teaching should be research based, and good research.

This chapter began with the articulation of deeply painful experiences that pushed at teacher's awareness of injustice and commitment to kindness. I do not, as noted, push teachers to mine for traumas. This can be inauthentic and even exploitative. Instead, I encourage teachers to simply name the experiences that drive them. Remember, Freire was moved by a simple act of caring attention.

Anne here is moved by a common and, in the grand scheme of cruelty, a lower-stakes example of injustice. Some might not even call it injustice and argue that Anne's parents were placing reasonable boundaries. Yet my purpose is not to judge the experience but instead to highlight that Anne's account of this moment motivated her teaching in important ways and pushed her to listen to children.

In drawing from her experience of injustice, Anne is not drawing equivalencies to racism. Instead, "smaller" injustice pushed her to pay attention and to be open to listening and learning about racial injustice. Reflecting on her experience pushed her to be attentive and caring when faced with the experiences of others.

Anne's conception is made up of a rich coming together of childhood experiences, her clear identification of needing further growth like attention to racial injustice, and, mentioned later in the interview, college courses and her parents' identities as scientists. As noted in my journal entry where I speak with Tanisha, Hugo, my ancestors, and my experience, our ethical origins are complex. This complexity appears again in Mattilda's and my poems in which we ground ourselves in experiences, texts, people, and physical places.

From a broad foundation that includes rooting in one's keystone experiences, teachers can then stretch and grow as they face disequilibrium. Doing so demands regular articulation of one's values, as described in chapter 1, and reflection on the source of those values as discussed in this chapter. As highlighted by Anne, it also involves so much more, and it is to those other sources that we turn in the next chapters.

YOU DO (IDEALLY DONE WITH A SMALL GROUP)

- Read the three "Where I'm From" poems referenced in this chapter.
- Using the refrain, write your own "Where I'm From" poem.

- Share with your group.
- What do you notice individually about the poems?
- What do you notice about the collection?
- Now connect with the values you identified in chapter 1. Where do you see your experiences informing these values?
- Does this reflection affirm and confirm your values? Are there commitments you are beginning to reconsider?

CHAPTER THREE

NO, DAVID! HERMENEUTICS

I have also really enjoyed watching the movies Mary Poppins, Peter Pan, and Inside Out from an educator perspective, and really diving into the values hidden within them.

—Katelyn Beedy, then preservice early
childhood teacher

Setting up the classroom immediately before winter break as a first- and second-grade teacher, I decided to place fairy tales at each table. I didn't have a detailed plan, but I did have a few intentions:

> Noticing that my students are confident discussing language but don't use terms to discuss plot or sustain plots in their own writing, I launch a study of fairy tales. I start the unit with a brief study of "The Three Little Pigs" because I have three versions of the tale in the classroom and I have some vague sense that the same story written in different ways should prove interesting . . . After reading a book from the wolf's point of view, the class seems

inclined to side with the wolf.[1] "Are you sure? . . . There's been so many more books written from the pigs' point of view. Isn't that [perspective therefore] right?" Some say no, some yes. Janie raises her hand, "Well, I think the wolf is just talking about sugar to make us like him, but we all know the wolves eat pigs, and therefore, he is just saying that to make us think he didn't just want to eat the pigs but he did."

The next day, they read more fairy tales at their tables, and in our meeting, I go over the idea of summaries. José immediately gets the idea, summarizing "Jack and the Beanstalk." Pretty quickly the whole class is offering summaries like there's no tomorrow. Max, though, remains perplexed,

"When you say summary, are you talking about summer?"

I am at a loss as to how to explain. He then states his second comment, referring back to Theo's claim from the day before that the pigs are going to hell. "They are not going to go to hell," Max says. "The pigs would go to heaven. The pigs were not bad." This leads to many children calling out theories on heaven and hell and the pig/wolf place in them. I end the period with a "by the way, some people believe in heaven and hell and some people don't," and they repeat the last phrase with me. "It's our job in this classroom to be respectful even if we feel different. Heaven and hell is just another one of those religious things."

"It is?" Carmen shouts out.

"Yeah," someone adds, "it goes with God."

"Oh, I knew that."

First let me note the combination of intention, following the children, and happenstance. I initially chose fairy tales because Max struggled with reading and writing comprehension and kept fairy tales that were too hard for him to decode in his book bin— poring over the pictures and remembering the plot from memory. He "wrote" fairy tales by drawing elaborate scenes during writing workshop—a daily extended period where children got to pursue writing projects independently. I thought he'd be happy to find the fairy tales on the table greeting him when he came back to school. Others would like this too, and it would be helpful for them learning to read for and write plot.

I also want to highlight the movement between developing skills and making deeper meaning and how the two are deeply interconnected.[2] Reading over my students' writing, a general issue had emerged—the stories often didn't seem to go anywhere, and when there was a plot, it would resolve abruptly. What better way to work on plot development than studying it in fairy tales that hinged on these relatively straightforward and dramatic storylines. With these goals, I placed the books on the tables for what I anticipated would be a few weeks of investigation.

Literary theorist, Louise Rosenblatt introduced reader response theory to describe the individual meaning that readers bring to a text. What we hear in a text is determined by what we bring.[3] As the kids gain fluency discussing plot, Max still struggles, and because there are opportunities to share thinking and ask questions, Max reveals that he is caught up on the word "summary" itself.

Where I officially developed the unit to focus on skills, the children and I are drawn by deeper questions. Culturally sustaining pedagogy makes room for children's cultural backgrounds and encourages children to draw from their backgrounds to make meaning.[4] From the very start of this study, we consider the nuances of who is good and who is bad. Theo introduces heaven and hell into the mix, and another child supplements my discussion of religion to add that it "goes with God." Building from their religious repertoire, children push my questions about the moral identity of the wolf deeper to think about heaven and hell.

Another key is happenstance. As I was about to leave the building for break, the art teacher, Patrice Lorenz, stopped into my room. Glancing at the tables covered in fairy tales, she asked me what my class was doing. Patrice worked in the basement, so she didn't usually pass my door. When I said we'd spend a little time studying and writing fairy tales, she immediately suggested that we should work together to create puppet shows. She had wanted to try a new puppet-making technique in the art room, and if I had the kids write the stories in my class, she could make the puppets in hers. This seemed like a big task and overwhelming. I had no idea how to support children in writing or performing shows, but I admired Patrice, and I liked fairy tales. In college, one of my favorite projects had been a paper I wrote analyzing "Snow White."[5] Some of my fondest memories in elementary school were writing either plays or songs and then performing them. "Sure," I replied and set out to figure out how to make this happen.

Working with my class to write fairy tales was exciting and complex. Here I explore one important and unforeseen element. As surfaced in the early journal entry, the project afforded the chance to consider and reconsider messages and morals. Over many months, we read countless fairy tales, including many versions of the same story. We unpacked stereotypes as we looked at phrases like "big bad" and context. When asked, "Where would you set a [urban] fairy tale?" the urban children replied, "In an alley."

When we began reading stories from other cultures, "the kids were taken with the more positive, generous, and subtle messages."

> After reading the Western story "The Magic Fish," where the fisherman's wife asks for more and more until she loses everything, the kids revolted. "She shouldn't have been so mean, but she shouldn't have lost everything," said Ellie. "It's not really fair that she gets so punished." "What's this tale trying to teach you?" I asked the class. "Not to be greedy," they responded. "Does it work?" I asked. "No," Elias said confidently, "it tells you everything you shouldn't do and you leave the story thinking about what you shouldn't do instead of what you should."

In contrast, the class loved Gail Sakurai's *Peach Boy: A Japanese Legend*, a retelling of a Japanese story that teaches generosity through positive example. They immediately connected the two tales. "It's just that in *Peach Boy*, you learn to be nice and generous because he's so generous," Shana said. "And that is why," I announced triumphantly, "when we're making rules at the beginning of the year, I have you put them in the positive and I usually focus on what you should do—be kind, walk in the hallways, be quiet so your classmates can read." I had been saying this all year, but finally they nodded, showing signs of comprehension.

After this moment, though still enjoying reading and hearing the Western fairy tales, the class was increasingly critical of their punitive and violent nature. They rewrote fairy tales again and again during writing workshop—often substantially changing the message.[6]

At the end of this account, summarizing this experience and referring to their own stories, I wrote, "They have claimed a right to revise."

The children picked up on the fact that stories convey values, values change over time, and the values we imbibe through stories may not fit with one's ethos. Rosenblatt stresses the "transactional" nature of the relationship between text and reader. There are certain parameters to each work that provoke readers. In turn, reading is dependent heavily on what we bring. My students discussed ethical quandaries in fairy tales because of their own interest in these topics *and* because the texts provoked ethical conversation.

What were the children and I doing in our readings of these fairy tales? What might a teacher need to be able to do to facilitate such conversations? How does a teacher choose books to provoke meaningful discussion? Next, I will describe our work using the philosophical term *hermeneutics* and argue that such conversations I had with the children are not only interesting but also important to digest cultural material in order to learn how to live well.

HERMENEUTICS

Writing about race and racism, activist geographer Ruth Wilson Gilmore writes, "Frameworks—or "paradigms"[7]—are not structures that emerge with spontaneous accuracy in the context of knowledge production. Rather, they are politically and socially as well as empirically contingent and contested explanations for how things work that, once widely adapted, are difficult to disinherit."[8] Reading and telling stories provides a paradigm, a way of making ethical sense of the world.[9] What teachers choose to read and how they approach these readings therefore have ethical implications.[10] Philosopher Martha Nussbaum argues that a difference between philosophy and literature is not in the kinds of questions asked but in the mode of asking the questions.[11] No exception, children's books have philosophical implications.[12] In some cases, the messaging is direct and pedantic.[13] In others, as is often the case with a work of philosophy, one is left pondering what meaning might be made.[14]

Philosopher Kate Manne writes that in "reading" Shel Silverstein's poem "Ladies First" and the book *The Giving Tree*, "I feel truly defeated: one of the chief dynamics underlying misogyny has been disseminated by means of popular children's poems and beloved bedtime stories. It has been dignified before children are even in preschool. And many people seem not to have noticed the gender dynamics at work here, even though they genuinely care about not instilling these biases."[15] Stories shape how people see themselves and communicate cultural norms and values.[16] The stories we hear as children can be especially potent, often associated with the comfort and security of family at bedtime. Picture books offer an especially powerful means of transferring views of the world and cultural values because they are heard, viewed, and read multiple times, engaging multiple senses.[17]

As a child, I loved *The Runaway Bunny* so much that I requested the poster when I was six that I kept on my bedroom wall for many years.[18] When I think about a children's book read to me countless times as a child, like *The Runaway Bunny*, I can picture particular scenes and hear the phrases. I know the cadence intimately. I even developed a unit for my first and second graders on Margaret Wise Brown that included *The Runaway Bunny*. Recently, though, I have read more about the book—the storyline comes from a song about a man who would not accept a woman leaving him.[19] Suddenly the message is very different. This theme of persistent refusal to respect someone else's desire to leave is reminiscent of romantic comedies I enjoyed when young where the man won't give up even after he has been rejected.[20] It is impossible to say whether *The Runaway Bunny* shaped my thinking about love and subtly influenced me to initially be intrigued by unrequited pursuit. That it is part of a culture where such dangerous pursuit is prized though is certainly true, and that it supports that culture in subtle ways among the very young also seems likely.

Manne emphasizes the power of children's books by noting her sense of "defeat" because such messaging is influential and "many people seem not to have noticed." In fact, it is common that children's messaging is imbibed without much analysis or attention. How might children, like those in my opening example, be supported in recognizing and then revising themes? How might the adults, to whom Manne addresses her passage, support children in this work as they too may not be alert to messaging? In this chapter, I turn to hermeneutics broadly and exegesis in particular.

Initially applied to biblical study, hermeneutics is the close study of a text in the service of making an interpretation. The interpretation can include both how the current person is making sense and the history of interpretations related to an item.[21] The philosopher Hans-Georg Gadamer uses the metaphor of the "horizon" to describe the extent and limits of one's sight.[22] As one engages with others around a text or topic, one's horizon grows and expands. Henceforth, one will always see further. Where philosophers tend to apply this careful and precise reading to texts, one can also take a hermeneutical approach to images and even lived phenomena such as teaching. As teacher writer Karen Hale Hankins explains: "I engage in hermeneutics as I make sense of events in the classroom, especially in regard to the things children say to me."[23]

An exegesis is a close reading to determine the messages of the text or, to use Gadamer's metaphor, determine the horizon from which one is seeing.[24] Taking an exegetical approach, a thinker describes the main ideas argued in a text as opposed to responding to those ideas. Often, an early step in the study of any given text is this exegetical take—a way of getting the lay of the land and mapping it for reference.

My first and second graders were upset with the fairy tales because they didn't like the image of human nature presented. They noted how different cultures consider behavior differently. They then connected the messages they were hearing in fairy tales with how we devised our class rules. They were able to do this complex thinking because they regularly engaged in exegetical analysis of text with attention to ethical messaging. Here I dive into how to cultivate that facility first by modeling an exegetical approach, the Descriptive Review of Work, to studying images and then picture books.

PICTURE THE CHILD

With the interplay of pictures and words, picture books sensually bring the child into the story, incorporating readers who see and hear the story.[25] I therefore begin with messaging in images. Namely, what do images of children tell us about societal values? Adapting and demonstrating the popular educational method *I do, We do, You do*, described in the Introduction, I scaffold an activity to help articulate the values behind an image.

A Descriptive Review of Work is a method of studying an item such as an image, text, or structure.[26] Educator Patricia Carini and museum curator Beth Alberty developed the process with colleagues inspired by practices in art appreciation and history where viewers closely studied images to consider the artist's way of making meaning.[27] The theory behind the Review of Work is that in studying a work descriptively with others, we gain insight into the work and, using Carini's preferred phrase, "the maker."[28] To get closer to the work itself and the maker's conceptions, we look descriptively. This helps us move past judgments, assumptions, and initial biases. Typically, a Review is done to learn more about a child's creation, but it can also be practiced, as done in this chapter, with adult work.[29]

Practicing a collaborative, oral inquiry, participants initially describe in a group what they see. Working in what are referred to as rounds, each person is expected to add, typically following the order in which they are sitting. Viewers share as literal a description as possible. One learns about the item by looking more closely and hearing other perspectives. It is only after much description, sometimes after multiple rounds, that inference enters into the commentary. When looking at a student's work, sometimes participants offer recommendations, such as *I see this child working in collage, and perhaps they would benefit from a closer study of the work of children's illustrators who do this*[30] or *Maybe they could apply this interest in gathering to writing found poems where they pull lines from a prewritten poem and rearrange as their own.*[31]

In the Theories class, students traced perceptions of the child through Western history. Launching this study, we looked at a

1520 painting titled *Portrait of Madeleine of France (1520–1537) 3rd Daughter of Francois I and Claude of France*, which depicts a stern-looking baby swaddled tightly.[32]

Just as blocks pushed aside preconceived assumptions about ability in chapter 1, I believed that this medieval image would help students describe without assumptions because the baby would seem so unfamiliar. Studying this image also provided a way of entering into another time and placed the author of our first philosophical reading, John Locke, within his cultural context. Because we would soon read about swaddling with Jean-Jacques Rousseau, I also sought a picture of a swaddled child to provide a mental image of this practice.

Describing, students were urged to be as precise as possible and to say no more than a few things. For example, participants might note that the figure has a multi-textured and semicircular item on their head. To signal a particularly striking feature, students could repeat a comment. This option supported particularly nervous students and those unconfident about their vocabulary.

After we described, I asked students to now make inferences based on our descriptions. I shared that aside from some general knowledge about the time period, I knew nothing about this image. Their inferences were as good as mine. In a traditional Review of Work, we share inferences in a round. When using this process with undergraduates, I often let students elect to speak for this inferential step.[33] Students typically don't find describing publicly to be especially stressful, but some get very anxious about inferences. While only a handful actively participated in the inferential round with the portrait of Madeleine, the conversation was lively. Students inferred wealth from the texture and detail of the clothes and furniture. Based on her physical location on the dais, students believed Madeleine was symbolically elevated, perhaps idealized in this culture. One commented that by placing a baby up high in that manner, you had to be pretty confident she would not and could not move. Any child who was comfortable confined and balanced up high would also be comfortable with stillness. Noting her expensive clothes, they commented with amusement that putting an infant in expensive clothes that would be quickly soiled could be signaling wealth. Asked to generalize what kind of philosophy this image might portray about children, they inferred that the image suggested that children should be seen but not heard, that they were ornaments and not people with a will.

WE DO WITH PEERS

After looking together at the image, students chose a partner and an image from a larger collection. The primary unifying criteria that often dominates my collections is that they include many images that I hope are familiar. In some cases, the familiarity is in the kind of depiction such as the family portraits in the *Kitchen Table* series by Carrie Mae Weems and images of parents and children such as *Young Mother Sewing* by Mary Cassatt.[34] I also want images that are actually familiar, such as one of Calvin from Bill Watterson's *Calvin and Hobbes*, a photograph of babies asleep on a shelf by Anne Geddes, one of Shirley Temple, and the cover of David Shannon's *No, David!*[35] I often pull from different historical periods, including images from Renaissance painter Filippo Lippi and contemporary artist Kadir Nelson.[36] The purpose is not to canonize familiar depictions but instead to avoid the fetishization that might come with unfamiliar images with students new to this process. Additionally, in studying familiar images closely, students think more about the cultural assumptions and dominant motifs they imbibe, and this, in turn, helps them potentially loosen the tether of assumptions.[37] Students were then asked to collaboratively

- describe the work;
- speculate on what might be the philosophy about children expressed in the work; and
- consider pedagogical practices that correspond to this view of children.

CHILDREN'S STORIES AS PHILOSOPHICAL TEXTS

After students analyzed images, they moved to picture books as philosophical works. Here I focus on three benefits of analyzing the messaging of children's books: (1) there is importance, as Manne points out, of being aware of the messages, both explicit and more subtle, that books convey; (2) books introduce us to new interlocutors who can help us think philosophically, grappling with big questions; and (3) picture books can serve as a step toward analyzing other kinds of texts including those that are more technically difficult. Following the same structure with images, in analyzing picture books, teachers were given a range of texts organized around the same theme.[38] (See the Appendix for further detail.)

Again, I build a collection from different time periods to show how visions of childhood both change and stay similar. Students are struck that in *Bedtime for Frances*, the father threatens to spank Frances when she refuses to go to bed. As with the images, I sought books students would know and be fond of. In my rural US context, Junie B. Jones texts and *No, David!* were mainstays, and I tried to introduce them to a number of high-quality texts that were new.

STORY ACTING INTO TEXTUAL MEANING

Early childhood educator Vivian Paley developed story acting to bridge how children naturally perform stories in dramatic play to formally tell stories. After children dictate a story, they perform it with peers.[39] As children enter each other's stories, Paley finds they join each other in community. Children also explore different ways of being together when acting. I also have students dramatize published stories. Here are some prompts:

- Select a text with multiple characters with bigger and smaller parts. I like *A Big Bed for Little Snow* and *Where the Wild Things Are*.[40]
- If the story is unfamiliar, read it ahead of time. If familiar, try a picture walk where students refresh their memory by describing each image.
- Students list all the characters (broadly defined) transcribed on the board.
- Announce that the class will perform this book and students can volunteer to be actors or audience members. Main characters, like Little Snow, can be played by multiple actors simultaneously, and some characters, like being snowflakes, lend themselves to many actors.
- Designate a specific location as stage. With children, physically marking off this space can help.
- Generate rules. *Audience and actors, what do we need from actors to be safe?* Responses usually include no actual touching, slow movement, staying in the boundaries of the stage, miming, and taking roles seriously. *Actors, what do you need from audience members to be safe?* Paying attention by watching the stage and being quiet, only laughing at intentionally funny parts, smiling, and showing support with your body language.
- Choose a reader. (This can be the teacher.)
- All actors step forward and stand still near the stage.
- Read and actors improvise their parts when described.

- Debrief:
  - What do you learn about the book from performing or watching?
  - What did you learn about the community or yourself? How did this feel in your body as an actor or audience member?

Much is always learned, but one element is that actors and audience members develop a more nuanced understanding of the characters. They typically feel the tensions of a text more dramatically—for example, Max's emotional growth hits home as they watch him move from being wild to peaceful.

TEXTUAL ANALYSIS

Teacher educator Patricia Cooper offers a useful "I do" with her close and powerful analysis of two books about children defying adult rules, *No, David!* and *Where the Wild Things Are.*[41] Analyzing these two books, Cooper highlights that Max's parent offers clear boundaries through swift and direct consequences. From adult clarity and support, Max grows and, upon growth, is forgiven. David is incorrigible, and his parent is superficially critical and ineffective and then accepts without caveats. David does not grow. The initial similarity between David and Max and the very different responses of the adults help students see the nuance in messaging.

Building on the same process used with the images, after reading Cooper's analysis, students do the following.

- They select a favorite picture book that features a child and bring it to class.
- In their letters, completed before they bring the book to class, they respond to the following prompts:
  - Summarize the text in your own words!
  - Provide an exegesis of the philosophy in this text.

– Why do you like this book?

– After analyzing the philosophy, how well does it connect to your own philosophy? Explain.

Having summarized a picture book and identified core values, then preservice early childhood teacher Katelyn Beedy wrote the following:

> I might read this book to a class if a situation arises where children are labeling each other as good or bad. I would definitely read this book as a reminder to my students (and future children!) that I appreciate and love them no matter how they act, because I know the person that they are underneath it all. I also believe that this book could be read to remind students that others can overhear your hurtful words even when you think you're being careful, so it's best to only say positive things about peers. I would connect this thought to the fact that if Mandy's mother hadn't been talking about and comparing her two children, then Mandy might not have been naughty in the first place.[42]

She then connected the book to her own previously articulated values:

> I think that this book reflects my own philosophy very well because one of my largest values is positive relationships because I believe it is the basis for growth. It is important to me that my students know that I care about them no matter what.

In many texts students like Katelyn chose, the parent is both frustrated and unable to change the behavior.[43] The child tended to be depicted in almost exactly the same way: a mischievous, constantly active being who faces a critical, irritated, and ineffective parent.[44] Students were struck when they noticed this—questioning the characterization of the child in many of their own childhood favorites and reconsidering how they might share them in the classroom.

At the start of this chapter, I described the powerful hold that particular motifs have on us as we navigate within a culture. As Hans-Georg Gadamer writes, "For the writer, free invention is always only one side of a mediation conditioned by values already given. He does not freely invent his plot, how much he imagines he does. Rather, even today the mimesis theory still retains something of the old validity. The writer's free invention is the presentation of a common truth that is binding on the writer also."[45] The stories we tell, both literally in writing but also how we orient ourselves, are inherited. As Gadamer explains with the word *mimesis*, much of storytelling is imitation even when we are unaware. As addressed in more depth in chapter 4, classroom management strategies depend on how children's behavior is perceived and the kinds of communities teachers hope to ultimately develop.

Further, the more a story is told, the more it is inscribed. As Gilmore writes, "to describe is also to produce."[46] The out-of-control child and ineffective parent form a dominant narrative.[47] This chapter focuses primarily on naming and describing so as to be alert to guiding principles of the stories we tell. Just as we focused on dominant discourses, it is also important to be alert to alternative schemas such as the messaging in the book Katelyn chose.

Upon describing the depiction of the child, we immediately move to discussions of what that account means to us. Similarly, when my first- and second-grade students analyzed plot, characters, and themes of folktales, they reflected about the messages. What, for example, did it mean to read harshly punitive tales when we sought to be a class where rehabilitation was the focus? One class immersed in Western fairy tales eventually decided enough was enough and that we should move to folktales that avoided binaries of good and evil. The same group expressed frustration reading about female characters who were either evil or bland.

PRACTICAL WISDOM:
WHY WE DID IT?/VALUES IN ACTION

Build from the Learner

As a reminder, psychologist Lev Vygotsky argues that you build new understanding off what a person already knows.[48] Psychologist Jerome Bruner further popularized this concept and introduced the term *scaffolding*.[49] Scaffolding depends on first knowing what your students can do. From a survey on the first day and prior experience with early childhood preservice teachers, I anticipated students in the upper-level Theories course would be intimidated about both reading and philosophy. Many needed an elective to graduate, and my course happened to be offered. Most were nervous about the class, and some were actually dreading it. The question became, How can I build from strength to try something new?

Studying children's artwork had been practiced and honed in previous courses.[50] A critical mass of the students would not only be very good at analyzing images by their junior or senior year but also feel confident in this skill. I had also taught a few of the students previously in an introductory freshman course where we had analyzed pictures of children. The lesson had gone well. As the class had been studying infants, toddlers, and young children now for nearly three years, they were familiar with elements of the content of the image I chose: swaddling, cribs, and infants.

Vygotsky again argues that our peers provide meaningful scaffolding.[51] Where I knew some of my students would find describing and inferring easy, some would find even the describing hard. Engaging in "We Do" and hearing the descriptions of nearly twenty others gave some descriptive language to those who might want it.[52] Analyzing an image of choice in small groups allowed everyone to practice this skill. Transitioning for homework from image to text after introducing textual analysis in class provided a jump to words that would ultimately take us to reading philosophy (see chapter 5).

Attend with Care

Students often carry strong feelings about their own capacity and aptitudes as readers and a host of often unexamined assumptions about how to respond to text based on prior schooling. For example, a first response to a picture book is to identify whether one likes it viscerally. Reactions such as "this is cute" are common. The capacity to analyze images has fewer preconceived notions as few students have been evaluated on this ability prior to class. Because they are rarely graded, images also have fewer preestablished ways of judging attached to them.

Interruption and Disruption

In an essay calling for the value of a scholar-activist, a category she identifies with, Ruth Wilson Gilmore describes her method in presenting information as "an attempt to make what is strange familiar, and what is familiar strange."[53] Playing with this tension, I chose the initial image of the medieval child. Swaddling is familiar and largely unquestioned as the safest and most effective method for helping infants sleep.[54] I suspected students would find the picture strange and even comical. Using a slightly funny (to the modern eye) image would bring some levity to our work. I also hoped that the image would be unfamiliar to everyone and chose one unfamiliar to me as well. While students and I were likely invested in swaddling, we knew little about and were not invested in swaddling in the way depicted in the image. If everyone, including me, experienced aporia and a lack of expertise, we'd be more at ease in describing without assumptions. As students considered what swaddling meant in other times, they could reflect on how it fit in present childcare.

Experiential Learning

In speaking to the value of the hyphen, the space in which one is dually scholar-activist and activist-scholar Gilmore, writes, "Here of course is where the question of *questions* comes most vividly into view. In the constant rounds of discussion and reflection through which engaged work proceeds, the strictly attentive practice of making the familiar strange is as important in extramural circles where projects come into being as it is in the halls of academia where scholar-activists struggle to legitimate our trade."[55] Gilmore's larger point in this passage is the importance of bringing together the worlds of scholarship and activism. That said, I draw on Gilmore here to emphasize Gilmore's method as opposed to her argument—namely, her belief that the capacity to work from the hyphen demands attention to method—the "questions of *questions*" and the "constant rounds of discussion and reflection."

Simply reading Cooper's article analyzing depictions of the child is provoking. Due to her close analysis of familiar texts, the teacher is invited to follow Cooper's arguments and consider their resonance. That said, the opportunity to try out Cooper's exegetical approach helps teachers learn to take an exegetical approach themselves and, ultimately, think more deeply about the messaging of texts they use in the classroom.

MESSAGING IN THE FIELD

I opened this chapter with how I closely analyzed texts to help my first- and second-grade students do the same. The children named their inheritance and rewrote elements that troubled them. I close with an analysis of both a picture book and a different kind of text teachers engage with constantly: curriculum. After articulating her commitment that a teacher "ha[s] to have the best interest of the child in mind," experienced early childhood teacher Juliet in her interview first says a teacher must have flexibility for children. Juliet then pivots to an example from her work in a dually public and privately funded preschool that served primarily children from low-income backgrounds:

> Teachers should have that flexibility too because they know what's going to be best for the students. The literacy curriculum was part of a city-based curriculum, which connecting that to [rural region] can be challenging. So, when I was teaching preschool, I would put my own twist to it even though that wasn't what I should be doing. However, we read a book called *Make Way for Ducklings*.[56] And that process, that idea of crossing the street is kind of vague to our students, so I brought my kids out to the parking lot, and we pretended to be ducks. And we walked across our road, and from there, we did a sound map.[57] And these are all things that weren't part of the curriculum, but it could increase their understanding of what that meant to be in a busy city and hearing those sounds. And talking about how living in [rural state] is different than in a city, or in [identifying small city] or wherever it is. And that's necessary, not necessarily something that I seek permission to do first, it was one of those things where I was willing to get the backlash because I could back up the why I was doing it.

First Juliet carefully read the book. *Make Way for Ducklings* centers on the duck's need for a natural habitat and the challenges of navigating a major city. Ultimately the ducks choose to live in the Boston Public Garden because it offers both a quiet refuge and bread from people. The city is a key character. Juliet read her students. Having grown up herself in a rural region and closely observed these children, Juliet understood that street crossing was central to the story and that this would be "vague" to her students. As such, Juliet created an experience for the children that helped them better understand the story. Juliet read the curriculum. The goal was reading comprehension and language with much emphasis on experiential learning.

Following a curriculum with "integrity" means understanding the structure and intention of the program well enough to make changes while keeping the "core elements stable."[58] Working from this core, teachers display practical wisdom as they tweak based on the children in front of them, their personal approaches, and outside influences.[59] Following with integrity, Juliet's modifications obviously made for better teaching.

Yet Juliet ends that she did not "seek permission first" and "was willing to get the backlash because I could back up the why I was doing it." The ability to read a situation and determine purpose helped Juliet affirm she was willing to take the risk. But why was doing right by her students a risk at all? An easy answer was that Juliet was required to teach with "fidelity" and modifying challenged that norm. But, again, why does "fidelity" dictate Juliet's moves? By way of a response, in chapter 4, we turn to a close attention to words themselves, including fidelity. In chapter 7, we then continue this exploration to consider more precisely where norms come from and, ultimately, how we might refine and redefine the norms (and stories) that bind.

YOU DO

- Create a collection of texts featuring a child (images, books, even movies).
- Zoom in on one. Using the steps in this chapter, do an exegetical analysis.

- Review the collection. What messaging stands out?
- What cultural norms do you see revealed in these texts? What norms are being reinforced? Challenged?
- What did you learn about analyzing texts?
- What did you learn about cultural norms?
- How might this influence your teaching?

CHAPTER FOUR

LANGUAGE GAMES: READING THE WORLD, READING THE WORD

As an educator I need to be constantly "reading" the world inhabited by the grassroots with which I work, that world that is their immediate context and the wider world of which they are part. What I mean is that on no account may I make little of or ignore in my contact with such groups the knowledge they acquire from direct experience and out of which they live. Of their way of explaining the world, which involves their comprehension of their role and presence in it. These knowledges are explicit, suggested, or hidden in what I call the decoding of the world, which in its turn always precedes the decoding of the word.[1]

—Paulo Freire

This chapter is about care and love and words. First, a distinction: I am defining *care* as a way of being with others. *Love* is a feeling that often guides that care and that teachers are often called on to have in order to guide actions.[2] I will focus most on care because it is more widely used in relation to teaching, and while I believe we can ask teachers to act with care, we cannot demand *that* they care or, for that matter, love.

Teachers are often characterized as care workers.[3] As I noted in chapter 1, new teachers regularly state, "I want to be a teacher because I love children," and I'd be hard-pressed to find a teacher who *doesn't* identify care as a key part of the work.[4] Asked which values they seek to exhibit in their classrooms in my interviews, teachers and teacher educators described being caring as a top priority. "Attending with care" is a core value for me.[5]

Preservice teachers can be quick and adept at identifying lack of care in their student teaching placements, and I typically agree with their concerns. Here is a story of one such instance that troubled both the student teacher and me. As a student teacher supervisor, I sat in a lot of classrooms, and I saw excellent and caring teaching. In many classrooms, I felt immediately at home—witnessing practices I would later adapt in my own teaching. In others, as described at the end of chapter 5, the teachers' style didn't immediately resonate, but I recognized and respected a guiding commitment to caring for children. In one early elementary classroom, though, I was upset.

Lina, the teacher, repeatedly professed a commitment to inclusion but constantly and loudly disciplined children who went against a narrow set of behavioral norms. Lina's classroom was punctuated by crescendos of noise and movement (the children's) and loud, firm, reprimands (Lina's). One such rigid norm that was constantly reinforced but rarely followed was that children had to sit still with legs crossed in the meeting area. Lina would quip, "Sit on your brain buttons" when asking children to readjust to sit with their legs crossed and on their bottoms. Philosopher of linguistics Sally Haslanger argues that terms assume particular meaning based on how they are applied in context.[6] In an example that resonates,

Haslanger explains that at her child's school, tardiness officially was defined as arriving after the late bell but in actuality it meant arriving after the teacher had filled out the attendance sheet (which was later than the late bell). It seemed, in Lina's class, that "sit on your brain buttons" was understood by Lina and her students and even the student teacher to mean sit still on your bottom and cross your legs.

The phrase rankled me as did Lina's rigid seating practices. The children did not appear happy or to be engaged in the meetings, and though they did change their physical orientation in response to her commands, they did not maintain her desired posture for long. The messaging of the words chosen also upset me, and that is the focus of this chapter. My close reading of "brain button" was that the phrase and the accompanying actions convey that (1) Our brains can turn on and off; (2) this is something we can control easily by pushing a button, and because it is easy, we should just do it; (3) sitting activates the button and therefore our brains; and (4) if we are not automatically learning when we are sitting, we are malfunctioning.

As a teacher who encouraged children to sit in a variety of ways, I thought the insistence that children sit in just one way was wrong. That your brain was accessed by sitting on your bottom was odd at best. Yet, though I've never since heard another teacher say "brain button," Lina was perpetuating standard practice that children sit in the same positions and fit with assumptions that certain ways of sitting yield better thinking.[7] The popular acronym SLANT describes what some charter schools have named as the optimal position for learning: "Engaged learners Sit up; they Listen; they Ask and Answer questions; they Nod when it makes sense to nod; and they Track the speaker—whether that speaker is a fellow student or the teacher."[8] A mind–body split is prevalent in Western thought and education. We think in our minds, and then our bodies simply execute what our minds have come up with. As such, the best thinking is done when our bodies are still so our minds can focus.[9] Just picture Auguste Rodin's *The Thinker*, a replica of which greeted me every time I walked to class or the library at Columbia University. Honoring this split, we must disconnect from our bodies to think and act.[10] This is false and leads to much physical discomfort.

In his story about his teacher, shared in chapter 2, Paulo Freire says, "I can speak of it now as if it had happened only today" because it influenced him that much.[11] I have been fascinated by Lina's classroom and have been puzzling over this story for more than ten years. Why? After witnessing Lina's constant reprimand of children to sit on their brain buttons, one response is to assume Lina is mean or wants to make children physically uncomfortable or doesn't really care about children's bodies or children period. Those would be easy explanations and, in a culture that often blames and shames teachers, probably the most common. But I actively resist. Lina was an energetic teacher, constantly bustling around the room to engage with students. She took time and energy to support student teachers and exposed her teaching to others, like me. In debriefs, Lina expressed deep-seated commitments to student learning and how much she liked her students.

Student teachers who judge cooperating teachers like Lina often go on to do things that, even by their own accounts, are uncaring.[12] Me too.[13] The morning I wrote this chapter I rushed my children into the car at *my* speed and wouldn't let one go back for a granola bar. We teachers (and parents) are Linas to varying degrees— committed, caring, talented, and also perpetually falling short.

Documenting how even experienced, talented, and caring teachers act in uncaring ways, teacher educator Carla Shalaby closes her book by calling upon teachers to "*be* love."[14] In a passage reminiscent of David Hansen and Julie Diamond's attention to detail with room set-up in chapter 1, Shalaby writes:

> I don't know what this public love will look like in every classroom moment. Problems of freedom in classrooms are thorny and complex, and we won't always know what to do. But teachers can ask, in those moments when they are unsure, what they could *do* to *be* love. How will you be love when you choose what to hang on your walls and how to arrange your desk? How will you be love when students who cannot afford lunch are watching you eat your snack? How will you be love when your colleagues tell you to lock your purse up in the morning because the students might steal from you? How will you be love when one child hits another.[15]

Being love is complicated and hard work and multifaceted. It demands that we live our ethics in the hardest moments with children who challenge us. It demands we recognize an opportunity for care—or love, in Shalaby's words—in instances where we may not have noticed it was at stake. It means we be love, be care, even as we shuttle squabbling children out the door when we are late.

To open a respectful conversation with Lina that supports ongoing interrogation of purpose and ethical practice, one could try activities from chapter 1. After reflecting on her goal with the phrase "brain button" and the seating requirements, Lina might determine that fundamentally she wants children learning in the meeting area. Based on their responses to her questions, regular wandering off, doing unrelated tasks, and frequent side conversations, it did not seem they were learning as much as they could be. From there, I could ask, *How might you meet that goal better?* We could then observe and assess the children's disconnection and come up with strategies built from Lina's goals. If these young children are having trouble sitting quietly, maybe pausing more in the lesson for discussion of questions with a partner (turn-and-talk) would help. If the children talking, wiggling, and wandering are having trouble understanding, maybe the lesson needs to be tweaked so skills and content are more accessible. Perhaps trying so hard to sit still is distracting to these children and movement-oriented lessons like the story-acting read-alouds in chapter 3 or the phonics lesson Hailey wrote about in chapter 1 could be adapted. Likely, all these factors were at play.

Alternatively, perhaps logic explains how within Lina's definition of inclusion, children needed to sit still on the floor. Many teachers in my interviews believed children should move but also felt pressure to prepare students to follow school rules and sitting expectations.[16] Identifying her ethical center might help Lina name and better advocate for seating practices that were more comfortable.

Lina teaches in a culture tightly tethered to controlling children's movement and with strong associations between sitting and thinking. Perhaps analysis of assumptions of what children look like when learning, as scaffolded in chapter 3, could help Lina unpack notions that thinking happens when a person is still and passive. Another line of analysis is to investigate *where did these commitments come from* and *what is the scope and foundation of these values?* These are questions we take up in chapter 7.

In this chapter, though, I focus in another direction: language use. Freire in the epigraph analyzes language to interrogate how words shape perceptions and argues that changes in words change the world.[17] As hooks writes: "Like desire, language disrupts, refuses to be contained within boundaries. It speaks itself against our will, in words and thoughts that intrude, even violate the most private spaces of mind and body."[18] Picture a child labeled "emotionally disturbed." Now picture one described as "having witnessed the death of her mother." Now try "selective mute." What about "autistic"? Do you see the same child? How has your vision changed? What if I have a particular child in mind who has had all these words applied to her at different times? How does it change our actions and this child's life when she is perceived through the different frames that these words provide?

Haslanger argues that sometimes our purposes with words and our actions are out of sync. Returning to Lina, an entry point might be to ask what she means by "inclusion," and we could then address whether requiring kids to sit on "brain buttons" fits the definition she generates. Often teachers use phrases like "brain button" without attention, and reflection on the words, a strategy modeled later in this chapter, quickly yields a desire for new language. Perhaps if Lina interrogated the link she was making between buttons, brains, and bottoms, she might reconsider the phrase "brain button," and, more significantly, a more thorough analysis of inclusion might help her stop enforcing seating in a particular posture as required for "activating" learning.

Sometimes, phrases like "brain button" are picked up without much reflection and then easily let go of after a quick analysis. Yet analyzing and addressing language can be arduous and complex work. Often, we struggle with words that are so commonly used that they, in philosopher Hannah Arendt's terminology, become "frozen."[19] Arendt writes: "The word *house* is something like a frozen thought which thinking must unfreeze, defrost as it were, whenever it wants to find out its original meaning."[20] "Frozen" words and thinking, according to Arendt, are dangerous because they encourage unthinking behavior. The antidote for Arendt is thinking—taking time apart from action to "defrost" and consider the nuanced range of meaning.

Shalaby surfaces contextualized challenges of living out a commitment to love. Adding another layer, philosopher Myisha Cherry describes the "love myth" as "that love can do no wrong, love is incompatible with blameworthy emotions, and love is all we need in the pursuit of racial justice."[21] Imploring readers to "look" "more closely," Cherry argues that love is attributed too much power and it is wrongly treated as an unquestioned good. Cherry calls readers to trouble and unpack both words like *love*, accepted as universally good, and words like *rage*, blanketly assumed to be problematic.

Arendt unfrosts by turning to "original meaning."[22] This can be useful but is only one limited approach to analysis. As argued in the epigraph, Freire encourages us to read the word and read the world in community. In coming to identify a concept that is important to and/or harmful to a community with that community, the group first better understands how they are making sense and second finds potentially new and more affirming ways of using language.[23]

I offer four collaborative approaches of analysis: considering words in the body, conceptual, descriptive, and ameliorative. While each of these approaches can be taken independently and need not build on each other, I find that drawing on a triangulated analysis by using these approaches in the order presented is helpful.[24] As such, in the pedagogy section, I draw all my examples from a research methods course for early childhood educators focused on care.[25] In choosing *care*, I opt for a challenging word that, like *love*, in Cherry's words is often seen as able to "do no wrong."[26] Unfreezing a word teachers are especially attached to, I showcase methods that can also help with words that teachers may be less familiar with or even find unappealing.

WORDS IN THE BODY

Patricia Carini writes, "Cliché and generalization obscure the particular, depriving the local, the immediate, of its power. This is not without consequence, for it is the particular's sensuous resonance with body and soul and the feelings that resonance stirs that jar complacency."[27] "Cliché and generalization" are what Arendt described in the previous section as "frozen," and both Carini and Arendt stress, in the words of Carini, the "consequence" of obscuring "particular" meaning. I therefore state front and center that unpacking words is emotional and political work.

As Carini notes, words sit, offer "sensuous resonance," in our particular bodies in particular ways. Soon after I moved to Maine, I was in a philosophy reading group, studying Ralph Waldo Emerson, and we were looking closely at a passage where Emerson used the metaphor of skating.[28] Having driven over slippery roads and with frozen lakes part of my daily walk, I sat with the metaphor of skating. What did it feel like, smell like, sound like, look like to skate in Emerson's world? How might skating matter to him? I read the passage radically differently when I considered that skating was not just an abstract metaphor but probably described an experience Emerson and his community understood in a more embodied way. To skate is to leave a temporary mark on ice, it is to embrace sliding, it involves risk of falling into ponds or losing control, and it is a means of moving fast. It happens in the cold. It can be fun. It is more fun in crisp, clear, cold weather. It can only occur in deep, cold winter, and so skating is time and context dependent. If you skate over someone else's marks, you can obscure them or, skating alongside, add to their pattern.[29]

About a year later, I sat pregnant and nauseated in an auditorium listening to a male philosopher who kept using pregnancy and birthing metaphors to describe the origins of *his* idea. As I popped almonds into my mouth to keep down waves of nausea and felt the pressure of the growing child moving independently within me and pressing on my bladder, I grimaced every time he invoked pregnancy. I thought: *I have written many things, and now I am growing a child, and these two experiences are not akin.* Having authored articles and books and birthed a child, I continue to feel strongly that the two are quite different. It matters when we use the word *skate* whether we've skated before, and I believe it matters more when we use metaphors of experiences shouldered by a particular community like birthing what our relationship is to that actual process. Arendt and many philosophers work largely in etymological origins, and these contribute much, but words demand body origins both for us and as we consider earlier uses.

Another layer. My grandmother grew up speaking Yiddish in the home, an Eastern European Jewish dialect with much overlap with German. Though we never discussed it, I imagine Yiddish was a language of care, familiarity, and safety for her. An oft-used word of affection with my grandfather was Yiddish, and the language served as their personal and private mode of communicating. In the concentration camps, my grandmother drew from Yiddish to learn German very rapidly. This was survival. German was the language of her tormentors. Moving to the United States, she didn't hear German or Yiddish often. When she did, in my understanding, German startled and frightened her. In fact, this fear passed into the next generations, and I had to consciously work to unlearn that fear. Words live through generations in our bodies and can terrorize. Recently, my six-year-old heard German characterized as harsh in a book, and he immediately queried, "Why would they say that? That's not true" and then referenced a friend at school who was part German. "She's kind," he said. Meaning lives and can be inherited, and meaning changes.

Writing of Africans forced from home to be slaves, hooks writes, "The very sound of English had to terrify," and yet "I imagine them hearing spoken English as the oppressor's language, yet I imagine also realizing that this language would need to be possessed, taken, claimed as a space of resistance."[30] Again, this fear and desire to retake passed through generations, pushing hooks to commit to speaking and writing in the rebellious "black vernacular" more widely.[31] It must be said again that words sit in our bodies and have embodied meaning. They have the power to terrify and harm. They can also, as hooks highlights and I discuss in the next section, be reclaimed, reformed, and reshaped and also put aside and let go.

In describing another attempt at cultural annihilation, ecologist Robin Wall Kimmerer documents a range of historical instances in which white settlers systematically tried to erase Indigenous culture and destroy Indigenous peoples. Kimmerer repeatedly notes how words are taken to harm and destroy and then can be taken back to affirm and reclaim.[32] Words give and deny ways of being in the world.

And one more layer. Radical teacher Lillian Weber called progressive teachers to work from the cracks—finding small spaces and expanding them.[33] I have long gravitated toward this concept. One year at the Summer Institute on Descriptive Inquiry, we first made collages around cracks.[34] Earlier that summer, as described in chapter 5, we had literally cracked mugs. As I listened to my colleagues' stories and processed my own, I felt the tear of the paper in my hands, the crashing of the mug after I had cracked it with a hammer. I saw the emotions on people's faces as they cracked mugs themselves. From this embodied experience, I saw that I had taken for granted that expanding cracks was good and my own experience had biased me from considering how those who might have built an edifice might feel seeing it cracked. I now felt cracks happen in fragile surfaces and that for anyone who wanted to push the crack, someone else might want to preserve the whole. Going forward, this shift in my understanding of the word led me to tread with more care about what was being taken apart and who might be invested.

We carry words in our bodies, and central to the pedagogy of this chapter, through our bodies, we can shift our orientations toward words.

THE CONCEPTUAL

With *conceptual*, Haslanger refers to our common and ordinary associations with a word.[35] She writes:

> In undertaking a conceptual analysis of say, F-ness, it is typically assumed that it is enough to ask any competent use of English under what conditions someone is F, without making any special effort to consult those whose daily lives are affected by the concept. However, if one is sensitive to the possibility that in any actual circumstance there are competing meanings (often quite explicit) that structure alternative practices, then it seems worth considering a broad range of speakers, who are differently situated with respect to the phenomenon.[36]

The goal is to get at the nuances of a word as defined in ordinary understanding, and this supplements official definitions and etymology. How does a particular concept live within a community and culture? How does a word live in someone's life?[37] As Cherry suggests with both "rage" and "love" upon interrogating, one tends to find both some of the power and the limitations of that word.[38]

THE DESCRIPTIVE

When taking a *descriptive* approach, Haslanger writes: "The task is to develop potentially more accurate concepts through careful consideration of the phenomena, usually relying on empirical or quasi-empirical methods."[39] Put differently, the goal is to determine how a concept lives in reality and in a range of realities, not just how we think it lives or ought to live. In her descriptive approach to misogyny, philosopher Kate Manne analyzes a range of sources including news articles and comments about Hillary Clinton, legal analysis of court cases centering on assaults, children's literature, and the language of those who have committed violent acts against women.[40] As previously referenced, Haslanger argues that we ought to understand tardiness through a range of contexts including how it is situationally defined (after the late bell or when the teacher has time to note it or both), how it is enforced with repercussions, and its role in the school day.

THE AMELIORATIVE

In a chapter titled "Language: Teaching New Worlds/New Words" hooks describes how those who were enslaved reclaimed English and calls us to attend to language and shift it for justice.[41] Quoting the poet Adrienne Rich, hooks then writes, "One line of this poem that moved and disturbed something within me: 'This is the oppressor's language yet I need it to talk to you.'"[42] Words shape us, and we depend on them. They can help us, and they can harm us. They can also be changed.

Describing an *ameliorative* project, Haslanger writes that the purpose becomes questions around "What is the point of having the concept in question—for example, why do we have a concept of knowledge or a concept of belief? What concept (if any) would do the work best?"[43] What happens when something like tardiness is defined based on a given teacher? What is the effect of enforcing tardiness at all? What does this enforcement say about the commitments and values of a school? I feel strongly that tardiness in an elementary school measures a parent's capacity to get the child into school. Does a strict policy send the message that school time is more important than parent time or that timeliness or uniformity is more important than the quality of a family's morning together?

Sometimes analysis proves a word need not be continued with or needs, as Cherry argues, supplementation.[44] Analyzing teachers' expressions of frustration in the workplace, philosopher of education Doris Santoro replaced the words "burn out" with "demoralized" to capture that teachers were not overextending themselves but wanting to leave teaching because of moral concerns. Teachers at the time of publication are required to teach curriculum to "fidelity." This term comes out of scientific research and refers to the capacity to replicate a study following an exact protocol. In a lab when someone is seeking to reduce variables, this approach is necessary. When administering things like the proper dosing of a vaccine, fidelity is also necessary. Classrooms, though, are not laboratories. Discussing this word with teachers, the general consensus is that if we are to be faithful, it is to families and children and ethics. Fidelity to curriculum violates that faithfulness to those in our care.

WE DO: WHAT DOES IT MEAN TO CARE?

Having introduced some frames for analysis, I now turn to employing these frames in the classroom. I look more closely at what it would mean to *be* care by showcasing how a group of teachers, drawing largely on the tools of analytic philosophy, began to think about what care even means and how it lives in, as Shalaby says, "every classroom moment."[45]

Seniors from the early childhood program where I taught take a research methods course centered each year on a particular topic. Over time, I observed that teachers generally and students in my program specifically needed more support in what they often referred to as "classroom management." My ethical compass is centered on the commitment that how we treat children in school is perhaps *the* most important lesson. From this core, one year I changed the research theme to *care* so that students would graduate having spent one of their last semesters thinking more deeply about what they mean by care and how they will enact it in schools.

CARE IN THE BODY

Let's begin with how we feel care in our bodies. How do we know we are cared for? I once saw somatic early childhood educator and dancer Alexia Buono lead a group of students as they danced their way into mathematical understanding.[46] Here is an adaptation that helps students get at care from another embodied space.

A Care Dance

In groups of three to four people, do the following:

- Take a moment to feel care, being cared for, caring in your body.
- Identify a movement that you think captures an element of how you perceive care.
- Share it with your group.
- Think about how you will choreograph these movements together in a three- to five-step dance.
- Each movement must be used, and you can repeat single movements or a whole series, all do the same thing, or have separate moves.
- Name your dance.

THE CONCEPTUAL

In chapter 3, I introduced the Descriptive Process, the Review of Work. Here I introduce a Descriptive Process for unpacking particular words and revitalizing their meaning, the Reflection on a Word. As described by longtime teacher educator and mentor of Descriptive Inquiry Cecelia Traugh, "The Reflection asks the group to focus on a word that is relevant to the group's inquiry and to think expansively about its many meanings. The aim is to deepen and expand the group's thinking about the ideas contained within the word and to push a context for the particular work of the group."[47] As with the Review of Work, participants collaborate to unearth meaning. In this case, a word is chosen, as Traugh explains, "that is relevant to the group's inquiry." Sometimes the group determines the word to focus on. Sometimes it is chosen by a community member, the session chair, or someone in the role of teacher. Here I give an overview of the steps. Using *care* as the word, do the following:

- Take a few minutes to jot down all associations with the word, such as etymology, common use, different forms, references in popular culture such as song lyrics, and famous phrases associated with the word. With those less familiar with this process and/or not confident in word play, I usually offer a little bit more time. Participants used to playing with words like professors of philosophy are given less time to inhibit overly long lists and treatises being generated.
- Share associations in rounds. A circular formation is ideal so everyone can see each other and turns are clear as you pass the word to the person next to you. When this is challenged by preset seating formations such as table groups, I ask students to rotate so they can see everyone, and then we "snake" the word around the room. The key is that everyone knows when their turn is, everyone takes a turn, and everyone sees each other.
- A predetermined chair takes notes. This is usually me until a community learns note-taking strategies.
- In what is called an integrated restatement, the chair pulls together themes. In order to code, I take notes by grouping ideas across a page and drawing lines between concepts. Participants are reminded that coding is subjective and just one read. To complement the chair's read, the group then adds in themes they have heard.

Figure 4.1 shows my notes from a Reflection on a Word *value* at the Summer Institute on Descriptive Inquiry that showcases both the range of responses and a mode of note-taking.

I often begin classes with a Reflection on a Word that will prove pivotal for the course, such as *play, literacy, community*, or, in this case, *care*.

As tends to happen with this process, when my class reflected on *care*, the results were intriguing. Many students voiced strong associations between care and self-denial. This struck me as significant and unsustainable. *If teachers saw care as key and as a sacrifice of the self, could they consistently commit to care? How would their self-image be impacted when they chose to protect their own needs? Might this link ultimately make them resent the children if they saw the children's care as taking precedence over their own?*

After culling themes orally, I encouraged students to reflect on what they noticed and begin to consider implications for practice. I noted in the restatement the frequent association between care and self-denial and shared an outlier that for some such as myself, care included looking out for the self. At that juncture, I shared that I defined myself as a caring teacher but saw my ability to care for children as closely linked to my capacity to care for myself.

Finally, as a caveat, it is also important to say that while the rounds process supports a diversity of perspectives entering in as equals, power differentials must be acknowledged. As Haslanger writes, "We would need to ask: What is the range of meanings? Whose meanings are dominant and why?"[48] Cherry's text highlights that *rage* means something different depending on the context and person. For example, a Black woman's rage at injustice is often read less sympathetically than the rage of a white man. At the Summer Institute one year, in a reflection on the word *community*, white-identifying participants in the group were overwhelmingly positive and shared warm associations with the word. A number

FIGURE 4.1 Reflection on a Word

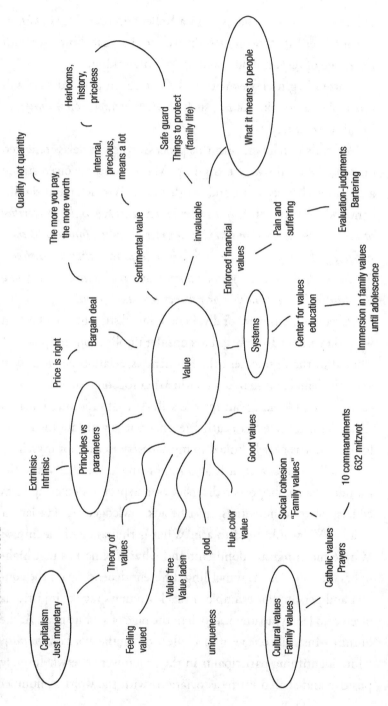

Source: Figure courtesy of Christina Lougee, created from the author's penned notes.

of people of color had a more nuanced relationship, seeing *community* as a term that could be used to place people on the outside or pressure homogeneity.

DESCRIPTIVE

In chapter 3, I began to explore some strategies for tracing a concept like childhood through a culture when relying on published texts. A number of wonderful books model descriptive attention to language and can help teachers start to unfreeze words.[49] That semester students read Carla Shalaby's *Troublemakers* and long-term teacher Vivian Paley's *The Kindness of Children*.[50] In another course on welcoming communities and families, students read *Respect: An Exploration* by Sarah Lawrence Lightfoot and used her portraits of individuals in a range of professions to see how respect manifests and could operate in their relationships.[51]

Children's books too offer a nuanced and multifaceted take on a word or concept. (See the Appendix for a list.) These books offer models from which students can capture their relationship to an important concept with their own books. For example, with family photographs, I've created a book inspired by Matt de la Peña's *Love* and a book about activities my husband and son did together based on Mary Murphy's *I Like It When*.[52]

As introduced in chapter 2, how one perceives is also influenced by one's personal experiences; racial, ethnic, and gendered positionality; and culture. As Shalaby highlights, to "*be* love" is a deeply contextualized action.[53] An Anecdotal Recollection is another Descriptive process. Highlighting the "structured" nature, the commitment to collaborative inquiry, and the attention to themes, Traugh writes, "Recollections are structured stories from life experience that participants in an inquiry prepare in advance to share with their inquiry group. The purposes of the Recollection are to give the theme of an inquiry meaning and to help group members connect to that meaning by hearing how the idea has been lived and experienced by group members."[54] In chapter 2, I argued that ethics builds from our personal experiences. Here Traugh explains how access to a concept emerges when we draw themes across stories from our lives.

The general guidelines for the Recollection are as follows.

- Prepare a story in advance in response to the prompt. [Sample prompts follow.]
- Give people a time limit of five to ten minutes.
- In rounds or when inspired to speak, tell your story. Time keeping is recommended with gentle warnings to ensure that everyone gets a turn.
- A chair takes notes. As with the coding in chapter 2 of the "Where I'm From" poem, particulars are referenced as they illustrate themes and not connected by name back to the original speaker.
- Stories stay in a group unless permission is granted, but themes can be shared.

When choosing a prompt for an Anecdotal Recollection, the group or presenter should do the following:

- Identify a topic, concept, or theme.
- Consider if there is a particular angle they want to discuss.
- Develop a prompt that is open-ended enough to get a broad response and narrow enough to keep the group grounded.
- Encourage participants to think of a story or two around the prompt.

I assigned three Recollections to unfreeze *care*:

Think of a time when you were tasked to care for someone and this posed a challenge for you. How did you deal with this challenge? How was it resolved (if it was)?

You have been reading *Troublemakers*. Now it's time to consider the themes more personally. Describe a time in your practice when a child was "disobedient" or resistant and you learned something from it or a time when your sense of "good" was stretched or expanded in some way by a child's "disobedience" or resistance. Tell what happened, how you responded at the time, what it brought up for you, and what, if any, changes this led to for you.

Think of a time (any age) when you really connected with peers in a school setting. What was the environment like? What kinds of activities happened in this space? What was the teacher like? How might these external elements have influenced your social development? What else might have influenced your ability to connect with others?

The Recollection offers a localized empirical way of drawing on first-person accounts to consider how a concept lives.

A broad range of research methods and studies offer a wider lens. Here I offer a very brief account of two. Another way to descriptively access a concept is delving into other people's studies. After narrowing the angle from which they would explore care, students then found and read related studies. As finding peer-reviewed articles and reading this kind of text were new, they were asked to find three to seven. Students considered care in relation to trauma, sibling dynamics, classroom routines, and discipline.

This prompt helped them analyze their findings to unpack the theme.

Literature reviews are written in many different ways.

Looking at the samples online and samples from class, what are features you notice about the literature review?

One way of organizing the literature review is the following (you may use this or come up with your organizational method):

Theme one: (Summarize how this theme is addressed by
different authors)
Theme two:
Theme three:
Outlier theme one:
Outlier theme two:

Students then conducted their own empirical research to explore the topic. They learned methods in class including surveys, sociograms that track interactions, interviews, observations, and work sample analyses. They then chose a method to pursue their topic.

In doing descriptive analysis of a concept, teachers must draw themes from the data—be they in an article or their own first-hand resource to push past preconceived notions. As Haslanger stresses, "In any descriptive project, intuitions about the conditions for applying the concept should be considered secondary to what the cases in fact have in common; so as we learn more about the paradigms, we learn more about our concepts."[55] As one example of how my own perception grew, I had previously assumed that the pressure to be selfless was external. Listening to my students' accounts of care, I was surprised that so many of their definitions centered on this selflessness. The question became, given this, did that account of the concept work for them even if it didn't work for me? This concern I take up in the next section.

AMELIORATIVE

Conceptual analysis is not simply an exercise; it is preparation for how to be, and be better, in the world.[56] This chapter is about helping educators not simply name their values and consider what they mean and how they are enacted but also unpack and challenge these values.

In my class on care, in addition to conducting research in articles and in the field, students read *Teaching Children to Care: Classroom Management for Ethical and Academic Growth, K–8*—a practical book on how to create classroom communities based around philosopher Nel Noddings's definition of care as an ethos that should be the foundation of schools and puts the needs of the child foremost.[57] Fortuitously (though exhaustingly), our class met in the evening at the end of a very long day for most students, and this led to management challenges. It was a long day for me too—something the students knew as many had been in classes with me starting at 8:00 that morning. Many of these college seniors were easily distractible, often goofy, resistant to focus on the work at hand, and straight-up tired and hungry. They were also self-aware; they knew they should be doing better and they were struggling. These conditions allowed us to test out the methods in the book and some of their articles as we tried to build a classroom community that was caring. Many nights, I would introduce a strategy for building caring communities and explain what I was doing and why I was doing this activity.

I often had to respond to the class with patience but also at times very direct feedback that they needed to stop what they were doing—*no side talk or giggling when others are sharing!* The class also gave me a space to directly explain how I was refining their (and Noddings's) definition of care to put more emphasis on the needs of the teacher, in this case myself.[58] I acknowledged moments when I found my capacity to care stretched by circumstances, including my own exhaustion. In doing so, care served as a public compass, guiding and righting me along the way.

Reflecting the social science emphasis in my department and education more broadly, students' research papers drew heavily on empirical findings and focused largely on methods proven to work for various purposes. Yet a key part of the project was putting together a definition of care that resonated for them. Over the semester, students identified, defined, and refined their understanding of care. They worked toward a definition that resonated, and they found practices that fit with their commitments so they could act as more caring professionals even in moments of difficulty. They processed their experience in words and readings, in research and stories, and in their bodies. In doing so, we all grew in our relation to care.

PRACTICAL WISDOM:
WHY WE DID IT?/VALUES IN ACTION

Integration Between Philosophy and Practice

The course on care developed after many years of hearing teachers use the word *care* in casual speech. Having witnessed teachers act in ways that I did and did not define as caring myself, I wanted to investigate with teachers what they meant by care and how they saw it playing out in practice. As Haslanger stresses, there is often a disconnect between what people think they mean and what they do, and identifying that disconnect is helpful.[59]

Attend with Care

In addition to the meaning made, the act of making meaning together in a manner that involves everyone is also key. Describing a class routine where each student writes a paragraph that they read aloud, hooks writes, "Just the physical experience of hearing, of listening intently, to each particular voice strengthens our capacity to learn together. Even though a student may not speak again after this moment, that student's participation has been acknowledged."[60] In listening to each student as they reflected on care and then shared Recollections, we unpacked our definitions and provided a space to attend to each person's perspective.

Picking up on distinctions from chapter 2, Anecdotal Recollections are not confessions. The reminder in my prompt to choose a story they are comfortable sharing is important. Building identities around care, considering a moment where you had trouble acting with care can be sensitive. Students used to being asked to reveal intimate information might do so not because they want to but to do well or please me. It was therefore important to stress that we came together around our experiences and did so not to reveal biographically but to make meaning together.

Build from the Learner

I focused my course on care having noticed a consistent disconnect between teachers' deep-rooted commitments to care and often uncaring behavior. We moved from the embodied to the more abstract (Reflection on a Word) to the Recollections regarding what care meant in their particular lives. As they moved in the Recollections from challenges with care to obedience and disobedience to friendship, they made sense of how care lived when it was difficult and the nuances of maintaining care in schools. As they chose their subtopics, teachers had the opportunity to build around their own concerns and challenges. Watching Buono's dance lesson, I was greatly impressed by the steps that made dance accessible and helped students feel successful and not self-conscious. The steps in the care research process help teachers gain confidence and skills.

Experiential Learning

Countering the issue raised in chapter 2 by hooks and Mary Midgley, that philosophy often represents a narrow slice of human experience because most philosophers are white men, the process of Recollection ensures that meaning is derived from a diversity of origins.[61] In hearing the themes and outliers when the Recollection is shared and then restated by the chair, listeners are reminded that concepts are subjectively derived. Deriving a concept self-consciously from a small group also gave me space to remind students that all concepts are personally motivated and subjectively derived to some degree. It is also important to raise attention in a group about who is in the room. Young white women from a rural state studying to be early childhood teachers often share approaches to care that diverge from other populations.

Analysis through a variety of modes helps teachers triangulate their understanding of a word. In this chapter, I focus on dance, analytic forms of analysis, collage, Recollections, and research. My students have also drawn alongside music to consider tone, written poetry into their understanding of particular words, and acted out concepts. In noting a range of ways one might experience a word, we were able to see and see past our own constructs.

Interruption and Disruption

To further what it meant to act with care, like Shalaby, I directed us to the place of tension: How does care live in moments that challenge the caretaker? Building on the tension that emerged in the reflection, I pressed on what happens when our desire to care pushes up against our desire for self-preservation.

Some teachers may resist considering how words and particular languages can hurt. It can be hard to accept that a language like English or even a word like *female* that you are attached to, could be more complicated and even hurtful to others. You are four chapters into this book. If you were in my class, we'd likely be a number of weeks into the semester. Trust and a relationship have been established. Building on that trust, I've told the story of my grandmother's experience learning German to illustrate how words that are treasured by one person can be painful to another.

BRICK BRAINS AND THE LIMITS
OF READING THE WORD

A cousin, Emmy, is distressed. Her daughter, Tanya, is regularly coming home crying. Tanya's teacher has been using "brick" and "bubble gum" brain to describe how people think and often calls Tanya a "brick brain" when she struggles. My first move is a conceptual analysis: "What does the teacher mean with this?" and "What does Tanya think they mean?" I believe the teacher is talking about "grit," but more information would help. Taking an ameliorative approach, Emmy and Tanya discussed whether "brick brain" aptly and helpfully described Tanya's learning. They determined that Tanya's openness to learning was situationally dependent and that, facing constant criticism, she was shutting down.

Yet the issue is not simply the meaning of the words but the way they are being used. As linguistic anthropologist Jonathan Rosa argues, terms take on a new layer when used as an epithet.[62] The teacher was labeling Tanya "a brick brain," and Tanya felt insulted.

When writing about Lina, I suggested that perhaps if she thought through her word choice, she might find it was not doing the work she intended. Perhaps "brain button" didn't describe how she saw the brain working. Perhaps, though, it did. What if Tanya's teacher did resonate with the metaphors of "brick" and "bubble gum"? The question might be how *to engage when a teacher's ethos conflicts with a parent's.* This we take up in chapter 6.

Finally, Rosa, alongside previous thinkers like Freire and hooks, emphasizes that while words and word choice matter and changing words changes worlds, words are not the only way worlds are constructed. Racist systems enact racism and must be dismantled. Words are tools within this system but not the only tools. Tanya found herself in a classroom that was hurtful. Being called a "brick brain" was just one of the ways, and while it would be good for that to stop, the issue was wider and needed a thorough redress.

YOU DO

- Select a word that resonates with and/or challenges a group.
- Try a Reflection on a Word or a Recollection and follow the prompts.
- After coding and sharing themes and outliers, what new insights do you have?
- Choose another medium to think with this word, such as a collage, song, photograph, dance, or poem.
- What does that work reveal about the word?
- What definition suits your goals? Does the word still work for you?

CHAPTER FIVE

TO BE A RESPECTFUL NEIGHBOR: WHAT LISTENING AND READING PHILOSOPHY CAN BE

*Locke and Rousseau have more in common than I would have origi-
nally thought, but this is good because I share many of their beliefs
as well.*

—Sasha Hampton, then preservice early
childhood teacher

Antonia seemed adrift in my elementary school classroom,
struggling to connect with me and peers. She seemed angry
in many of our interactions, and the sounds she made, such as
chicken noises, made teaching hard. Initially, with Antonia, I had
few roads by which to travel. Neither Antonia nor her family spoke
English. I knew very little about her country of origin, and few in
my school had much to add to what I knew. Her home language was
not spoken by many in our school nor widely in the city. It wasn't

clear to me what interested Antonia or what she liked. I struggled to draw her into activities that enticed other children.

Trying to find my way to Antonia, I wrote in my teaching journal:

> Reading [a picture book that took place in Antonia's country of origin]. I become lost in a world as I have not been in a long time and the magic of that universe . . . the pictures and the words pull me into the country of magic. It took Andrei [another student from the same country in the school] to lead me to Antonia and a bit of [spiritual text for adults from Antonia's country of origin] which I have put down but will pick up again, I think, because it has sounded and resounded in me. It took [other students from the same community] to let me see Antonia and cherish her and they to get me to get the book and the book to suddenly tell me that the magic goes two ways, and they are as much the magic as I am. That we spark each other back and forth. And somehow between them and Quakerism and my reading, something can come. The magic that is creation and I think of [the children's book author] merging his tradition with those of the story and me merging America and Jewish and Catholic and all these worlds into some kind of potion that might ignite or explode.

As discussed in chapter 4, words convey an idea, shape perspectives, and open up new vistas. Philosopher María Lugones draws on the metaphor of *pilgrimages* as a vista for traveling to the "worlds" of others.[1] With pilgrimages, she suggests the sacred and collaborative nature of journeying to another. The journey and those on the journey matter, as does the destination.

For Lugones, an important part of world travel is a reciprocated and loving relationship that can and should be "playful."[2] With playfulness, Lugones clarifies that she does not mean "frivolity." Instead, "when one considers the many crossings, I think it is important to cross, to go through, in uncertainty, open to risking one's own ground, including one's own self-understanding. An openness to uncertainty, which includes a vocation not bound by meaning and norms that constitute one's ground, is characteristic of what I identify as a playful attitude. It is that openness to uncertainty that enables one to find in others one's own possibility and theirs."[3] World travel demands openness. Facing Antonia, my first protective instinct was to focus on who I was and what I needed and, in doing so, be closed off to Antonia's world. I had to risk my own comfort by opening up. To become open to Antonia, who challenged me so much, "took" other interlocutors such as Andrei, who encouraged me to begin the journey by helping me be more curious about Antonia's experiences. It took a published children's book that encouraged that curiosity more. Openness is "risk[y]" in that when we truly take in another perspective, our own will be challenged and altered. Being open often demands an alternative way of considering oneself. Namely, a commitment to openness leads to a more permeable and adaptable identity that is not "bound by meaning and norms."

With pilgrimages, Lugones offers a powerful metaphor for embracing others. Traveling to Antonia, I, like a pilgrim, was enriched by the journey that was taking the time and paying attention to get to know someone else. There are reciprocal benefits in this journey. I ultimately joyfully grew as I learned from Antonia, from the books, and these new (to me) worlds "spark[ed]" with my own background.

Further, not taking this time to attend posed a grave injustice and danger. A lack of attention to another, such as Antonia, is deeply hurtful.[4] Not listening or listening only to hear oneself echoed back is a violation.

The inability to listen is harmful to individuals and communities. It breaks down the fabric of relationships, including those needed for democracy.[5] Socrates seeks out Alcibiades, worried that the young man sees himself as not only far superior to others but entirely independent of them. He writes: "You say you don't need anybody for anything, since your own qualities, from your body right up to your soul, are so great there's nothing you lack."[6]

In the passage about Antonia, I converse with other students, children's authors, and a philosophical text to find my way forward. In this chapter, I focus on listening to books and philosophical texts specifically. Just as fellow walkers on a pilgrimage offer insights and companionship, texts offer us a crucial friendship.[7] Texts gave me entries into Antonia's culture I could not access otherwise. hooks writes of her long-term textual and then in-person interlocutor, "Finding Freire in the midst of that estrangement was crucial to my survival as a student. His work offered both a way for me to understand the limitations of the type of education I was receiving and to discover alternative strategies for learning and teaching."[8] Freire offered another world, one that hooks preferred to inhabit. In this chapter, I offer methodologies that help readers listen to and honor complicated writings with the hope that learning to read philosophy provides a way into philosophy *and* a way to better travel to the complexity of another.

Before proceeding, a bit about the ethics of this engagement. The Haudenosaunee Confederacy is an alliance among six Native American nations. According to Robin Wall Kimmerer, the Haudenosaunee have crafted a Thanksgiving Address as "a statement of identity and an exercise in sovereignty" that is communally recited in schools each morning.[9] Kimmerer writes:

> Living as a neighbor to the Haudenosaunee, I have heard the Thanksgiving Address in many forms, spoken by many different voices, and I raise my heart to it like raising my face to the rain. But I am not a Haudenosaunee citizen or scholar—just a respectful neighbor and a listener. Because I feared overstepping my boundaries in sharing what I have been told, I asked

permission. Over and over, I was told that these words are a gift of the Haudenosaunee to the world. When I asked Onondaga Faithkeeper Oren Lyons about it, he gave his signature slightly bemused smile and said, "Of course you should write about it. It's supposed to be shared, otherwise how can it work? We've been waiting five hundred years for people to listen. If they'd understood the Thanksgiving then, we wouldn't be in this mess."[10]

This book is premised on the need to be "a respectful neighbor"— someone who listens and listens well. We visit other worlds, including the worlds they offer in text, not to colonize or take over or take away, or appropriate as discussed in chapter 6, but to listen with care and grow with them. Philosopher William Paris writes, "By presenting reading as a form of bodily constitution, I urge readers to move away from metabolic reading of incorporation (absorbing what one wants while discarding the rest) and towards excorporation (slowing down and learning to learn how to read differently)."[11] As Paris highlights, slowing down to read and listen challenges dominant norms in which we read to possess and "incorporate" but not honor the other.

Attending is always hard work, demanding constant practice.[12] It is difficult intrinsically and difficult because many of us are taught to read as colonizers—to "master" a text or grasp what serves us and leave behind the rest. In a context where we are trained to listen for what we can "take away" from the engagement and where our attention has constant demands, attending is all the harder.

Attending is also hard because it involves traveling to worlds with unfamiliar terrain. Lugones writes, "The first way of being at ease in a particular 'world' is by being a fluent speaker in that 'world.' I know all the norms that there are to be followed. I know all the words that there are to be spoken. I know all the moves. I am confident."[13] When I first read a philosopher or meet a person, for that matter, I typically have trouble understanding them. Once

I read more, I become familiar with their rhythms and cadence, and I hear better. This is all the more challenging if a philosopher or, as Lugones describes, a person hails from a different cultural background. Sometimes, I find their thinking particularly hard to follow. Other times, I think I understand and am reading too superficially.

Another layer of fluency needed is with reading philosophically itself. Listening well demands exercise.[14] Kimmerer models respectful listening to the Haudenosaunee Thanksgiving Address, interweaving the address with her experiences and her philosophy to tell a story about the address and gratitude more broadly. This interweaving is akin to philosopher Karen Barad's "diffracted reading"—a mode of reading that acknowledges how, as we engage with an idea, ripples are unleashed, with the reading cascading across our experiences, perception, and other texts.[15]

Cristina is an early childhood teacher I interviewed who was working at an Applied Behavior Analysis center where children identified with autism are taught with direct and precise instructions. She explains:

> I have a little boy I work with. And right now we're working on him being able to wash his hands independently. And he's been kind of stuck on one step of the programming. So, we had to reevaluate what we were teaching him and we started out with modeling and then a visual schedule as far as how to wash his hands and the steps it takes to wash his hands. Right now we kind of go hand over hand to help him learn how to dry his hands . . . It's a slow process. Realizing when it's time to modify the original plan and just go with the learner's pace and not rush it and just really take a step back and slow down and reevaluate where he's at and plan out a more helpful procedure.

For most, handwashing is relatively straightforward—so obvious we do it in a habituated manner. In fact, the task is deceptively simple as it was a skill relearned at the height of the Covid-19 pandemic. For each child, though, at some point, it is learned, and for Cristina's student, it is difficult. One response to difficulty is to be frustrated or assume incapacity in the learner. With faith in the child's ability, Cristina breaks down what for the child is a complex task. To break down reading philosophy into concrete parts, I offer methods for reading somewhat akin to that of Kimmerer and Barad. Drawn primarily from the Descriptive Processes of Patricia Carini, I showcase a slow and purposeful moving between listening, diffracting one's experiences, and attending closely to the language, syntax, and ideas of a text.[16]

MOVING INTO TEXT

It is summer, and I am sitting around a small table in Bennington, Vermont, with a group of teachers and teacher educators at the Summer Institute of Descriptive Inquiry, a group that convenes every summer to study teaching practice, student work, and philosophy together. The first part of the week is always devoted to a three-day study of classroom practice. It is Thursday, the day of transition to a close study of a philosophical text. We are reading philosopher Ernest G. Schachtel's account of perception in *Metamorphosis*.[17] The text is dense, and Schachtel is new to me. Despite being a relatively confident reader of philosophy, I am not especially engaged.

We will be discussing the text in small groups, chaired by facilitators (in this case two veteran teachers and teacher educators) who have co-planned together. That morning, a group of mugs and small paper bags sat on the table in front of our facilitator. Gina Ritscher with some assistance from Bruce Turnquist has planned this activity. Bruce is my facilitator and instructs us to choose a mug. Dutifully everyone does. Mine is green and white with zigzags. Bruce, gently and, I think, nervously, tells us to look at our mug and simultaneously warns us not to get too attached. Going around in a circle, we each share an adjective about our mug. Then Bruce gives us the paper bags. He, again nervously, draws out hammers and instructs, "You will stick your mugs in the bags. Then you will smash your mugs with the hammers. The bags will catch any loose shards." We do so, some gleefully, some with horror. (Two in Gina's group outright refuse.) Passing out glue guns, Bruce then tells us to reconstruct the mugs in whatever way we see fit.

After smashing and reconstructing our mugs and then reflecting on that experience, we dive into close analysis of the text. Using the process called a Descriptive Review of Work, we slowly parse the text, passage by passage and even line by line together. The learning from this activity is not the activity itself or even Schachtel. Once, I had planned to do the exercise, but as I was standing in a used goods store and lifting a mug, another patron exclaimed over how nice it was. I just couldn't smash something that someone else felt they needed and loved.

That said, breaking and reconstructing my mug allowed me to enter the philosophy with more depth than I had before. I now read the book viscerally, feeling in my hands what it means to both break and create, to perceive one way and then another. Analyzing the text closely through Descriptive Processes added another layer. I felt that day that philosophy can (and for me should) be read as embodied experience. Reading philosophy as a teacher among teachers at the Summer Institute added something deep, powerful, and important that my academic training had not offered.

As noted, while teaching Theories, each week I'd pre-read course readings on Friday and then I'd practice yoga on Saturday. I moved in my yoga class into new meanings of the text that I would then bring to my students. For example, much philosophy calls for moderation—finding the balance between conflicting or extreme perspectives. To work with John Locke's *Treatise on Education*, preservice teachers were offered this series of prompts:[18]

- Stand next to a wall or a solid table.
- Please place your feet firmly on the floor. Get a sense of the floor. You may remove your shoes, but you do not need to.
- Find a steady spot to rest your eyes. This should not be another person. They will likely prove unsteady.
- Put your weight on the leg you feel is more sturdy. Use the wall or table if helpful.
- Slowly lift the other leg and hold the position.
- Lower your leg.
- Play around with different ways to balance. Perhaps lift your other leg up. Perhaps raise your hands. Perhaps close your eyes. Explore.
- Consider these questions:
  - How did it feel as you did this activity?
  - How did balancing affect your ability to think and focus?
  - What might balance have to do with teaching young children?

Grappling with equilibrium physically helped the students think through Locke's arguments and legacy. Some questions emerged: *What does a sense of balance do for us? Where is balance helpful? What does disequilibrium do? How might it help? Can balance be achieved without symmetry? What might this mean in other contexts?* Responses to these questions lead to considerations of balance and equanimity as they manifest in current educational discourse. For example, much social-emotional curriculum focuses on maintaining balance and emotional equilibrium. There are other ways to engage with emotions.

WHAT IS THE TEXT TO ME?

We read the world and the word through our experiences. Early childhood curriculum often emphasizes "text-to-self" connections as an entry point. Experiences can also be blinders. In chapter 2, I read Tanisha's comments about Martin Luther King Jr. through my family's losses in the Holocaust. Often a first step in a Review of Work, a process introduced in chapter 3 for studying items people have made, is the Anecdotal Recollection introduced in chapter 4. Hearing peers gives us more experience to rest on and helps us see beyond our own biases.

The Philosophy Fellowship, a teacher group of folks who engage in Descriptive Inquiry, met monthly to study philosophy, Descriptive Inquiry, and teaching together. Entering into Lugones's *Pilgrimages*, a text participants found so challenging and helpful that we stayed with it for multiple years, Cecelia Traugh and Gina Ritscher constructed this Recollection to think about world traveling:

> Think of times when you tried to travel to other's "world." Select one to share with the group.
>
> • What was the context?
> • How did you try to understand the "world" of the other person?
> • How far did you get in understanding what it is to be that other person?
> • How far did you get in understanding what it is to be ourselves in their eyes?

I don't remember what I shared. I do remember grappling with a moment when I felt traveling to someone else's world put my own sense of security at risk. I wanted to discuss how one handles that danger both in relation to Lugones's text and in relation to teaching. I also remember being moved and pushed intellectually in hearing other people's stories and primed to enter Lugones's work more deeply.

IDENTIFYING PASSAGES

This step moves us more directly into the text and maps onto Karen Barad's "diffracted" reading.[19]

- Choose a passage that resonates. One might choose and write about it in advance. Passages can also be chosen on the spot.
- Everyone reads their passage and tells why they chose it, perhaps in rounds or collect all the page numbers of passages ahead of time and share in the order in the text.

CLOSE READING: CRACKING OPEN THE TEXT

Here I offer the steps of a close reading with an excerpt (abbreviated here) from Lugones that proved pivotal for the Philosophy Fellowship.

- Identify a passage. Somewhere between ten and fifteen lines is ideal. This could be a passage that someone chose in the previous activity.
- Read out loud the passage. Now someone else read it out loud.

According to Marilyn Frye, to perceive arrogantly is to perceive that others are for oneself and to proceed to arrogate their substance to oneself (Frye 1983:66). Here, I make a connection between "arrogant perception" and the failure to identify with persons that one views arrogantly or has come to see as the products of arrogant perception . . . The identification of which I speak is constituted by what I come to characterize as playful "world"-traveling. To the extent that we learn to perceive others arrogantly or come to see them only as products of arrogant perception and continue to perceive them that way, we fail to identify with them—fail to love them—in this particular way.[20]

The following steps are typically done in rounds:

- Read the sentence and paraphrase as I have done with the first sentence: *In the thinking of feminist philosopher Marilyn Frye, to look at someone from a place of assumed superiority is to view that that person exists for my benefit and, acting accordingly, I possess that person's essence for my own purposes.* Do ask the group for help on words. I needed to look up *arrogate*. Some words might even be identified later for a Reflection on a Word. We reflected on *arrogant* and *pilgrimages* among others.

- Move sentence by sentence describing features. You can also go back. Some features I note: quotes and frequent citations, long multi-clause sentences, dashes. From Traugh and Ritscher's notes from review with the group, shifts between "one," "I," and "we" and "several clusters of related words that were repeated, although used in different ways: *identification, fail/failure, perceive/perception.*"

- Now make connections and inferences: *What do you now think having listened to the author? Where does this work provoke you further? What more do you want to know about their work? About your own? How might this passage relate to the rest of the piece? To previous discussions?* Arrogant perception as a contrast to world traveling stayed with me. This Review of Work helped me better enter into other sections of Lugones's book when she describes her relationship with her mother and how white women sometimes treat her. It helped me identify that sometimes my children approached me physically and I felt like a tool, my body treated as a means to their end. This didn't feel good. Other times, we joined each other in a hug or handhold or even just resting together, and I felt like we were traveling to each other's world with love.

- Close with a reflection on the process: What did you notice from reading in this way? How might this support your independent reading? Did you honor the author? The work? Did you honor each other?

Even as an experienced reader of philosophy, a Review of Work helps me enter challenging texts and offers a new way into texts where the meaning might initially feel obvious. This careful and attentive reading expands the text. It presses me to listen with respect.

Such reading serves as an exercise. Formally, I practice the Review of Work infrequently but bring this kind of close attention and care back to independent reading. After engaging in the Review of Work as a community together, students can be directed to reading on their own. Here I scaffold moving from the shared close reading to a more independent one as students take on a short assigned reading:

- Take notes as you read. Write in the margins or use sticky notes. Pictorial notes help me as do definitions of terms.
- Collect quotes as you read. You might underline, use a sticky note, or type them out.
- Mark key ideas and quotes that support.
- Identify five big ideas presented in the piece. Collaboratively generating a list is helpful here.
- Try to articulate the thinker's philosophy based on what you've read so far.
- Connect the thinker's philosophy to other readings.
- Give an example from practice of how this lives.

Here is how then preservice early child major Sasha Hampton analyzed a short section of John Locke's vision of education after collecting and paraphrasing key passages and summarizing the passage:[21]

Locke's Philosophy:

> I think Locke believes in the child to decide what they want to learn on any particular day, and the teacher is there for guidance. I see this because he mentioned multiple times in this reading that children should learn what they have a disposition for, and the teacher, parent, role model, etc. shouldn't put certain learning topics upon them.

E. Connecting philosophies:

> Locke's philosophy strongly correlates with my philosophy, especially now that I've learned more about progressive education. I strongly believe that children should be the ones (for the most part) to choose what they learn about. For example, if I were to force them to learn about the rainforest when they really wanted to learn about Egypt, then they'd possibly end up resenting the rainforest as well as me. Personally, I think you can pull any subject (math, science, social studies, etc.) out of any topic the children are interested in, so why not go with the flow of the classroom and their inquiries? [MY NOTE IN MARGIN: Yes. I agree. Many would say that the "content" is less important than the concepts developed through that content.] I know that I learn best and work a lot harder on projects if I'm genuinely interested and intrigued in them, so why would it be any different for young children? I think if Locke were here today, he would agree with me and I with him. [MY NOTE IN MARGIN: :)]

F. Example:

> A better example than what was given in the last section would be something like a few children from your classroom coming back

from recess excited about seeing the buds of blooming flowers in the school garden. They may ask questions to keep this interest of theirs going or the teacher may, but I'm sure a long conversation occurs once the whole class is back in the room from recess. This strikes you, the teacher, because the children had never shown any interest in flowers, gardens, or plants before, but you notice it as a great learning opportunity. So, instead of beginning your pre-planned lesson on mathematics that afternoon, you begin making a KWL chart with your class about flowers, plants, and gardening. This could lead into a large class project. The class could even create their own class garden, have daily journals to write in or draw pictures of what they see, and each child could even grow their own plant in a small cup on a windowsill in the classroom. This is how great learning and great projects begin and come alive. The teacher just has to be able to notice a great learning opportunity as well as be flexible. [MY NOTE IN MARGIN: Exactly. With the younger grades, I think almost all your curriculum could connect back to a theme. With older grades, some elements of math need to be taught independently. This is at least how I found it.]

Sasha builds on the text she has closely studied to infer, commenting that Locke believes the teacher should guide and follow the child's lead because "he mentioned multiple times in this reading that children should learn what they have a disposition for."

Sasha then builds from both Locke and previous reading on "progressive education" to define her own philosophy. Speaking to this confidence, she connects Locke both to other philosophers and also to herself as a philosopher. Putting herself forward as an interlocutor, she concludes that section, "I think if Locke were here today, he would agree with me and I with him." Finally, showing how philosophy could live in the present and in practice, she closes with a detailed and, in her words, "better" example of how a curriculum could be developed around children's interest.

SHAPING SELF AND SHAPING PRACTICE

For Socrates, as we come to know another, we have the chance of ultimately finding our own thinking.[22] After a multipage analysis of Locke, early childhood major and college senior Erin Silver writes:

> An example of what Locke's philosophy looks like enacted is in the book *The Boy Who Would Be a Helicopter* by Vivian Gussin Paley. [MY NOTE IN MARGIN: Awesome to see you connecting across classes!] In one specific part of the book, Paley describes a scene where two preschool-aged boys are engaged in fantasy play. The boys are able to choose what to play, and while doing so, they learn some very important concepts. The boys discuss "too many" and "both" by working out a plan of who will play what role in their pretend play of dad and brother police officers. The boys go back and forth debating how many police officers is too many, to which they finally decide that if they are both police officers, it will not be too many.
>
> Paley argues that no adult would be able to explain these concepts to the boys as effectively as their child-initiated play taught them. She goes on to add, "This is why play feels so good. Discovering and using the essence of any part of ourselves is the most euphoric experience of all. It opens the blocked passages and establishes new routes. Any approach to language and thought that eliminates dramatic play . . . ignores the greatest incentive to the creative process," (Paley, p. 6). This directly relates to Locke's philosophy of allowing the children to be in control of

their learning. The boys in Paley's example used their interests, playing police officers, to learn about abstract concepts, without even realizing they were learning at all. [MY NOTE IN MARGIN: Very strong example and well explained!]

I found that reading this excerpt from John Locke's *Some Thoughts Concerning Education* helped me to further my understanding of my own personal teaching philosophy. I realized that I do agree with Locke that children should learn through their interests and that the teacher should observe the students to determine when is the best time to teach them certain concepts. I also learned that I do not necessarily think children should have all the rights that adults do, but that they should gain these over time. This does not mean that I do not think children should not have any rights, or that the teacher should be a dictator in the classroom. [MY NOTE IN MARGIN: This articulation might be helpful for your final reflection.] I instead feel that the children should develop more rights, and they themselves grow. I also think that the classroom should be a democracy, with the teacher having the right to veto anything that they feel may not be in the best interest of the class. [MY NOTE IN MARGIN: Yes. Your thinking reminds me of a piece of writing by Hannah Arendt. I will get you a copy. She worries about the tyranny that can take place when children are given complete control.] I would not have known any of this about my own philosophy had I not read Locke's and analyzed it thoroughly. This is a perfect example as to why it is so important to research other individual's philosophies, in order to build on one's own [MY NOTE IN MARGIN: I agree.].

As with Sasha, Erin places herself as an interlocutor alongside Locke. Erin pushes back on Locke more directly, commenting earlier in her analysis, "After completely analyzing Locke's philosophy, I have decided that I agree with him to an extent." Striking here are Erin's philosophical acumen and ability to note subtly. By carefully looking at the nuances in Locke's arguments through analysis of quotes, she, in a Socrates-like move, is able to see where she joins Locke and where she diverges.

As with Sasha, Erin brings Locke into contemporary conversation—in this case, drawing extensively from a text from another class, *The Boy Who Would Be a Helicopter*.[23] Mirroring the attention to language she has applied to Locke, she quotes and analyzes Paley with precision, demonstrating her fluency applying close reading skills across texts. Erin specifically brings in Paley as "an example of what Locke's philosophy looked like enacted," showing fluency moving between philosophy and practice.

Erin finds that Locke has "helped me to further my understanding of my own personal teaching philosophy." She then goes on to explain exactly how Locke's ideas have helped her do so. She concludes, "I would not have known any of this about my own philosophy had I not read Locke's and analyzed thoroughly. This is a perfect example as to why it is so important to research other individual's philosophies, in order to build on one's own." Erin highlights both the careful listening that comes from closely analyzing philosophy and how through that careful listening she has grown as a thinker because she was exposed to another's way of thinking.

Similarly, in her final course reflection, Katelyn Beedy shares how reading philosophers both complemented and supported her growing commitments.

1. My core values for teaching include positive relationships, viewing the child holistically, and learning through experiences. I think that my value for positive relationships comes from a very personal place, knowing that my best years in

school were my best years because I had a strong connection with my teacher. I believe my value of viewing the child holistically comes from Dewey, and my value for learning through experiences stems from Locke.

2. As mentioned above, I really enjoyed translating and interpreting the works of Dewey and Locke because I found that I shared a lot of values with them. It helped me to deepen my understanding of why I have those values, and also how my values can be enacted in my future career. I have also found it valuable to read about philosophers who I don't agree with as much as Locke or Dewey. This also helped to shape my values even more. The more I learn about philosophers in this class, the more I seem to learn about myself. [MY NOTE IN MARGIN: That's wonderful. That's why I love philosophy. It gives me a language for thinking about the world.]

Here Katelyn attributes to Dewey and Locke two core values developed over the term. Describing the listening exercises as "translating and interpreting," she acknowledges the close attention to their ideas that she has cultivated all semester. She also notes the power of other perspectives, "philosophers who I don't agree with as much" who "helped to shape my values even more." She closes affirmatively, "The more I learn about philosophers in this class, the more I seem to learn about myself." As with hooks, as with Kimmerer, as with Socrates, as with me, Katelyn finds herself thinking with a community, and through that community, she comes to know others and herself.

In chapter 4, I used the metaphor of words as tools that help us operate in particular ways. Of course, we've all used tools for purposes not intended—we regularly unlock stuck doors with paper clips in my house—but with tools, there is a use, and generally a tool does that activity best. Writing of the power of study—engaging with ideas and practice collaboratively—philosophers Stephano Harney and Fred Moten offer instead *toy.* Harney says, "To me, it's picking up different toys to see if we can get back to what we're really interested in."[24] Toys bring forth imaginative and playful element of engagement. Toys can influence play in the sense that a baby doll may guide a child toward caretaking. Toys are also deeply pliant. In my son's hands, an earring becomes a Transformer. Picking up a concept, a word, a conversation, an author, a text, a philosophical approach, we have toys, and as we play, we grow to move in particular ways. Reading philosophy, we all played, and with the toys offered by each thinker, we uncovered new ways of being.

Build from the Learner

I have read philosophy with people from a range of academic backgrounds with the Descriptive Review of Work. The process is amazing, making accessible that which tends to be evasive and bringing together readers with different levels of experience as peers. As psychologist Jerome Bruner argues, most anyone can learn most anything if it is scaffolded well, and learning to slowly take apart a text is an invaluable part of literacy development.[25]

Parsing a text step-by-step, the teachers picked up strategies that supported their reading. The structured questions scaffolded reading and gave teachers an entry into philosophy. As the teachers repeatedly testify, reading philosophy itself is valuable. Yet an additional benefit is the opportunity that reading philosophy afforded to showcase methods that would help teachers slowly work through texts. The process supported the confidence and the skill that they had a way into the hardest texts and that they could share with children.

Experiential Learning

Dewey argues that we learn to swim by swimming.[26] The workshop model is premised on a similar belief. If we practice reading and writing every day, both alone and with others, we will become readers.[27] That said, throwing someone into a lake and saying "go" is not responsible teaching. Neither is simply handing someone a text.[28] Proponents of the writing workshop, Katie Wood Ray and Lisa Cleveland, give discrete steps to set up a workshop so children slowly acclimate with confidence to the work. Responsive Classroom offers a similar approach to management and conflict. Before you hand children glue sticks, you teach them how to open and close the cap, take just enough, and put them away in the right bin in the classroom. As Cristina illustrates with handwashing, not knowing how to do something suggests that one needs, often very precise, supports.[29] The step-by-step structure of the Descriptive Review of Work scaffolded reading for students and gave them an entry into it.

Attend with Care

The scaffolded reading process helped students feel powerful and successful. In a mid-semester assessment, Katelyn writes:

- I am particularly proud of my newfound ability to translate hard-to-read philosophy passages! I am surprised with my ability to focus on one text and pick up on the meanings of the main points of a text. In a way, it has made me feel powerful. [My NOTE IN MARGIN: So glad! That was one of my hopes with the course. You guys are powerful!] I think this is a great skill to have!

Katelyn is ready to take on the world, and in the next bullet of her response, she expresses pride in participating regularly in class and wanting to keep growing in her power to share her values with others going forward.

Again, honing one's reading skills is valuable, as is the process of working toward something hard. As literacy educator Timothy Shanahan says of learning to read, "Intellectual persistence—an intensity of purpose—is really what I'm talking about. What underlies that is having techniques and skills: What do you do when you come to a sentence that you can't make heads or tails of, or when you come upon a word that you don't know? What do you do when you read three paragraphs in and you're not sure where you are?"[30] Grit, the capacity to stick with something hard, is not a feature of one's essence. None of us are "brick brains." Instead, staying with challenge is a capacity that one learns over many experiences where one successfully works through adversity step-by-step.[31]

Just as Cristina modified the steps by attending to her student to support his handwashing, none of the practices in this chapter (or this book) are perfect. Students were encouraged to diverge from the form as long as they wove in each component. Erin, for example, opted to write her responses to philosophers in paragraph form, paraphrasing and analyzing in a more integrated fashion. Understanding the assignment, she adapted it with "integrity."[32]

When doing the Descriptive Review of Work, some people get very anxious during the paraphrasing round when they come to words they don't know. I've adapted this process with larger groups and undergraduates by often suggesting we do this part collaboratively or encourage people to request an assist on any word.

Interruption and Disruption

At the beginning of the semester, many of the students expressed trepidation about the Theories course. Many did not actually take it by choice but because they needed *an* elective and this one was offered. Learning to listen to philosophers was transformative because the language is so obscure and challenging. As one works through philosophical text, considering the meaning behind each word, one is habituated into attending to language. Reading this way then transfers to reading other types of texts, including the words and writing of children.

Reading a text closely, one becomes attached and feels connected. Having invested this kind of energy in an author, one is more likely to try seeing from their perspective, to consider openness as a stance. In other words, by reading this closely, one travels to another world and, in doing so, likely grows and changes.

BEING A GOOD NEIGHBOR

Freire writes: "If I am prejudiced against a child who is poor, or black or Indian, or rich, or against a woman who is a peasant or from the working class, it is obvious that I cannot listen to them and I cannot speak *with them, only* to *or at* them, from the top down."[33] Many teachers are prejudiced against philosophy, assuming it is too hard and too esoteric. As they learned to listen to something they had dismissed, I hope that they became better listeners period and that this capacity to listen and be open carried into their relationships with other people.

In closing, I will tell one more story. As in chapter 4, I bring you into the classroom of a teacher I observed when supporting student teachers. Entering this classroom, I was put off by what I saw as the teacher's fierce adherence to routines and structures. Her class was incredibly orderly in physical presentation, her movement through the schedule, and her adherence to curriculum. On the other hand, I was drawn by how this teacher always used a soft, gentle voice with children and listened carefully to them. When she redirected, it was done quietly and with affection. The children looked safe and seemed eager to live up to her high expectations.

Honoring children's work, she often had them write and draw with Sharpies—trusting their control of a tool that could be very messy. The permanence of the ink added gravitas to their work, and the children seemed empowered by the pens in their hands and took on the responsibility of the Sharpies with serious intentionality and intense focus.

Her way was not how I showed care, but I came to believe that the rigidity and clarity that the structures brought allowed this teacher and the children to calmly find their voices within the space. Within strict boundaries, there was in fact much freedom that honored the children's need to feel safe and explore and to take creative risks.

A nuanced and expansive understanding of the word *care* helps me see this teacher's work as caring and try to help the student teacher enter in. Listening as a respectful neighbor, I saw an ethos I valued. Yet a student teacher I supported in this classroom felt strongly it was not inclusive and struggled. Aristotle says that a true friend is one who sees you and is able to give critical feedback.[34] In fact, one of the key ways practical wisdom is cultivated is with true friends who help you reach your goals with critical feedback. As noted, Katelyn speaks proudly of her ability to speak up in class and wants to continue to foster this capacity in the field. She also recognizes this as an area to work on that feels challenging. I never pushed the structured teacher described above on her rigidity and felt that wasn't appropriate as a guest in her classroom. I also didn't work with the student teacher to open up a dialogue between them about their differences. But I now think we need more guests who listen and give feedback too. It is to disagreement that I turn to in chapter 6.

YOU DO: READING PHILOSOPHICALLY IN COMMUNITY

- Create spaces for reading together, such as reading groups, conferences, and study groups in schools.
- Introduce protocols that support reading such as those described in the chapter.
- Be prepared to translate ideas, experiences, and words across fields.
- Anticipate, sit with, and reflect on moments of challenge, confusion, and even frustration.[35]

CHAPTER SIX

COLLABORATIVE GRAPPLING IN CULTURE CIRCLES

At recess I've become known as one that you can go to because I'm not just going to tell you to hush up and go. And I'm also not going to let the kid off the hook. But I'm also not just going to dish out a punishment and walk away—we're going to talk about it. I think responding to conflict is where I get the most chance to use the values that are harder to include [such as "affirming that children are humans"].

—Anne, third-grade teacher

One day in my first and second grade class, Lisa told me that her classmate, Janie, was crying because Lars had said something mean. Janie repeated Lars's comment. It was very mean. A common teacher response would be to, in Anne's words, "dish out a punishment." In keeping with our legal system, I would first determine who did what and assess the severity of the harm. Then I would select a just response that adequately punishes the wrongdoer. Lars did not deny his comment, and many children heard it. Janie rarely instigated, and not even Lars accused her of doing so that day. If I follow that line of thought, the question becomes *what is the appropriate punishment?*

But as a teacher I am responsible to each child and their growth and happiness, not to some external notion of justice. Prison abolitionist Mariame Kaba stresses that those who commit crimes tend to have been victims themselves.[1] In every crime, victimhood is far more complex than a simplistic good/bad or victim/perpetrator dichotomy. Lars often bemoaned feeling lonely. He had trouble joining other children. Though he was usually not unkind, his classmates seemed not to know how to engage with him. Janie was popular—able to move smoothly between different children and generally included by her peers. Janie was one of the few children who actively included Lars. In contrast with Janie, Lisa rarely engaged with Lars and complained about him often. Asked what happened, Lars readily admitted to what he said but countered that they weren't including him. I suspected this particularly stung since Lars was often excluded by Lisa and rarely by Janie, and he lashed out with the cruel comment.

I sympathized, and I could, again in Anne's words, "let the kid off the hook." This didn't seem right either. A harm had been done. Janie needed something to heal. Her classmates witnessed this harm. Lars struggled socially for a variety of reasons but sometimes because he was, in fact, not very nice to his peers. I wanted to be clear with everyone that what Lars did was not okay. I cared about each child. How could I resolve this situation with that care? My students were learning how to be friends and care for others in turn. How could I ensure that while fairness was achieved, growth was as well?

In a management curriculum used in my school, Responsive Classroom, when children had a conflict, each child was asked what they needed going forward to feel better.[2] With Lars, Janie, Lisa, and the rest of the class, though, determining what was needed was not so clear.

Philosopher Kate Manne writes that "there is nothing conceptually difficult" in recognizing that someone who hurts others might have also been harmed.

> But these ideas are not easily incorporated into the narratives that script many of our *reactions* to wrongdoing. We only have one set of eyes, and hence can only occupy one point of view at once, plausibly. Similarly, our points of view are typically total, rather than partial. So, if empathy requires perspective-taking in a rather literal (though of course not necessarily visual) sense, this may limit the number of characters in a story who we can empathize with simultaneously—especially when they are somehow at cross purposes.[3]

When our view is narrowed to only see one perspective at a time, the other is occluded. Through sources ranging from children's fairy tales to our legal system, the dominant cultural narrative is one in which justice within demands a victim and a perpetrator.[4]

Further, Manne argues that when someone can see the perpetrator with any sympathy or even see their humanity, this can supersede their ability to appreciate that despite some sympathetic qualities, someone did indeed perpetrate a horrendous act. Considering simplistic narratives that paint a person as either good or evil, Manne writes:

> You might wonder if these narratives are the problem. I think they are a problem, but I doubt that we can give them up completely. Would that we were better at recognizing that someone can be both threatened and a threat to others, both wounded and lashing out, and both vulnerable and hostile. I believe we need to think seriously about how to do justice to the duality

and ambiguity of our moral roles, perhaps by dint of more nuanced alternatives to the fairly crude, Manichean moral narratives that are currently our primary cultural recourse for interpreting wrongdoing. But at least as importantly, I think we need to get better at recognizing the fact that there are often multiple overlapping narratives that cut against each other.[5]

One issue at stake is the kinds of stories that make up our cultural orientation as discussed in chapter 3. Yet Manne also identifies that sometimes the issue is not simply the narratives we are conducted into but the fact that in life situations are often complicated and it is truly challenging to hold two perspectives at once. One can dually feel bad for Lars and acknowledge that what he did was wrong.

Longtime teacher Karen Gallas argues that we shouldn't treat children's actions the same as adults' because they don't carry the same intent. On the other hand, she emphasizes that children's actions can be read as experiments that slowly become habits.[6] As children navigate daily conflict, they are learning ways of being in the world. Helping children navigate these moments in a manner that holds space for nuance, complexity, and different perspectives grows people able to respond with more nuance to each other as adults. My task with Lars and Lisa was not to determine what was fair and mete out justice but to help all the children learn to engage with more kindness going forward. This demanded that I, as the teacher, hold multiple truths in my mind at the same time. In teaching this capacity, I call for broadening perspective and building on this expanded perspective to reframe a situation so the context is less stifling.

MULTIPLE PERSPECTIVES IN CULTURE CIRCLES

How does one learn to hold multiple perspectives at once, to turn a situation over and over to see multiple layers? A key to this work is engagement with ethical questions, what I have elsewhere termed with math educator Shannon Larsen "collaborative grappling."[7] The capacity to grapple collaboratively is strengthened when practiced with dilemmas regularly and over time.[8] To grapple with dilemmas in low-stakes situations offers an "exercise" to draw from amid challenges.[9] For example, regularly listening to different perspectives when the stakes are low—such as discussing a read-aloud—prepares students to listen in the midst of actual conflict.

As longtime teacher Cornelius Minor explains, "Class meeting might happen in line as we walk to lunch or the gym; it might happen on the bus on the way to a field trip or during a class transition from one activity to the next. If I have done this well, the kids don't even know that we've had a 'meeting.' This should feel like we're just talking. Because we are."[10] The more a community meets to discuss all kinds of topics, the readier they are to have serious conversations about weighty issues. The exercises in this chapter are based on the contention that engaging in regular collaborative grappling must be "intentional" and that, when practiced regularly, it can be drawn on constantly. Such responses to conflict begin to "feel like we're just talking."

What exercises encourage collaborative grappling? Ethicists of education Meira Levinson and Jacob Fay suggest discussing normative case studies to jump-start teacher reasoning with analysis from a range of experts (faculty, practitioners, administrators).[11] Cecelia Traugh and I have described how Descriptive Inquiry brings teachers together as equals to think through a shared question or look at a topic or piece of work.[12] The phrase *culture circle*, which I adapt because of its roominess, comes from Paulo Freire and describes community engagements in which the learners set the parameters of the conversation.[13] Freire provides no precise method. He does emphasize that the meaning must come about democratically, with participants coming together around a particular topic of importance to the community. From this definition,

I believe that the methods described by Levinson and Fay and Traugh and me can be engaged as culture circles. The core elements from each approach to collaborative grappling are:

- a shared concern or question derived from a community or determined as relevant to that community
- a structured method for participating that encourages each person to weigh in as equals
- analysis of the discussion to determine findings

In this chapter, I showcase how culture circles can be scaffolded so they can be drawn on both with preplanning and, as Minor notes, spontaneously. Finally, I want to emphasize that this work is challenging not only because assumptions may be upended (such as stories about justice) but also because in making meaning with students, we step into the unknown. I focus primarily on whole-class engagements but reference some other ways where the ethos of the culture circle left its mark in smaller-group interactions.

CULTURE CIRCLES: SETTING THE SCENE

Culture circles help build interdependent communities. They also depend on a baseline of respect that includes the capacities high-lighted in chapter 5 to both speak and listen for the sake of making meaning. Here I describe a series of structures that can help prepare a group for meaningful and frank dialogue.

Names

In chapter 1, I emphasize the importance of the learning environment. One of the most important environmental factors is knowing people's names.[14] In my interviews, longtime secondary teacher educator Beatrice describes how she communicates "I really care about names" by "spend[ing] a lot of time on names" and giving a "fake low stakes quiz" to "hold" "students accountable." After describing the efforts he takes to ensure that students learn names, philosopher of education David Hansen argues that name work "facilitates whole- and small group discussion. I also believe that using names regularly in classroom talks supports the emergence of a humane environment or, phrased differently, an environment that humanizes."[15] One must be in a "humane environment" to think well with others.

To know each other intellectually, my students begin a semester-long ritual the first week called "Big Ideas" in which we close each week with every student saying what they will take from our work together. Often students are asked to speak when their comment fits with the one that went before it. This encourages careful listening and connecting in some manner, including disagreement.

Seating

How we orient physically also matters immensely. As Hansen describes in chapter 1, placing chairs in a circle fosters the democratic community he seeks.[16] In a culture circle with preK students processing the Boston Marathon bombing, teacher Dana Bentley moved from her chair that elevated her above the students to the floor. This signaled that she was participating as a group member in the conversation.[17]

For culture circles, I move the class from the chairs where they are spread out widely and have desks separating them from each other. We push back the chairs and desks, and most sit on the floor, though everyone has the option of a chair. The switch in location showcases that we are doing something special since we usually sit at desks. The floor itself is more intimate—we find ourselves closer to each other, and students sometimes even take the liberty of leaning on a friend. Additionally, it is hard to bring paper, computers, phones, water bottles, bookbags, and so on to the floor. Leaving behind accessories signals an emphasis on listening to each other. As with Bentley, I signal my own place among the group by sitting among the students on the floor.

Interdependence

Using the analytic attention to language of chapter 4, philosopher of education Sigal Ben-Porath notes how describing contemporary discourse with language like "cancel" and "war" suggests that participants should annihilate those with different perspectives.[18] Knowing each other's names and seating arrangements that encourage democratic engagement counter this destructive impulse. Those with different opinions are, as Hansen says, "humanize[d]."[19]

An additional key element is building trust and reciprocity—a sense that we are interdependent and no one should be removed. This too requires intentional instruction. Elementary teacher educator Sam said the following:

> One of the things I almost always open up with is developing a web of interdependence. It's a simple activity that I've seen done in many places, but I bring a ball of yarn that I actually spun from the wool of the sheep that I raised. I start with a ball of yarn, and I will share something about myself, who I am, and something that I feel passionately about. Then I throw it to the next person and the yarn spins around the circle and it builds this web. And then I ask a few students to drop it. I talk about the integrity of the web and what's happened now that a few people have dropped their hold within our community. That leads into a conversation of the ways in which we're all needed to contribute to the community.

As with my collaborative block building in chapter 1, Sam's web leads to a class experience that illustrates a way of being together, sets a tone, and ultimately proves a touchstone to reference as a reminder of everyone's role.

Educators Chip Wood and Peter Wrenn encourage teachers to make a list of all the children in their class and next to each child write something that they know about them. They then ask the teacher to consider whether the child knows they know and, if not, to take the time to tell the child. In this way, the teacher dually ensures that they are paying attention to their students and the children know they've been seen. I share this activity with my students and then tell them to look around the room—going person by person to see if they could say something positive about each classmate and whether that classmate knows they know. I tell them to pay attention and over the course of the semester subtly share what they've noticed with the peer. If we are to listen to others, seeing them as people we know and even care about supports the process.

Participation Structures

Different modes of conducting discussion lead to vastly different participation.[20] If a conversation is carefully structured to promote equity of voice, people who do not know or feel connected to each other can become connected through the conversation. The capacity to make meaning together can be cultivated quickly through participation structures that invite. Intimacy and community often follow.

In my first college teaching gig, my colleague and co-teacher at the time, education professor Wanda Watson, suggested that I stop calling on students and have them lead the conversation for some of our class discussions. I found the proposition scary and frankly a little unappealing. I worried about what would happen. As a graduate student faculty member, I had just established a new realm of authority (teaching adults), and I didn't want to let go of my role in the group as arbiter and "wise" commenter.

From the student perspective, I had also always found it hard to jump into conversations that were not regulated by some person. I had been assigned the role of lead faculty for this particular class, and so the ultimate decision was in my hands. That said, I respected Wanda and our collaboration very much. I felt I needed to honor her suggestion regardless of how nervous it made me. The result was amazing. Removing myself from the conversation led, as Wanda of course knew, to a much deeper conversation. It also led to much more participation—the burden of long pauses now on the students instead of me.

Since then, I have included student-facilitated discussions in every class. Every semester, I worry, likely because I have been habituated into a desire for control and certainty, that without my guidance nothing will happen. Yet these conversations tend to be the most meaningful. Along the way, I've picked up a few strategies that address some of my initial misgivings about particular people dominating or not behaving in ways that encourage sharing and listening:

- Have the class establish ground rules for how people will elect to speak. For example, the person who just spoke can call on someone with a hand raised. Students might also speak in the go-around with everyone having a clear time to speak.
- Every student is encouraged to regulate participation by reflecting on their obligation to the community. Quiet students are encouraged to speak up and talkers to pause before jumping in to make sure others have a chance to contribute to the conversation. As demonstrated in Sam's keystone activity, if anyone drops the thread, some integrity of the conversation is lost.

- If a group wants them or needs them, we make rules about participation explicit. My students tend to prefer listening to speaking. Occasionally the rules require that everyone participate at least once. Some noisier groups might want their peers to participate only once.
- Sometimes it helps to generate open-ended discussion questions ahead of time, especially if the class is building the discussion around an assigned reading. Small groups can devise questions or find quotes they want to discuss and post them on the classroom boards. During the discussion, students can then voice predetermined questions or come up with new ones.
- To keep myself engaged but not dominating, my job, which I explain ahead of time, is to take notes. Often I will provide an integrated restatement either orally in the moment or typed the following day noting themes and outlier comments.

To give a sense of this practice in action, I will analyze one provocation for a culture circle I like to use early on. I will then give an overview of the range of topics covered in culture circles.

WHAT TO DO ABOUT COYOTE?

In my classroom, children had the opportunity to choose books that interested them and read books to support skill development. As noted in chapter 1, with teachers I create collections of picture books loosely assorted around a theme for an independent exploration.[21] Teachers keep track on a What We Read chart of books they want to use in their future classrooms with the following prompts:

- What We Read: Title, Author, Illustrator
- What makes it valuable to me?
  – Values it conveys?
  – Skills it supports?

- Something I liked about it?
- What does this book include? (consider topics and context)
- Who does it include and leave out? (consider the identity of those depicted as well as the identity of the author)
- How might I use it?

As noted in chapter 2, as students read, I ask them to share, discuss, and recognize what they do and don't like with the right to disconnect emphasized.[22] Introducing the What We Read chart, I focus on attention to who is included. No book will include everyone, but a classroom library must reflect windows and mirrors so children see themselves represented across a range of books and are exposed to other communities.[23] My library and curation are imperfect and ongoing, and each student reviews my collections and discusses who is well included and who is absent. Over time, some holes students have identified that I've worked to address include the presence of military families and books featuring characters who identify as lesbian, gay, bisexual, transgender, and nonbinary. In one assignment, students research for books that "tell a story they wish had been present in their own classroom."

Every semester, it is inevitable. One day, I hear a yelp. When I approach and ask what's going on, the student will express outrage, disturbance, frustration, or disbelief about a particular text. Their unrest is followed with something like "I cannot possibly imagine sharing this with children." "Why not?" I query. Typically, their answer follows one of three tracks: the book is morally suspect because characters are not nice to each other or behaving in ways deemed unappealing, the topic is perceived as controversial such as a book that offers a secular take on the Old Testament, or the text handles topics deemed inappropriate for young children such as jail, death, or slavery. As calls for book banning spread through the country, in my classes responses to books are stronger and students are less tolerant of ambiguity. Where my students, at least with me, reject overt censorship, concerns about appropriateness and fear of how others might respond to a text are widespread.

When my students challenge a book, I am relieved because it opens up the space to discuss. Here I discuss one such offending book that consistently yields rich discussion: *Coyote: A Trickster Tale from the American Southwest* by Gerald McDermott.[24] I begin with an ongoing dilemma. When I became a teacher, I discovered McDermott's folktale "retellings." I knew to also seek out and include folktales authored by those from the culture from which they came. However, I didn't interrogate McDermott's tellings to the degree to which I should have, and I purchased a number of his texts and centered them in the folktale curriculum discussed in chapter 3.[25] I have since listened when interlocutors have challenged McDermott's and others' retellings. I would no longer make these books the focus with children. At the time of this writing, I still share them with teachers in part as a chance to discuss appropriation and incorrect portrayals of the Indigenous communities McDermott borrows from.[26]

Yet in raising my children, teaching my classes, and writing this book, I find a remaining dilemma. Do I remove McDermott's books entirely from my library and stop reading *Coyote*? Or do I continue to include the books but do so centering Indigenous critiques? As indicated in the What We Read prompts, every text in a classroom demands consideration of authorship. At present, I have determined the following about *Coyote*. As summarized by professor of sociology and equity studies Judy Iseke-Barnes, rewriting the stories of another culture is wrong for many reasons, including that doing so easily misrepresents, tends to be superficial, often degrades and can be racist, and is a "theft."[27] *Coyote*, contrary to the full title, is not a trickster tale from the American Southwest. It is a story that McDermott wrote that takes components from Indigenous tales from the Southwest. *Coyote* includes superficial depictions of Indigenous culture that need naming and challenging.

Writing this chapter, I have also debated whether to devote so much attention to a text I no longer highlight with children and find so problematic, but I think sharing my journey away from this book as a white educator is useful. Additionally, as a teacher and parent, I don't forbid but I do engage in critical conversations about resources.[28] Finally, *Coyote* is fairly unique in that children tend to love the narrative and adults, as discussed, become very upset by the characters' behavior. The narrative pushes students of all ages to talk in more nuanced ways about inclusion and kindness. With caveats and concerns, I've opted to include the book.

Blue Coyote, the protagonist (or maybe antagonist), "has a nose for trouble" and "always finds it." Coyote wants to fly with the crows. Begrudgingly consenting, the crows each take a feather and affix it to Coyote. This is painful, making Coyote "cringe" as they stab the feather into his side. Coyote flies but not particularly well, and unable to keep up, he whines. The effect is that he, as child readers point out, ruins the crows' game. Frustrated, the crows retrieve their feathers from Coyote mid-flight, and he falls. From this episode, "to this day" he is permanently gray.

I've read this text countless times to children and teachers. My older son relates to the rule-enforcing crows, and my younger son seems to identify with a mischievous Coyote who wants to be included. I wrote the following in my journal after reading the book with third graders:

> They worked really well together and had good energy. We read *Coyote* today which led to some good discussion about inclusion and exclusion. Armen said he liked the story because he, like Coyote, has a nose for trouble.

Tiana did a beautiful job explaining the positives and negatives of the book—that the crows are kind of mean but that coyote is pretty frustrating.

Children, as captured here, find the book engaging and consistently note the nuances in the relationships. They also often can see both sides, as Tiana does. When the birds stick their feathers into Coyote, teachers recoil. Adults tend to be critical of the book (even angry) and its message. One teacher expressed anger and horror that after his engagement with the mean crows, Coyote had been permanently changed. Teachers often worry the book will promote bullying. To address this text philosophically in a culture circle, I have the following routine.

- I share issues with cultural appropriation.
- I have the class join me on the rug and read out loud.
- Students turn and talk with initial impressions. Sometimes I give permission to not like the book.
- Students share in the full group. Typically, the class is at first unusually quiet. Sometimes students look for the positives about the book even though in partners they were critical. Once one person expresses dislike, the floodgates open, and the majority of students have a negative take on the plot.
- Once a number and range of impressions are aired, I pivot beyond opinion to consider the message of the text. *How many of you think that Coyote was wrong? How many of you disagree with the crows? Why?*
- I then tell students that I will keep quiet, and a nuanced and animated discussion tends to develop.
- Wrapping up, I share that when reading moralistic texts about the value of inclusion, my first and second graders tended to take a righteous stand, making claims like "I would never exclude anyone." This book allowed us to talk more deeply.

Teachers often describe this discussion as transformative. As then preservice elementary student Jada Richard reflected:

> While my classmates saw how mean and rude both the coyote and crows are I saw the nonfictional component of the book [the coyote and crows were behaving somewhat like the animals they are based on]. I really like the concept of people seeing different things from the same readings and I would definitely make that part of my teachings. Finding the morals and themes of things is so fascinating to me and I know that heavily influences how I teach. Connecting to personal experience both influences my writing and reading. I fully believe that if a student can connect something they read or wrote to something personal they will understand better. It's another core value I have for literacy. If a student was picked on when they tried to join a group of people they can relate to the coyote in the book.

For Jada, bringing in a range of "themes" or topics becomes a keystone of her reading identity. In fact, Jada did a self-directed project researching books that featured characters from communities often excluded from classrooms and decided to create a calendar that highlighted these books. Instead of running away from controversy or banning certain topics, Jada leans into them.

Noting the value of perspective, Jada celebrates the opportunity to read the same text and, after close analysis, take away different meanings. For Jada, closely reading a text, with strategies modeled in chapters 3 and 5, allowed her and her classmates to read closely for the message(s) of a text and then determine where they stood.

Reading *Coyote* and discussing it in a culture circle paved the way for deeper analysis of the messaging in books as well as more nuanced discussions of right and wrong. As showcased by Jada's reference to reading *Coyote* months later in her final reflection, the book and conversation proved a touchstone to reference as we discussed other picture books with difficult themes.

The discussion of teasing offers us a soft launch into culture circles. While teachers vociferously object to the relationship between Coyote and the crows, another layer of concern is McDermott's appropriation. Here I add the next and more challenging layer, ideal to be taken up soon after the original read.

- Read aloud *Creation* by Gerald McDermott, which is a retelling from the beginning of the Old Testament.[29]
  - What is your response to hearing this text told as a story?
- For homework, read the article about appropriation of trickster tales and gather quotes related to the ethics of reading McDermott's tales.[30]
- Share meaningful quotes from the article.
- Using the culture circle format, address the following:
  - What are the ethics of teaching with these books?
  - What are the concerns?
  - How might you handle texts such as these in the classroom?
  - How does this conversation fit within larger commitments to culturally sustaining pedagogy?
- Role-play: Students break into groups of two or three. One person will be the teacher and the other children and/or parents. With language focused on the grade they teach, practice presenting to children and/or parents' concerns about McDermott's presentation of the Indigenous origins folktale.

WELCOMING PROVOCATIONS

The capacity to live with the conundrums is not a one-time lesson but a daily way of being in the classroom. Writing from the kindergarten classroom, Vivian Paley comments, "Whenever the discussion touched on fantasy, fairness, or friendship ('the three

Fs' I began to call them), participation zoomed upward."[31] Young children and their teachers are perennially concerned with fairness and friendship. In the case of *Coyote*, the provocation was planted intentionally by me because the issues raised by the book are always timely.

Discussing *Coyote* early sets the tone for students to raise disagreements and concerns as the semester goes on. What proves provocative for a given class then varies considerably. Often student behavior leads to the provocation needing discussion. For example, in one early childhood literacy course, a critical minority were resistant to reading. Perceiving this tension, I asked students to respond to the question *what is literacy?* Though the conversation was only about ten minutes, it was rich and wide-reaching with students considering what it means to think without words and the range of activities associated with literacy. This early conversation laid out many of the themes we would address that semester, giving me a touchpoint to regularly return to. In Theories, students read an article about children given yoga balls to sit on instead of chairs. The argument in the article was that the children would be able to concentrate better if they could move. One student challenged this practice, saying that teachers should instead create a more inclusive interactive space in which children don't need yoga balls to sit still because they are sitting less. She phrased her challenge as the question "Are the yoga balls really necessary?" and I turned the question to the class for discussion.

VALUES IN ACTION

Build from the Learner

I have encouraged different perspectives and disagreement in my classes. Yet I have found that despite encouragement, students tend to resist controversy and seem to believe that, in spite of my claims otherwise, there is actually one right way of doing things.[32] It seems no surprise that in a culture where disagreement is often described as "wars," my kind and non-dominating students would avoid anything hinting at conflict.

Engaging in culture circles on a regular basis creates a space for grappling with the unknown and a format to support that work. My first and second graders would not have been able to have an honest and productive discussion about friendship on the first day. It came from building relationships and structures for speaking with each other. In beginning with planned (and lower-intensity and lower-stakes) provocations, we exercise capacities that can be drawn on in unplanned and often higher-intensity moments such as how to respond to racism or school shootings.

As an entry to discuss perspective, I like starting with a book and *Coyote* in particular because it focuses on a kind of mundane meanness that is recognizable to children and those who work with children. No class has yet to come to a clear-cut conclusion about who has acted justly, though some individual students feel strongly about a particular character. It allows us to first wade into discussions of controversy and practice our capacity to think together with low stakes and then to take tensions on more directly as we discuss McDermott's appropriation.

Experiential Learning

In grappling collaboratively, students experience sharing and hearing different perspectives on a broad range of topics. In doing so, they seem to find their own perspectives as well as note those of others. Students must experience welcoming different ideas. They must feel the power and potential of disagreement as it occurs in a safe context. For example, after having engaged in culture circles multiple times and then led a collaborative storytelling activity with a peer, then preservice teacher Mattilda Rice says, "I think using these during circle time or other activities is useful and allows for every child to have a chance to add in their thoughts. It is a great time to bring the group together and talk about something that we have done or something that is important to us while allowing everyone to have a fair share to add in or choose to just listen." Here Mattilda showcases not only what she learned by engaging in culture circles but, through experiencing this, the value of creating similar spaces for children to express themselves.

Interruption and Disruption

In a culture that values conformity and agreement and sometimes shuns people when they express opinions or misspeak, listening and responding to others can be scary and intimidating for teachers. Experiencing conversations with disagreements and learning structures to support these conversations make them less scary.

In starting with reading *Coyote*, sharing my own and other students' mixed responses to the text and my regret that I included the book initially without attention to appropriation, I lay the groundwork for disagreement and even dislike of particular ideas and resources. I see this as granting permission for the risk taking necessary for both speaking and listening that a democratic society depends on. As my colleague Wanda Watson showed me so many years ago, taking myself out of the conversation and setting some ground rules does much to encourage the risk of participation. Without an obvious authority, me, lending weight to an idea, students have more room to enter in with their own voices. That said, I do weigh in directly about concerns with cultural appropriation because I want to protect and amplify what I see as the more vulnerable perspective of an Indigenous community that has often been silenced.[33]

Given the chance to practice speaking out throughout the semester, then preservice teacher Kiley Chambers expresses pride in her participation:

> I feel that I had beneficial things to add to the discussion and honestly felt like a leader at certain points during in-class discussions. I felt confident in what I had to say and felt I was able to start discussions as well as bounce off of what others had said . . . I feel that I gave my classmates the space to be able to speak their thoughts too and think I did a good job being an active listener. I am not trying to toot my own horn by any means, but it is often difficult for me to be an active participant in class, but in this class, this semester I am very proud of myself for all of the participation . . .

Interrupting old patterns of behavior, Kiley feels the reward of being a "leader" and developing confidence. Just a few years later, Kiley is a teacher with her own classroom, confidently speaking up to administrators and parents as she works to navigate what she believes is right. Having learned to take risks as a student and shift communication patterns, she now continues to do so as a teacher.

MY CLASS IS TOO NICE

Now returning to Lars, Janie, and Lisa. Lars's class had read and discussed *Coyote* in much the way described in this chapter. While initially quick to condemn exclusive behavior in theory, after reading *Coyote*, they recognized that they sometimes acted in exclusive ways and behaved in ways that frustrated others. As a class, we identified in *Coyote* where things could have gone differently and re-storied the book with a resolution where everyone was treated better.

Processing Lars's conflict with Lisa and Janie, I blurted out to my principal, "My class is too nice!" As the words came out, I recognized that following my lead, my well-behaved, conflict-averse students were choosing politeness over honest communication. Lars would benefit from clearer feedback from peers. Building on the foundation of talking about how we treat others, soon after the conflict with Lars, Lisa, and Janie, I did something many would find controversial. I called a class meeting. I told the class that I noticed that when children didn't like what their peers were doing, they acted politely and then avoided that classmate. I acknowledged that I too tended to avoid people when they upset me. Yet not confronting people when they upset us, as the class discussed, makes people lonely and deprives them of a clear sense of why they were left out. As described in chapter 5, a true friend supports us in our projects and gives us honest and sometimes critical feedback.[34] My class decided to give each other clear feedback to support acting as better friends. Going forward, they did. Over time, Lars was not simply tolerated but became a valued friend.

Freire conceived of culture circles as a space to name the world with all those who have a stake in a situation, and the goal in naming is change.[35] In closing, I highlight that the capacity to see wider, to expand our vision and grapple with nuance, gave my class and me an entry to act more justly with Lars. We moved past niceness to friendship. Yet, despite supports like Responsive Classroom, my and Lisa's initial reaction to Lars was to follow judicial logic and punish. Even though I believed in talking through conflict and even taught this with picture books, the conflict between Lars, Lisa, and Janie made me see I was not living this value in pushing my students to prioritize niceness. Why were my commitments and my daily practice out of sync? In chapter 7, I turn to how one recognizes the culture where one sits and how this influences values.

YOU DO

- Make a list of thorny challenges in your classroom (or school community). Some of these might be particular to this year. Others might be perennial. Stick with conflicts and situations where multiple goals are at stake and you suspect a way forward demands forging a new and nuanced path.
- Using the hermeneutical tools of chapter 3, analyze a few of these conflicts to think about what deeper issues might be at stake. For example, is your class struggling, as mine often do, with a tension between forging close and somewhat exclusive friendships and pressures to welcome everyone?
- Now use the same tools to find a story that grapples with similar issues. Perhaps it is a published book, or maybe you have a story from your own childhood that is fitting.
- Ask your group to gather in a circle.
- Set the rules with them for engagement. Will everyone respond in rounds? Will they call on each other? Must everyone participate?
- Begin with a question that will help them consider the nuance of perspectives in the story.
- Once students have discussed the issues at length and raised a range of points, ask them to write a new ending or way forward. How could this story move on so everyone feels okay?
- Now (or maybe the next day), ask the students to connect their resolution to an actual situation in the classroom. How could they take what they learned about perspective to better handle this thorny conflict in a manner that keeps everyone, using Sam's metaphor, holding a string in the web of the community?

PART 3

TEACHING FROM ONE'S MORAL CENTER

CHAPTER SEVEN

WHOM DO YOU WALK WITH?

One day,
your legs will have power
to break through vines
that bind old growth
and block your path forward

The trees may whisper,
we know the way,
but follow your own, sweet boy,
Your heart is a compass
that will guide you.

You will shift the stories we tell . . .

—Joanna Ho[1]

As a first- and second-grade teacher, I had students who wouldn't write. This was frustrating. I was passionate about writing and saw writing instruction as an area of practical wisdom. I pulled from best practices and innovated. One child, Amanda, had lots to say (orally), was creative (when drawing), and had decent spelling, punctuation, and pencil grip. Amanda spoke with a flair for narrative construction. In other words, she had all the competencies I initially looked for when troubleshooting. Still, Amanda would not write.

One problem-solving approach was through a lens of efficacy. Perhaps other genres were more enticing. Research both supports the curriculum I used and challenges it. Perhaps she needed more choice?[2] Following that tack, one day, I cut out pictures from magazines and glued them into the picture spot on a page with lines for writing.[3] I suggested Amanda and her classmates make up stories about the picture. She did, writing pages and pages of fantasy. It turned out many but not all of Amanda's classmates preferred writing fantasy too.

Yet something nagged at me. More was at stake than simply finding methods that worked. At the time, I was rereading *The History of Sexuality*, Michel Foucault's philosophical genealogy, a concept I define in the next section.[4] As I followed Foucault's careful tracing of the lineage of confessional practice from the church to the law to secular practices such as psychoanalysis, I wondered, *Was asking children to write personal narrative in some ways akin to asking for a confession? Was I demanding an exchange of personal stories for the approval of the teacher?*[5] Perhaps Amanda wasn't writing because she didn't want to share intimate details with an authority figure.

Foucault helped me think through an ethical challenge in the classroom by unearthing some surprising links.[6] Reading Foucault alongside Amanda's resistance, I saw a society that asked people to share biographical information with the promise of some kind of gain, and this worried me.[7] Having named and described the idea and seen how it lived over time, I now took an ameliorative approach to confessional discourse. I queried, *is it just to ask children to share their home lives as part of a school assignment?* Or, put more broadly, *should people exchange biographical information for gain?*

We often talk about whether a child's peers are a good influence. Anthropologist Pierre Bourdieu describes habitus as the habituated ways in which people go about their daily actions.[8] He argues that these grooves are personally developed and also culturally derived. We think in the patterns of our forebears and community or, put more positively, stand on their shoulders. Our peer influences are both in person and cultural, contemporary and historical. As Robin Wall Kimmerer writes, "The questions scientists raised were not 'Who are you?' but 'What is it?' No one asked plants, 'What can you tell us?' The primary question was 'How does it work?' The botany I was taught was reductionist, mechanistic, and strictly objective."[9] Western science treats plants as an object to be colonized. Potawatomi science engages them as peers to be engaged with. We learn these different perspectives from the communities we think with, and these different perspectives encourage different practices.

Approaching retirement, historian and philosopher of education Robbie McClintock taught a course at Teachers College, Columbia, titled "My Canon." [10] As a doctoral student, I was unable to take the course, but the premise intrigued me. I had always been interested in people's libraries. I anticipated students in the course would make their way through McClintock's canon, a fantastic list of books shared in the course description. Yet I became more intrigued when I learned that though McClintock would share the books that he traveled with, he invited students to consider their canons in the course. This resonated with another idea I was playing with at the time, David Hansen's call to teachers to consider their handbooks.[11] Writing of the ancient Greek philosopher

Epictetus's "Handbook," Hansen describes it as "a set of his views on the art of living put together by one of his students" that "was meant to be carried around by the learner: to be held by hand, kept in hand, in order to be ready at hand."[12] We keep thinkers with us, often in the form of books, so we can live better.[13]

Whom, McClintock's and Hansen's work makes me wonder, does the teacher carry in hand? To determine who will help us live up to our ethos, we must interrogate those we think among. In this chapter, we investigate influences, chosen, inherited, noticed, and under the surface. In doing so, I take a historical and contemporary perspective to bring together a number of activities previously introduced, and I add a few more. Before diving into exercises, I offer another layer to the philosophical framing of this chapter to help perceive the influence of heritage.

"WHAT FLASHES UP"

While I was finishing this book, my father left a phone message. "Everyone is okay," he prefaced, "but . . . I need to talk with you soon before you read a troubling email." When I called, my father explained that a relative had found records of the murders of "Jew Furman," my great-grandparents, and the discovery of unmarked graves. The news hurt. We all knew my paternal grandparents were murdered by Nazis, though the details were nebulous. After the Second World War, when my grandfather tried to return home, a neighbor reported that his parents and a brother had been murdered and that the family property had been repossessed by neighbors. *Don't return*, he was admonished. *The new owners will kill you too.* Thus, my grandfather, weary from war, learned of the loss of his family and his home alongside a threat to his life. He turned around and left the country, and none of us ever returned. Locating what had long been denied us, an acknowledgment and account of the murder and the location of graves, helped me feel oriented, but it was a painful and grief-filled orientation.

In an essay titled "What Flashes Up," philosopher Karen Barad describes how elements of the past emerge and become prominent in a particular context.[14] Barad draws on the metaphor of constellations to describe how multiple beings create a shape despite existing at different times. Barad offers a visceral and political engagement with the past.[15] The past doesn't just influence the present; it lives with it, and how it lives poses ethical concerns. As described in chapter 2, my great-grandparents and their murders often flash up to make claims on and in the present, influencing my ethos.[16]

At the opening of this chapter, the regulatory nature of confession "flashed up" in the personal narrative curriculum, pushing my students to share stories in a manner that, despite the best of intentions, left them exposed. The past cannot be simply left behind. It is present regardless of intent, and it surfaces in noisy and unexpected ways.

As the past lives in and influences the present, an important part of locating oneself is tracing origins. Language and literacy professor Gholdy Muhammad calls teachers to historicize, by which she "means to connect a topic to history or to represent it as historical. I often suggest to teachers that they teach history and meaning of their discipline during the first days of school rather than beginning with Chapter 1 of their textbooks, which may do little more than teach skills in isolation."[17] As philosopher Alasdair McIntyre argues, we are "part of a history and that is generally to say, whether I like it or not, whether I recognize it or not, one of the bearers of a tradition."[18] We draw stability and a needed context when we historicize. As McIntyre writes and Muhammad suggests, "Deprive children of stories and you leave them unscripted, anxious, stutterers in their actions as in their words."[19]

A philosophical genealogy, an approach associated with Foucault and Friedrich Nietzsche, traces a particular idea or way of thinking and acting.[20] For example, Foucault traces morals, sexuality, punishment, and confession to see how each has lived and lives. One looks both at what has been said about an idea and at the apparatus and practices that construct it. Confession, Foucault finds, lives in church documents, in a particular way of being with a priest, and the schema later emerges in the relationship between therapist and patient.[21] In mapping a genealogy, one looks for a schema passed on such as how confession involves sharing biographical details in exchange for either religious or emotional absolution. In confessional relationships, the person who shares is in some way dependent on the other person who is silent. The context changes from the confessional to the therapist's office, but the relationship and the power dynamic are much the same.

A genealogy is not typically seen as evaluative or subjective.[22] Yet, as I hope my story reminds, biological genealogies are not just innocuous tracings of lineage. They are often racist works. Bloodlines are revealed to determine caste, and revelations can be dangerous if not deadly.[23] Tracing and erasing lines of thought can also be a powerful means of domination, oppression, and enacting white supremacy.

Kimmerer describes having account of plants diminished by a botany professor: "I didn't think about it at the time, but it was happening all over again, an echo of my grandfather's first day at school, when he was ordered to leave everything—language, culture, family—behind. The professor made me doubt where I came from, what I knew, and claimed that his was the *right* way to think."[24] When one is part of a nondominant culture, being denied one's cultural orientation is brutal, often leaving the individual adrift and shamed. Native Americans were killed in battles but also with blankets laced with smallpox. This is to say that deadly destruction happens in acts as seemingly banal as handing over a blanket or teaching someone the "correct way to think." Sometimes cruel viciousness is even laced in claims of kindness. This is not to say that Kimmerer's professor sought cultural annihilation in his actions. It is to maintain that silencing a way of thinking can be rooted in a larger system that destroys cultures through a variety of means and Kimmerer's professor was operating within and as part of that structure.

Originally a religious term, *canon* refers to a body of texts or images deemed sacred or essential. Talks of "canons" tend in the words of postcolonial scholar Gayatri Spivak to "secure institutions as institutions secure canons."[25] The question is not whether canons influence us but instead how they change us and who gets to choose what works have influence. A canon does not simply offer a genealogy it can erase and inscribe.

In "I Am Where I Think: Remapping the Order of Knowing," philosopher Walter Mignolo challenges the Western norm that posits "First World zero point epistemology" as the location from which all other thinking must respond and react.[26] What does he mean with this challenging phrase? First, let's utilize the strategies from chapter 5 to paraphrase. "First World" refers to countries in Western Europe and the United States that dominate the global market economically. "Zero point" references the position on a map where the longitude and latitude degrees start and from which the rest of the map is organized. *Epistemology* is a word for ways of knowing and organizing thought. Put together, Mignolo is critiquing a worldview that privileges ways of knowing from one community, namely, the West.

This Western dominance is often conscious, hierarchical, and intentional. It can also be oblivious—a perception that there is no other way.[27] Either way, when the zero point epistemology obliterates other perspectives, as it often does, it is destructive and harmful to cultures and people.[28]

Years ago, I was disturbed reading a German author who wrote about World War II and made no mention of Jewish people because I couldn't imagine a Jewish person writing about that time without including a German.[29] While those who come from the "zero point" can construct canons that ignore the rest of the world, everyone else cannot fully ignore the legacy of the "zero point epistemology." As social justice activist and professor of education Denise Taliaferro Baszile writes, "Moving toward a pedagogy of Black self-love requires first and foremost that we be able to identify and deconstruct the master narratives that often colonize our thinking."[30]

Educational scholar Lisa Delpit famously writes that access to power demands that one knows the cultural "codes." She calls teachers to directly teach and deconstruct codes in behavior and language so that students, particularly those of color, who don't grow up at the zero point can acquire fluency in the language of those who have power. Direct instruction also helps students, such as those who are white and middle class, for whom the zero point culture is intuitive to see that their ways of being are not a given.

Adding a layer of nuance, philosopher Eddie Glaude calls us to attend to the past and past ideas and see what is useful in navigating the present.[31] With a rich and complicated work, there may be something to be gained while other elements should be left behind. Further, some thinkers or ideas work in one context but lose their resonance in another. Glaude argues that marching was a particularly powerful literal and symbolic resistance to Jim Crow laws that controlled physical space and suggests that other oppressive contexts may benefit from different forms of protest.

In a chapter titled "When We Dead Awaken: Writing as Re-Vision," poet and essayist Adrienne Rich writes, "Re-vision—the act of looking back, of seeing with fresh eyes, of entering an old text from a new critical direction—is for women more than a chapter in cultural history: it is an act of survival. Until we understand the assumptions in which we are drenched we cannot know ourselves . . . We need to know the writing of the past and know it differently than we have ever known it; not to pass on a tradition but to break its hold over us."[32] As with Baszile, we must read backward to liberate us from oppressive culture. As with Glaude, we must read carefully to see what is worth taking. The question becomes how might "we dead awaken" so as to prepare for and engage with what "flashes up." How might dead awakening help us then also create something new? A question becomes, how do we name the harm and hear what might benefit in a way that can be liberatory? How can we do so without pretending the harm isn't there or simply lifting ideas we like from a larger text (context)? How can we join, as described in chapter 5, as a good neighbor who can hear well and, in hearing well, push back so we can think better together?

Finally, sometimes it is also necessary to create and name alternative lineages. Muhammad's genealogy of Black literacy is a story of commitment, inquiry, and genius in the Black community.[33] Historian of education Jarvis Givens offers a genealogy of the Black teacher as rebel and antiracist.[34] Muhammad's and Givens's stories have been hidden to perpetuate negative stereotypes. Documenting these stories is also challenged because of evidence both never saved or lost.[35] Surfacing and sharing these genealogies inscribes a new order.

MAPPING

My friend and colleague nature-based educator Patti Bailie introduced "sound mapping" as a staple from her preschool.[36] Here is an adaptation:

- Identify the five senses as a group: sight, touch, smell, taste, hearing.
- Take a notebook and pencil and walk silently outside. As you walk, take in the experience through the five senses.

- Locate somewhere with natural features. In my classes, if we didn't have time to walk to a park, we went right outside and stood at the edge of a parking lot, which overlooked a stream and trees.
- Find a spot where you can see the rest of the group and hear me. You will stay for five minutes, so get comfortable.
- On your paper, make a person, your initials, or an "X" at the center to represent you.
- Every time you hear a sound, make a mark on your map.

Once the group has been regathered, the teacher makes a chart of the five senses with space under each for notes.

- Share impressions sense by sense.[37]
- Reflection: *What did you notice about yourself from doing this activity? How did your body feel before and after? What did you notice about your surroundings?* Invariably students are amazed at how much sensory stimulation they take in even in a relatively secluded environment.
- What insights from this activity can you bring to thinking more broadly about your relationship to space and environment?

I WALK WITH . . .

In the wordless picture book *I Walk with Vanessa: A Story About a Simple Act of Kindness* by Kerascoët, when a new girl is teased, another child leads her peers and walks with her to school.[38] The protagonists have brown skin and brown hair, and the teasing boy is blond and white. The book ends with the protagonist girls sitting together and talking. I have always read "I" to be the "friend" girl and Vanessa to be the new girl, but by rereading, I note that this is not actually indicated in the images. I can identify "I" or

"Vanessa" with both characters, and the effect is that I can more easily take on the experience of either.

After "reading," I then give this prompt:

- Write down who walks with you.
- Whom do you walk with?
- Think of family, friends, teachers, and classmates.
- What about books? Ideas? Movies? Characters?
- How are you influenced by those you walk with?
- What do you notice about your list?
- How did making this list make you feel?

BECAUSE

Bringing together personal biography and cultural heritage, Mo Willems's *Because* follows the arc of a "how the world came to be" story tracing the origins of a musician. Repeating the word *because*, Willems begins, "Because a man named Ludwig wrote beautiful music/a man named Franze was inspired to create his own" and moves us to the near-present with "Because someone's uncle caught a cold—/ someone's aunt had an extra ticket for someone special." After "someone special" is "changed" by the "beautiful music" and "worked very hard," she becomes a composer. At the end, listening to her "composition dedicated to the uncle in Row C, seat 14," "someone else was changed."[39] After reading aloud *Because,* I tell my own *because* story about how a series of happenings, intended and not, shifted and changed me. Then I prompt as follows:

- With words or images, mark yourself at the bottom right corner of a piece of blank paper.
- Choose an origin (in personal or world history). Mark it at the top left.

- Think of the route. How many stopping points would you like to include?
- Using the phrasing "because," write out the story.
- Share. You can read the whole thing or share key points on your map or selected points.
- Reflection: What do you notice about your journey?

WHAT IS A CANON?

Educators and practitioners of Descriptive Inquiry Alisa Algava and Rachel Seher coined the term *Reco-flection*: a merging of the conceptual analysis of the Reflection on a Word with the descriptive analysis associated with the Anecdotal Recollection. Try this Reco-flection:

- Consider the word *canon* in relation to texts you've read or heard about. What does it mean to you? What does it invoke? What does it open up? How might the word limit?
- Now consider the phrase "my canon." What would be on that list?
- Reflect on your choices. What do you notice about what is there? What do you notice about what is absent?

Responding asynchronously to a similar prompt to launch an educators' Philosophy Fellowship, I wrote the following:[40]

> When I think of a canon, I think of the works that link a community. This relates both to how a community is preserved and also how ideas can become codified. In college, I took courses almost exclusively in the Western Canon. I didn't always like what I encountered but I felt intuitively that I needed to know what that white Anglo Saxon male voice was all about

to survive. Did it help me survive? I don't know. I didn't really learn to write essays until I started reading modern feminist theorists and the writings of teachers. I think about professors' offices as physical traces of personal canons (and people's home libraries). Whenever I go to someone's house for the first time, I find myself studying their books. Before being a professor, I had this fantasy of sitting in my office and talking to students and retrieving relevant books from my shelf. I suppose this is something I do. In academia, I think about the way that ideas are literally passed along in this way (how many times was a book handed to me from someone's shelf and how threads of ideas are connected in real conversations between people and then on paper). I think about how for teachers these threads also exist but are not as likely to be documented (the way an author like Karen Gallas made it into my hands through ETN [Elementary Teacher Network, a teacher group] or I met Sarah Lawrence Lightfoot's work first in a quote from a session that Cecelia [Traugh] ran and how I then gave one of Lightfoot's books to my advisor as a gift and had my students read something by Lightfoot.

WHEN WE DEAD AWAKEN

Muhammad argues that courses should begin with the history of a discipline, and her book offers one such powerful entry into literacy.[41] In the Theories course, I had the rare opportunity to focus a class around philosophy and where ideas come from. Seeing this as my chance to show both the future teachers and my colleagues that philosophy was meaningful, I wanted readings to be accessible, feel linked to practice, and get us all thinking about the quandaries of education. In another example of canon exploration, in the weeks before a presidential inaugural address my first and second graders used the Descriptive Review of Work to familiarize themselves with often narrowly excerpted speeches by Presidents Abraham Lincoln and John Fitzgerald Kennedy and civil rights leader Martin Luther King Jr. In both cases, as my classes constructed meaning with challenging influential texts, we "dead awaken[ed]," explored, and unpacked the canon.[42] When introducing and unpacking canons here are some principles to consider:

- Who are the thinkers and lines of thought that are frequently referenced and/or guide how a community operates?[43] Philosopher John Dewey, psychologist Jean Piaget, and physician and educator Maria Montessori are all frequently referenced and rarely read in early childhood circles.
- Keep the scope narrow. In the course listed as "Theories in Early Childhood Education," I focused specifically on philosophy associated with progressive education. As illustrated in previous chapters, I also narrow by topic such as the child, care, or conceptions of play. In other words, I ask, what does a group of thinkers think about X?
- Rely on primary source documents.
- Select excerpts based on importance to argument, length, readability, and the ability for the writing to speak coherently out of the textual context from which it was pulled.
  - Short passages allow us to look more closely at difficult concepts and syntax.
  - I want students to construct their own meaning, and so the more a piece needs wider context to follow an argument, the more I undermine students' sense that they can interpret.

My elementary school students listened to a recording of King's full speech and then we did a Review of Work on a passage.

- Supplement with texts that provide an overarching narrative. *Loving Learning: How Progressive Education Can Save America's Schools* is a thorough and readable overview of educational movements, and Little expertly connects theories directly to teaching practice.[44] *Martin's Big Words: The Life of Dr. Martin Luther King* provides meaningful context to studying King's speeches.[45]
- Over the course of a study, have students parse a new text, compare it to those they have previously read, and give examples from their experiences as learners and teachers that illustrate that philosophy in action. Thus, the thinker is placed within a genealogy and in the present context.

Over time, then preservice early childhood teacher Katelyn Beedy teased out the subtle nuances of philosophers to consider the implications on her own practice. In a journal entry that asked her first to analyze and then contrast Dewey and Montessori, Katelyn writes:

> Some similarities that I see between Dewey and Montessori is that they both see the child as a capable and complete being. I think that they both value the child and understand the child. It is also very clear to me that they both value the importance of observation as an educator. However, I get the notion that Dewey seems to view the teacher as more of an active participant and influence in a child's learning experience, while Montessori clearly says that the teacher plays a "passive" role in the classroom. I think it's important for me to realize that I have never really liked the idea of Montessori education, so my views may be biased.

In this passage, Katelyn builds from her close reading to tease out the nuances of two thinkers associated with learning through materials and learning by doing. Doing so helps her better locate herself and specifically, perhaps, gives her a more clear understanding of why she "never really liked" Montessori education.

RECLAIMING CANONS

Canons need not only unpacking but also revisions and nuanced new stories of lineage. Here I describe how one community, associated with the Institute on Descriptive Inquiry, worked through works that sustained us and the fact that, as dear as we held many of the titles, our canon was limiting. In sharing, I want to note that this work was necessary and hard. We weren't dismantling some faraway canon imposed by others or one used to oppress. We were revisiting a collection of texts that had empowered and sustained a community but that we now felt needed revision to better welcome and center people of color.

As an example of how we might collectively consider and reconsider canons, I offer an invitational letter I sent to those joining the conversation after we had been working together for two years.

> We began the Philosophy Fellowship in 2020 with the purpose of revisiting and reinvigorating the canon. At that juncture, two elements seemed key. The first was that people in the organization's relationship to texts was possibly changing with fewer books read in full and many in the community feeling nervous around philosophy. Core texts ranging from Dewey to Carini to Merleau-Ponty were less familiar to many of the younger community members and many of the older community members were less active. It seemed that if these books were to continue to matter to us, people needed to revisit and begin their own relationships with the texts.
>
> Secondarily, there was concern about the Whiteness of this canon. This is not to say that texts authored by a broad diversity of authors weren't always widely read or influential on thinkers

such as Patricia Carini. That said, when "philosophy" texts were chosen, they tended to be written by White Western men as were many of the authors whose work proved foundational. We as a community needed to be reading more widely and to revisit the processes in relation to this wider reading.

Norms

Book Selection

We spent some time working through norms. For example, and key, we initially voted to select texts but worried that perhaps following a majority might re-inscribe some of the norms we were pushing to move past. Based on a suggestion from Alisa Algava, we shifted to having someone propose a book and to follow that text for as long as the group felt energized around it.

Chairing

We rotate chairing, typically selecting a general frame and a chair the session before. We try to have co-chairing whenever possible to ease the pressure and have multiple perspectives. Notes have been taken at sessions and these detailed notes have been "Works" themselves with a lot of care going into that.

Reading Approach

We typically draw on the Descriptive Processes. Sometimes we modify, for example, encouraging people to ask for assists when paraphrasing in Spanish. We also have sometimes deviated by doing summaries of a text at the end of a reading.

Connection to Institute

We try to encourage overlap with the Institute, suggesting texts, bringing Institute readings back for a session in our group, and encouraging participants to help chair institute sessions. Co-Directors of Institute 2 both attend regularly.

Group

Anyone with a relationship to the organization, members, long-term connectors etc. People come as they can come.

How the Work Lives

For many of us, this work has proven transformative in our teaching lives and for those of us who are also writers, in our writings. Since beginning the group, a number of publications have resulted that have in varying degrees leaned on our work together and many in our group have recently published.

Finally, we hope the work will live beyond this group. I therefore encourage folks to donate any texts they are done with to the community's library or others in the group so that folks can read books they have not yet been able to read.

Something that must be noted: our organization has a majority of white-identifying participants, although there are many people of color. Nearly every text we read was written by a Black, Latinx, or Indigenous scholar, and we also focused on women and LGBTQ+ authors. Reading offered a means of bringing in other perspectives without forcing the people of color in our community to constantly represent themselves and sit through our blunders.[46] A hope was that this project would pave the way for a more welcoming and diverse community going forward, one that we hoped for but hadn't yet reached. We read with a constant eye toward making institutional and cultural shifts in our organization. In reading and reading differently together, we wrote new ways forward both together and apart.

Sometimes, as Hansen notes, we find texts that serve as "handbooks" that we walk with and keep close.[47] The Philosophy Fellowship stayed with María Lugones for two years, finding we needed to keep talking with Lugones for a long time. The authors we read as a fellowship have all influenced this book in significant ways. They and my reading colleagues have been important companions helping me do better work.

THE COMPANY WE KEEP

Where Socrates's interlocutors tended to be his contemporaries in the agora, in most subsequent philosophy thinkers create conversations across time and space. As quoted in the epigraph in chapter 5, Sasha Hampton declares, "Locke and Rousseau have more in common than I would have originally thought, but this is good because I share many of their beliefs as well." Connecting with Locke, Katelyn comments:

> I really enjoyed reading and translating Locke's text because I felt as though we have many similarities in philosophy. One of my most prominent values which I have talked about in past journals is the importance of positive relationships with children. I believe that Locke shares this value as I mentioned above when Locke speaks of how one must have a respect for the child in order for the child to convey the same respect back to you. Another area that I have mentioned in this journal that I strongly connect with is Locke's value of the child's interests in his education. In my future classroom, I intend to base as many lessons as possible off of what I observe as interests in my students. I agree with Locke that if children have an interest in what they are learning, it is infinitely more meaningful to them. This point is proven in my own life with this class in particular. I find myself more engaged with class discussions, and my desire to understand the content and perform to the best of my abilities is greater because I genuinely enjoy learning about philosophy; including the philosophy of others as well as

discovering my own. This only amplifies my desire to bring the same enjoyment to my students.

Katelyn saw philosophy as accessible and interesting. Speaking to both the challenge of the texts and her capacity, she writes, "I really enjoyed reading and translating Locke's text because I felt as though we have many similarities in philosophy." Able to translate Locke's thinking, Katelyn places him alongside herself: someone who shares "many similarities in philosophy." She then demonstrates her fluency, giving examples of what Locke's thinking looked like in practice.

At the beginning of the chapter, I described how reading Foucault's genealogy of confession helped me identify what troubled me about asking children to write personal narratives. Put differently, like Katelyn notes with Montessori in a previous quote, I initially had misgivings I had trouble articulating. Years later, reading Foucault on truth telling further helped me think through this complicated topic and added a layer of nuance to my understanding.[48] Foucault distinguishes between a personal share for the sake of confession as opposed to an intentional, worked-through, and crafted personal share for the sake of telling a hard truth that the teller believes ought to be known. Literacy professor Elizabeth Dutro helped me further think through the nuances of testimony.[49] She encourages welcoming and supporting whatever stories children want to tell, including personal stories of loss, but stresses that the purpose in doing so is not to offer therapy nor should children be required or pressured to share. Dutro instead argues that in creating art as storytellers, children have a way into telling about their experiences and thinking with them that can be empowering. Finally, hooks and Lugones firmly pressed that philosophy is always rooted in the personal, and we must recognize those roots as we unpack canons and consider new ways forward.[50] Walking with these scholars and peers alongside my teaching, I created a new canon around testimony that has helped me better live my ethical commitment of honoring students.

PRACTICAL WISDOM: WHY WE DID IT?/VALUES IN ACTION

At this point in the book, I typically analyze why I did activities in relation to core values. Toward the end of the semester, I increasingly turn ethical analysis over to the students as they claim their own voice. As such, I do so here.

YOU DO: PART A

- Pull out the What We Did chart introduced in chapter 1.
- In the first column, list activities in this chapter that interest you.
- Move to the "Why We Did It?" section. Using the categories I have worked with—*Attend with Care, Build from the Learner, Experiential Learning, Interruption and Disruption*—make a note of why I might have done these activities. Add in some of your values. Why might you do activities?
- For "How I Might Use It," how might you modify activities with the age you work with.
- Now, thinking about canons, apply some "Learning Standards." Do these standards resonate with your purpose? Do they reflect your ethical center? Are you adding them in but actually doing the activity for a different purpose?

WHOM DOES SHINEAD WALK WITH?

Asked a few years after graduation what helps her stay true to her ethical center an in-service teacher, then teaching second grade in a charter school, Shinead immediately orients around philosophers she had read as an undergraduate:

> I think a lot of it was influenced by the courses that I took at [university]. I think definitely the philosophies of education class that I took with you was super beneficial. And I know I talked to you, when I took that class that I wish I had taken it, or it was offered when I was a freshman even because I went through many years of college, not knowing that there are different types of education, and that you develop philosophies based on the different types of education and also different experiences. And so, a lot of it came from learning about progressive schools and other types of education that aren't like the typical public school—a go in, just teach your subjects and then leave kind of kind of thing.

Shinead then pivots, "But then I'd also say a lot of it came from just experience." She then focuses primarily on another interlocutor:

> I had a wonderful mentor teacher when I was a student teacher, and she was the epitome of calm, cool, and collected. And she taught me, I don't think I included this earlier when I was talking about values, but we also do a mindful minute. After recess, they come in, they close their eyes, and I walk around and ring a chime. Their goal is to just focus on the chime. And then when they can't hear it anymore, they raise their hand. They do that like three times. So that they're just focusing on "okay, there's other distractions around the room,"—maybe someone's tapping their foot, or someone keeps coughing, but just focusing on this sound. We talk about how, when you're in the classroom learning, there's going to be a lot of distractions so focus on that one thing that you need to be doing. And then after they have a

chance to color or draw for five minutes to just kind of recenter themselves. So, she taught me that. And she just had a wonderful philosophy of, "okay, we're in a public school. Yes, it's mandatory to teach these things. But there are little pockets in the day where you can squeeze in the social emotional skills that, again, schools just kind of assumed these kids already came to school with."

This book opened with David Hansen and Julie Diamond, two highly experienced teachers, describing in minute detail how they set up the room for an optimal environment in contexts where they had considerable freedom. Here, Shinead, just a few years out in a highly restrictive context, offers the same attention to detail in service of ethics. Bringing together mentors ranging from Dewey to her mentor teacher, she finds ways to live her values in "little pockets."

Describing her capacity to live these values, Shinead begins by acknowledging how much support she does get from her school but then pivots:

> But does it fit completely into my philosophy of education, and my values, as an educator? Not really, no, because I'm not able to mold the curriculum around the students. That is the big thing about progressive education, they value choice and they value students' opinions, whereas in the typical public school, that's not the case. There's a set curriculum either by the state or by the school, and that's the only thing you can teach. So, a lot of times, I just feel like I've settled. I got a job. It's not the job that is my dream job, but it's a job, and I get to work with kids. I think every once in a while . . . I'll read an article online, or I'll pick up *Love of Learning*. I have a John Dewey book that sometimes I read to just remind myself that this isn't . . . that I'm still young, I can still work towards working in a progressive school or even trying different types of schools that I didn't know about because I think philosophies of all types are always changing and growing,

depending on the experiences you have. But I think that part of me still really believes in progressive education. And I just wished that other schools and other teachers were even just aware of it because I think it would be really beneficial for everyone to incorporate some progressive education into the schools.

In closing, let me note a few things. First, faced with a context where her values are not always realized or developed, Shinead turns to texts as interlocutors—both finding new ideas online and returning to her handbooks, *Loving Learning* and Dewey. She read an excerpt of Dewey's in my class but ended up purchasing a full book the next semester to read on her own. Second, Shinead also talks with a colleague, her mentor teacher. Thinking about that colleague inspires Shinead to center children's emotional needs. Third, Shinead does not reify progressive education. She acknowledges the appeal of this lineage and notes that other ideas might also be emerging that she should follow. Fourth, Shinead wishes that others knew this lineage; she wants a way to make people "aware," believing that they might then "incorporate." Finally, I note with sadness and some anger Shinead's idealism as a new teacher and her wistfulness. Shinead loves working with children, and she is prepared to do so in accordance with her ethics. Yet she is not able to teach from her values to the degree she wants and knows how. She, like many of the teachers in this book, have potential and skills that are not fully being realized.

YOU DO: PART B

- Reflect on your canon using the Reco-flection.
- What do you notice? Who is present, and who is absent?
- Who walks with you, and how does that influence you?
- Are you pleased with that influence?
- Are there other influences you might bring into the mix?

CHAPTER EIGHT

PRACTICAL WISDOM: AN ETHICAL COMPASS TO NAVIGATE ALL TERRAIN

I am where I once was
I stay rooted in my past
I grew toward the light
I am rooted in life
From living for my own growth
To providing life for others
I acknowledge my past
As much as I accept my future
I am now hollow
But full of new life
Where my bark once laid
New life takes hold
Moss and mushrooms now cover my surface

Dotted with holes from the bugs
That made me their home

> —KB Dunham, Hailey Hall, and Jacie Nickerson,
> then preservice elementary school teachers

I begin this final chapter with this poem for a few reasons. First, the process that the students underwent in first studying a fallen tree and then writing the poem mirrors the process that I argue supports reading and making sense of philosophy as it lives in context and in texts: they closely analyzed and then made it their own. Second, the poem offers in a nuanced and original way an integration between past and future, individual and context, that I have called for throughout. Turning to this decaying tree, they begin by highlighting a rootedness in the past, "I am where I once was / I stay rooted in my past." Speaking to the movement toward new life they then offer, "I am rooted in life." The tree they describe is no longer alive itself, but "New life takes hold / Moss and mushrooms now cover my surface / Dotted with holes from the bugs." We are given a vision of new and different life that grows from the old. Last and most importantly, I share this poem in full because I want to end this book with the powerful and creative voices of teachers.

How do teachers build from ongoing philosophical reflection to grow and regrow as they face and navigate new terrain? By way of response, I now add more of my own teacher stories.

As a first- and second-grade teacher, I taught reading and writing with what is broadly called the workshop model.[1] The general premise of this model is that students learn by doing and then reflecting.[2] In my classroom, I had long stretches of independent writing and reading. Children chose books at their level that interested them, listened to a steady diet of high-quality read-alouds, and engaged in a lot of direct skill instruction in phonics, handwriting, and grammar.[3] Read-alouds throughout the day focused on noticing the author's moves as a writer, discussing the text in depth, comprehension, and sometimes phonics skill work.[4] The reading workshops themselves typically began with brief mini-lessons about reading skills or comprehension, and then children read pre-chosen books from individualized book boxes independently (a few in partners) for thirty to forty minutes. During the workshop, the room was quiet and still, and children tended to be intent on what they were doing.

While they read independently, I'd read with individual children, assessing and giving a few tips.[5] With the very beginning readers, I'd meet nearly every week. More fluent children and I met for longer but less frequent meetings. Sometimes I'd lead small "guided reading" groups that worked on phonics skills. I also led book groups that focused on discussion and comprehension.[6] At a separate time in the day, I gave direct instruction in phonics that was differentiated to what kids were working on. I also guided the children orally through handwriting exercises as they practiced at tables.

The workshop model was rooted in a Deweyan philosophy I referenced in chapter 5—that children learn to swim by swimming in the pool and learn to read largely by reading.[7] Children could choose from a large variety of relatively easy texts that were "leveled" according to an alphabetic schema. This scaffolded and accessible approach to new material I also agreed with.[8] By finding books at their coded level, children could independently select books and build stamina in reading. This autonomy and space for choice too fit with my values.

This system has flaws and following curriculum associated with this approach to fidelity yields problems.[9] One issue, much on my radar as a classroom teacher, was that when asked about the kind of reading they did or what they liked to read, children labeled themselves according to the alphabetic level. This was reductive and drew attention away from capacities that better described what a child could do in terms of both skills and their wider relationship to reading.[10] Asked about one's reading, a more helpful description than, "I am an E reader" is "I know a lot of words automatically, and I can decode one- and two-syllable words, and I am passionate about nonfiction and fiction books about trucks. I have trouble sitting for long stretches of time, and so I need to take frequent breaks from reading, but I know how to quietly do so and pick up where I left off." The latter was a way of talking about reading I taught.

Levels are an assessment tool, and sharing the levels made it easy for my administrator to see how fluent my class was at reading. However, that ease also encouraged students and families to measure children against each other or predetermined norms. This led to shame, worry, and even teasing. One way I challenged this was I let children put whatever books they wanted in their bins as long as some of the books were at their reading level.[11] Children could spend much of the forty minutes looking at any book as long as they spent a core amount of time working through the text they could independently decode. As I suspect you experienced in chapter 5, working through a challenging text is exhausting, and most readers read quite a bit that is easy for them. The challenge is compounded for new readers, whose texts are both very hard and so basic they are boring. Ten minutes a day of intense focus decoding something hard with thirty minutes browsing picture books meant my students quickly grew as readers.

Another significant issue I had more trouble articulating at the time but that has since become national news is that the leveled books I taught with were written to support a cueing system that relied on repeated phrasing and pictures and drew attention away from decoding.[12] I was often frustrated that while

I taught phonics directly during a period we called "word study," I had trouble finding books that reinforced the phonics they were practicing.

Luckily, I was a teacher with a clear sense of what mattered to me. I was firm on my commitment to following children's interests, helping them develop a robust passion for reading, and not labeling children. I was committed to lots of opportunities to experience firsthand reading (including listening to books), choice, autonomy, joy, *and* direct skill instruction on discrete tasks. I was also a teacher with a broad range of methods at my disposal. This came from a very strong teacher education master's (thank you, guys) and the chance for regular and meaningful professional development, both supported by my school and done on my own time. I also read professional books constantly. Finally, I was a teacher with community, mentorship, and freedom to explore (thanks again, guys).

Further, aware that our workshop reading curriculum did not include direct skill instruction, my school supplemented it with a phonics and also a handwriting curriculum. Students practiced phonics and handwriting separate from the workshop times and during them in the context of reading and writing.[13]

When I couldn't find a book that met a child's interest and worked on the skills they needed, like "long e," I made one. If I didn't have an activity, I made a game or the kids made one. If an activity didn't work, I tried something else or modified it. The phonics curriculum I used involved cutting out words, multiple days of sorting words, and then pasting them. Simply laminating the sorts and passing them out to reuse worked better.[14]

I also made some major changes. One summer, I re-sorted my library to set it up not by level but by topic. The books still had the levels written on them, but a child would then shop for their level in a bin labeled something like "animals." I then worked harder at the beginning of the year to "identify a just right book" so that

within a basket children could find what they could read by trying a book and not just looking at the Sharpied level on the front.

Practical wisdom is knowing the right way to act in context.
Bringing together my values with methods and constant observation
of children's learning, I listened to the curriculum to see what worked
and also what needed modification. Thankfully, I had the freedom
and the capacity to modify well. Put differently, instead of teaching with fidelity, I taught with integrity, and because I did so, my
students learned to read and learned with joy.[15] Had I been required
to follow the curriculum to fidelity or not had adequate phonics
understanding to supplement, I might have been one of the teachers
I've since heard now lamenting years spent not teaching children to
read because they followed a limited curriculum to fidelity.[16]

Another story: I began this book describing the ways in which
I needed to center myself after returning from my first maternity
leave. Returning from my second maternity leave was more challenging. This time, halfway through the semester, Covid-19 was
thrown into the mix. As happened across the country, abruptly
I found myself teaching my last face-to-face class. Covid hit our
remote location somewhat slowly, and we had a moment in class to
say goodbye. The night before that class, as cases worldwide began
to swell and fear escalated, I wrote:

Dear Class:

As you must have read now, we are moving to remote classes
for the semester. We will talk about what this means in some
depth in class tomorrow, but I want to begin the conversation
now with some framing. What worries me the most about this
move? Frankly not the content (I can find a way to share this).
What worries me is the students who will need to go home but
do not have a comfortable home to go home to. I am worried
about students being disconnected from a part of life that feels

positive and safe, which I know this university is for many of you. I am worried about the lack of social contact some of you will experience. I am worried about hunger. With this in mind, if you need help, please reach out to me and reach out to each other. I urge you to maintain some social distance physically but not emotionally.

Regarding what we will cover . . .

Let me begin by saying that we cannot predict the curriculum that will be our lives. Things happen (personally, locally, nationally) that mean that what we thought we were going to be doing changes abruptly. This semester, will we learn exactly what and how I intended us to? No. We will not. But fundamentally, we never do. We will learn something valuable, though, about flexibility, working through difficulty, and supporting each other in difficult times, and frankly this is more important than anything I planned for us at my computer when I prepped the class last summer.

What does this mean for you as a teacher? It is our job to support our communities in difficult moments, to be aware of some of the hidden ripples of moments like this. When I was in the classroom, a huge hurricane hit my city. The principal opened up the playground of the school every day so families had a place to connect. The PTA explored what people needed by way of food, furniture, and clothing. This part worked well. That said, suddenly, my school was dealing with homelessness in a way we had not before. The ripples of these kinds of events can be quite troubling. You cannot prevent the ripples from occurring, but you can be thoughtful, caring, and knowledgeable.

As a teacher, as some of you know, I worked quite a bit with children in crises. At some point, I noticed that people were always running to situations. I stopped running. I drank tea all day and carried it in my hands when I was called to a classroom situation. As I walked calmly, I readied myself for the intensity I knew I'd find. A few situations demand running. Most don't. Practice moving slowly. Be thoughtful about when you run.

Just as we have only so much hand sanitizer, emotional resources are not unlimited. I intended to focus my energy on helping you all stay emotionally connected. Whatever I decide to do for class technologically, I will keep it as simple and accessible as possible.

For most of us, this virus will be an irritation and produce some inconvenience. For some of you, this may pose a real challenge. As you sort through your situation, consider which category this is for you. If this is an irritation, consider being calm and supportive of others. If this is a crisis for you (and it might be), reach out to the rest of us for help.

See you tomorrow and wash your hands.

Radical educational philosopher Patricia Carini writes:

To be in the habit of questioning, of exercising a philosophical attitude, is invaluable in times of duress. It is by sustaining a philosophical attitude, by reflecting, recollecting, questioning, that it is possible to face threatened loss and to reach decisions on when to resist, on how not to give one more inch than necessary, and on how to make what inches you have count for a lot. I can't have choice time. Perhaps I have said the day I give that up is the day I leave teaching. I am torn. So: What is choice time anyway? What does it mean for the learner to have choice? Where can I continue to create spaces for choosing and to free the child's own capacity for making knowledge? Where can I still catch glimpses of this child's interest, of that child's strengths? How can I, and others, keep choice present even in these tightened circumstances? How can we keep it talkable? Can this be a recurring conversation in the school—or if not in the school, with other teachers who share this commitment?[17]

What Carini describes here is a systematic rooting in one's values that can yield practical wisdom. Faced with different, and sometimes jarring and painful, changes, how do we act? How do we stay true?

In considering how to go forward amid the pandemic, the questions *who cares? does it matter?* and *if so, why?* became my constant refrain. Do I continue to focus on phonics in the midst of a pandemic? Yes, the children they teach will need to learn to read, and a background in phonics is necessary for teachers to do this well. Did we need to meet through Zoom that first semester? No, my students were grappling with family obligations, jobs, and problematic internet access and told me in our last face-to-face class they'd rather meet asynchronously. Did I need to have students do paperwork for national accreditation? I decided no, this was not a semester that should be measured, and the students had too much stress as it was. I advocated that we waive this requirement temporarily, and my request was granted.

That semester and those that followed, I affirmed that I cared a great deal about relationships with me and more so with peers. When mostly teaching virtually, I established mandatory tutorials twice a semester in which students met with me one-on-one. When we returned to class, the breakdown was their relationship not with me but with each other, and so I shifted those tutorials to be peer-to-peer opportunities to talk and socialize.

When students unloaded in class the degree they felt anxious and depressed, I asked them how they could help children manage worry and anxiety. I was stunned when all responses focused on normalization of therapy and a medical approach. "Yes," I responded, "those are good, but what about recess?" I asked, "What about friendships?" I began bringing toys like colored pencils, paper, Legos, and blocks to class and urged the students to play and talk before class and during breaks. I told them they could play with the materials throughout class if they could do so without distracting anyone. They did and commented on how relaxed and even happy doing so made them.

A key element of being able to hit the ground running in both adapting and explaining my adaptations to students was that I had worked out my core values and could articulate them. In my reading curriculum, making shifts was relatively easy. Bringing together what I knew about methods with my values, I had the freedom to change, and I did. Parents, colleagues, and administrators supported me and even rewarded me by praising and thanking me for my work.

In navigating Covid, change was harder. So much of what I knew and valued deeply was undermined and in danger. My typical commitment to sharing physical space and closeness could endanger the health of my family and students. Physical safety won out. Rooting in my core, I found ways to reclaim the relationships I typically cultivated face-to-face. That said, when we finally returned with masks off, I felt a tremendous relief and joy. As teachers, we can work around all kinds of things—faulty curriculum and even pandemics—and no context is perfect, but that doesn't mean we should have to adapt to everything.

My third example offers a different kind of malaise. Doris Santoro writes that demoralization happens when a teacher can't realize their ethical vision.[18] Recently, as a professor, I found myself similarly gloomy. As I talked it through endlessly with friends and colleagues, I was at a loss. I loved teaching, and yet I was dragging. What was wrong? As I parsed through what I valued about my job, it was clear: I loved being in class with students. This was fun and energizing. I liked the students themselves. I was passionate about the topic I taught, literacy. I loved my colleagues. Two frustrations emerged: student recalcitrance and grading. I found nagging someone to do something, especially something that will serve them such as learning phonics so they can teach, truly tiresome. bell hooks writes of opting out from being a professor: "My first awareness was that I did not want to teach in settings where students were not fully committed to our shared learning experience. I did not want to teach in settings where individuals needed to be graded. To me the best context for teaching was, of course, one where students chose to come because they wanted to learn, from me, from one another."[19] Having reflected on my values with others, including hooks, I was now aware of what was core for me: being part of a community of learners where we attended to each other. From there, I worked to convey my needs more directly with students: *I do not want to nag you to do your work, and in fact, I won't.* I set boundaries: *I am not available outside business hours.* I set clear times of availability: *I will be advising in this location at this time. Come. Otherwise, you will need to create your schedule.* I developed changes and implemented them with colleagues who felt similarly frustrated. In this way, we used our combined experiences to make more effective changes, and we were prepared to support each other if changes didn't go well. They did.

In regard to grading, I revised and revised a grading contract to make it more clear and had students fill it out themselves. Again, I was direct in my explanations: *This is a contract and not a description of your worth. If you do x, you get x grade. That's pretty much it. I will still like you very much if you do C work, but you will get a C. C work does not mean you are a C person. I don't grade people.*[20]

Writing of Nazi-occupied Europe, Hannah Arendt argued that witnessing outright resistance not only led to more resistance movements but also caused even Nazis to begin to change.[21] I have taken this to mean that even in the most oppressive contexts, resistance is beneficial and powerful and that I, in a context where I face no real threats, must resist constantly and loudly when I witness injustice.

I believe most grading practices are dehumanizing, and so, after testing grading contracts out one semester to make sure work still happened and was quality (it did and the quality was actually generally better), I have since shared this practice widely and loudly. Most loudly, I've written extensively about my shifts in grading in documents I submitted for tenure. Sometimes practical wisdom demands outright rejection and resistance of norms. Knowing where one stands ethically helps with that resistance, and it helps articulate that resistance.

In a chapter titled "An Offering," Robin Wall Kimmerer describes a daily ritual in which her father would pour the first cup of coffee out on the ground and declare, "Here's to the gods of Tahawus," the Algonquin name for what is called on US maps Mount Marcy. Kimmerer goes on to explain that this was her father's ritual, not an ancestral ritual, strictly speaking. Of the rituals, she writes, "their rhythm made me feel at home and the ceremony drew a circle around our family" that highlighted and reinforced the family commitment to gratitude.[22] Beginning the day this way, Kimmerer's father later confesses, was initially logistical, a clearing of the pot to make way for the better coffee, but coupled with the gratitude, "it became something else. A thought. It was a kind of respect, a kind of thanks. On a beautiful summer morning, I suppose you could call it joy."[23]

Kimmerer then concludes, "That, I think, is the power of ceremony: it marries the mundane to the sacred. The water turns to wine, the coffee to prayer. The material and the spiritual mingle like grounds mingled with humus, transformed like steam rising from a mug into the morning mist."[24] Seeking to be a good neighbor, let me first say there is much to focus on in this story. It is a story of gratitude and community with family, with ancestors, with mountains and lakes and loons. It is a sacred story—a religious ethos mixed with daily banalities. It is also a story of racism and some recovery. At the time her father performed this ritual, he did not know the ancestral ways of giving thanks as they had been "taken" from her family at the boarding schools.[25] Yet Kimmerer feels that somehow this ancestral way was in his being and inspired him.

Elizabeth Dutro argues that we can witness by giving testimony in which the details of a story are different but elements of the essence correspond.[26] In this book, I hope I have offered a testimony in witness to Kimmerer's. Like her, I believe the banal is not only potentially sacred but also central to doing good in the world. Goodness and cruelty happen in the mundane. Like Kimmerer, much is at stake. Like Kimmerer, in daily rituals I seek to not only preserve my own ethos but also do right by others. Finally, like Kimmerer, I feel that the ways we ground ourselves are key and that we need, if not daily, constant opportunities to reaffirm what it is we hold most dear.

In this final chapter, I offer concluding methods for articulating and reflecting on one's values as a teacher. I build on many of the philosophers in this book to argue that clarity about one's ethical center serves three distinct and essential needs:

- It helps the teacher make daily ethical decisions around practice.
- When forced to shift gears, as one often is, it helps the teacher to find a way forward that takes what is essential and adapts.
- Stating one's values is a form of self-affirmation that can bolster a person in difficult contexts and demand change.

As philosopher of education Megan Laverty explained at the start, philosophy helps us name, articulate, explore, and interrogate our values, and it helps us determine whether conduct fits with those values.[27] As then preservice early childhood teacher Katelyn Beedy writes in her mid-semester reflection: "I believe that I have exceeded my own expectations for myself in this class, as I am learning about things that I am genuinely interested in. I suppose one area I'd like to improve on is my confidence about my own values and defining them more sharply." Learning about philosophy and practice, Katelyn thrives, "exceeding" her own "expectations" because the work interests her. As she finishes out the semester, she wants to feel more "confident" in her values and also keep "defining them more sharply." It is to goals such as these that I turn.

This book began in chapter 1 with conducting a values interview. In articulating one's ethical center, I first encourage returning to some of those exercises. How did you answer the questions when you began reading? Do you answer in the same ways? Having thought more about the topic, do some of your answers change or get further refined?

Here are a few more activities to help with this articulation, bolstering, and affirming.

VALUES WALL

Teacher educator Fred Korthagen introduces the "teaching wall," where students get a set of paper "bricks" on which they write core values to help them consider what makes up their foundation.[28] As with word sorts, having a physical material to move easily and manipulate can be helpful. My two favorite "bricks" are colored index cards cut into small rectangles or using the sticky note feature on a digital whiteboard.

- Make a list of core values—one per brick. Typically, I share mine first.
- Arrange the values in an order that has metaphorical meaning for you.
- Share your values wall with others.
- Go back to your work and see if you have anything to add.
- Then give examples of practices that you enact or want to enact that will correlate with the values.

My values wall is shown in figure 8.1.

FIGURE 8.1 Values wall

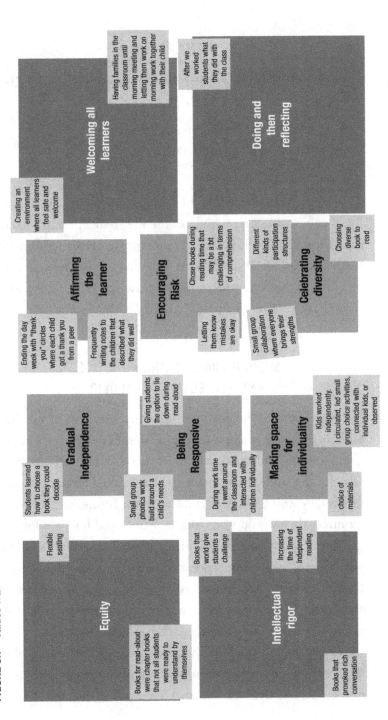

Welcoming all learners

Having families in the classroom until morning meeting and letting them work on morning work together with their child

Creating an environment where all learners feel safe and welcome

Doing and then reflecting

After we worked students what they did with the class

Affirming the learner

Ending the day week with "thank you" circles where each child got a thank you from a peer

Frequently writing notes to the children that described what they did well

Encouraging Risk

Chose books during reading time that may be a bit challenging in terms of comprehension

Letting them know mistakes are okay

Celebrating diversity

Different kinds of participation structures

Choosing diverse book to read

Small group collaboration where everyone brings their strengths

Gradual Independence

Students learned how to choose a book they could decode

Small group phonics work build around a child's needs

Giving students the option to lie down during read aloud

Being Responsive

During work time I went around the classroom and interacted with children individually

Making space for individuality

Kids worked independently. I circulated, led small group choice activities, connected with individual kids, or observed

choice of materials

Equity

Flexible seating

Books for read-aloud were chapter books that not all students were ready to understand by themselves

Intellectual rigor

Books that world give students a challenge

Increasing the time of independent reading

Books that provoked rich conversation

"I AM" POEMS

"I am" poems follow a repeated refrain and fill-in-the-blank prompts:

> I am (two special characteristics you have)
> I wonder (something of curiosity)[29]

. . .

As illustrated in the poem in the epigraph, after describing an item like a painting or a tree, students use the "I am" prompts to consider the item in another way. As a rooting in values activity, after teachers create their values walls, they then articulate and affirm by filling in the blanks to describe themselves. Hearing these read aloud has the effect of an affirmation.

MERGING VALUES AND PRACTICE:
THE REFLECTIVE PORTFOLIO

For many years, I assigned two final assignments, answering a series of reflective prompts in relation to the content and one's ongoing learning and a resource binder that included activities, work samples the student had made (which I called artifacts), assessments they would use with children in the future, and purchased resources they would want such as games and books. One year, my doctoral advisors philosophers of education David Hansen and Megan Laverty convened a conference named Reimagining Research and Practice at the Crossroads of Philosophy, Teaching, and Teacher Education, where they invited collaborations between faculty affiliated with philosophy and education and those affiliated with teacher education—both broadly defined.[30] Thinking about the artificial binaries between philosophy and teacher education during this conference, it occurred to me that despite seeing myself as occupying the crossroads of philosophy, teaching, and teacher education, my formal assignments were re-creating exactly the binaries I felt needed to be taken down.

I returned, mid-semester, to my teaching, told my classes about the conference, and asked them to join me in an experiment. Their two final projects would be merged into one—a reflective binder. I promised them I would be lenient as we all figured out how to talk in this way. With some trepidation and unease, they joined me and did fantastic work.[31] Here I share later, revised iterations of this assignment in a K–3 literacy class. Of note, this permutation brings in observations of a child based on a process called the Descriptive Review of the Child.[32] As such, the project helps students enact practical wisdom as they bring together values, content, and context.

HUMAN–CENTERED PORTFOLIO

Here is the assignment as introduced in the syllabus:

> Strong literacy instruction is based on practical wisdom: knowing one's values and strengths as a teacher, knowing children and context well, and knowing the content. In this class, we will be working on these three areas both individually and drawing them together. Your final assignment (worked on throughout the term) will bring these areas together. Most of the content of the portfolio will come from work done over the course of the semester. You will also be given a variety of reflection prompts. We will go over this at length. Save all of your assignments and in class work.

And here is the full assignment (students drafted each section in journal assignments throughout the semester and got feedback):

Part 1: Who are you as the teacher in the classroom?
1. What are your core values about teaching literacy? Use the texts we've read this semester to back these up where applicable.

2. What are some activities we've done in class or things you've watched or read about that have particularly resonated with your values this semester? Add hyperlinks here to the following:
   – the What We Did chart with standards
   – any activities and two or three work samples you want to take with you such as your phonics scavenger hunt

3. What will literacy look like in your classroom?
   – Share some books you hope to have in your library? Make a copy of the book collection document [a slideshow of books on themes created collaboratively] and include any slides of books you are excited about or the What We Read chart.

4. We've talked a lot about culturally sustaining pedagogy. How might this fit with and inform your values?

5. Is there a time you've experienced a disconnect between your values and/or practices and something you've read or done this semester? If so, please explain.

6. You've done a lot of reading and writing this semester. How would you describe your current literacy identity and how will this influence your teaching? Add the following hyperlinks:
   – two or three artifacts you want to share with children such as poems or picture books you made either independently or collaboratively

7. What are you particularly proud of that you've done this semester?

8. What is one area you'd like to improve on as you prepare to go forward as a literacy teacher? What will you do to improve in this area?

Part 2: Child study

1. Please include your revised Descriptive Review of the Child with links to any assessments or work samples you want to include.
2. What did you learn from studying a child closely this semester?
3. How will that help you with future students?
4. Please include links to at least five assessments we used in class or you used in the field that you found particularly helpful. You can download the assessment folder in handouts [a virtual resource collection] or take a picture from the hard copies handed out in class.

Part 3: Bringing it all together

1. Imagine you are the teacher (with all your values and aptitudes) and you have the child you studied full time in your class.
2. Name three big structures and/or practices you would bring in to create a meaningful literacy environment for this child.
3. Name three activities we've done that you would love to try with this child and explain why.

ETHICAL INTERVIEWS

Korthagen argues that the practices teachers pick up while learning to teach tend to be those they rely on in the field.[33] In the earlier passage, Kimmerer speaks to the strong foundation of learning gratitude from her father's rituals. She also emphasizes that this was a daily way of greeting each morning. Gratitude, as such, was enacted anew at the foundation of every day.

Throughout this book, I called upon exercises engaged with in community. In this final section, I share how what began as a research study on how ethics lived in teachers' practice has illuminated for me a way of engaging with teachers in a more meaningful ongoing way. Here are the general prompts:

Complete a values wall (see figure 8.1)

- List the values that inform your teaching.
- Arrange them in a manner that expresses how they interact with each other.

Interview Questions

- What values inform your teaching?
- Please give specific examples of how these values live in your own practice.
- Describe where you picked up these values. What informs them?
- How are your values reinforced and/or challenged in your current teaching placement?
- What supports reinforce/stay true to your values?

COMMUNITY AROUND VALUES EXERCISES

Hannah Arendt argues that when we come together around "words and deeds," we grow in practical wisdom, and we leave the encounter feeling seen and heard.[34] Similarly, as noted at the end of chapter 5, while Aristotle is vague about how practical wisdom is cultivated, in addition to learning from experience, he argues that we grow through critical friends.[35]

Throughout the interviews, teachers described a key mentor and/or colleagues who served as interlocutors and helped the teachers sort through their values, think of methods to support them, and confidently stay true when they felt challenged.

Teachers talk all the time, and this talk can be incredibly meaningful and productive. It can also be consumed by logistics, activities, lessons to prepare for the next day, talking through emergencies, and even expressing frustrations. A little formality can help support the conversation.[36] For example, when students share their values walls or interview each other as Katelyn and Sasha did in chapter 1, they get ideas about what matters to them. Sharing with colleagues, one sees both congruence and differences, and that can help one recognize in more sharp focus one's own commitments.

I offer Ana's story from my interviews to showcase the potential of a structured collaborative reflective process to explore values. Ana began her interview, even before the recording went on, expressing frustration with her school year. Her class was wild, and she didn't feel especially effective. As I turned on the recording, I was nervous. How was this going to go? Would anything positive come of the conversation?

On the cusp of a transition, long-term progressive educator Julie Fournier tells a story she titled "Conviction: The Teacher I Want to Be." She concludes: "Writing this, reading it, and rereading it, has driven home to me how truly child-centered this education was. Virtually *every* decision was based on the children we were teaching at the time"[37] Like Julia, as the interview rolled out, Ana seemed to talk her way into conviction. As Ana stated her values and described all that she was doing that was in sync with them, her voice took on confidence, and a picture of a very successful new teacher emerged.

Ana began the interview with some specific frustrations: children not listening or following rules and her sense of being pressured to indulge misbehavior and not set limits. She closed with examples of figuring out how to help children follow her expectations in a manner that honored what both she and they needed in the classroom:

> I think all my values definitely come into play this school year.
> I feel like last year, I felt a little over my head as a first year

teacher, going from preK to first grade and then you know all the guidelines and all the quarantines and not having kids for such a long period of time. I think my brain focused a lot on if I was doing the right thing last year, and not knowing what I should be doing, and this year, I feel like I have a firmer ground of this is what I want my classroom to look like, this is how I want it to go. This is what I want my kids to get from this school year.

As with Fournier, telling the story of what she valued and how she was accomplishing so much, Ana seemed to notice that though the year was imperfect, she was doing quite well.

Advice to teachers is notoriously unhelpful with outsiders offering remedies to situations the teacher might not see as a problem or suggesting practices the teacher either has already tried or would not do.[38] Writing about teacher development, Michael Fullan and Andy Hargreaves emphasize, "What matters here is *not just whether the particular model is valid or not, but how it connects to a teacher's overall sense of purpose in the particular situation in which he or she is working.*"[39] I would add that whether an approach is valid (as determined by a range of sources) matters too, but certainly the teacher's purpose and the context should be a top priority.

In her interview, Ana identified a challenge. She wanted kids to have autonomy and choice over seats. Her students weren't using freedoms well, and her colleagues advised her to limit choice. After listening to what Ana valued, a description of her class, and practices that were working well for her, I suggested she might talk directly with the children about her desire to give choice and her concern about behavior and ask them if they thought they could handle this responsibility and what might help them be successful. For suggestions and changes to practice to be both ethical and effective, they must correspond with what the teacher is hoping to accomplish.

Reflecting on values does not just serve us to adapt, it also helps us identify when we must stand up and resist. Throughout my interviews with teachers, a common refrain was that they were constantly assessing whether a placement worked for them and either making changes or, if changes couldn't be made, leaving. As first-grade teacher Jenny responds when asked how she stays true to her ethos:

> I would say, just being able to talk about it and finding even just one person that has similar values as you do, and just being able to share ideas, but also be like *this happened, what do you think?* That's helpful. And then I think also sometimes I have to take a step back and be like, I know that this is best for my kids. So it might not be best for you, but it's best for my kids. So I'm gonna go ahead and do what I think is needed here . . . I've heard from several other teachers that their school often doesn't necessarily support them. I said, you know, nothing's holding me here. So, if I ever do feel that way, then I can just test out a different school.

Jenny reiterates the power of someone to discuss values with, in this case, someone with shared commitments. This clarity helps her do what is "best for my kids" even if it goes against colleagues or administrators. Finally, this clarity supports Jenny in assessing a context overall. She confidently concludes that "nothing's holding me here."

Thinking philosophically as teachers helps us stay true to our commitments, it helps us find joy for students and create spaces of joy, and it helps us navigate all kinds of terrain. This is not easy work, but it is meaningful. In the Introduction, I began with a quote from a new preschool teacher, Liz, in which she affirms that she must stay true to her values to teach. I will close with an exchange with longtime preK teacher Nina. Having witnessed Nina's teaching for nearly ten years, I have always been amazed at how ethically grounded and gifted she is and the countless ways she exudes practical wisdom in her daily engagement with very young children. Nina came to my math methods class with an associate's degree and many years of experience. She knew as much about teaching math and B–5 children as I did.

We approached each other as colleagues with whom we could learn and excitedly talk about teaching. That semester she was attentive to coursework, considering what worked for her and then immediately adapting and trying activities with the children in her home day care. After she took my class, I invited her to give a guest lecture in one of my classes, which she did brilliantly, and I visited her at one of her teaching placements. I was very impressed and brought back some practices she used to my classes.

Given her constant thoughtfulness and acumen, I shouldn't have been surprised, but I was moved by the following exchange. I asked her at the end of our interview if she had anything else to add:

Nina: I don't know if I have anything to add in just that I've spent the last week really looking at . . . just thinking about my values and journaling about them and reflecting on them at home and in the classroom. And I don't think I ever realized how much my values are reflected here. Like, I know I value the connections with our families and making them part of what we're doing. But I'm just like, oh, that's, I love Bronfenbrenner, so that's why I do it. But really, it's just more than that. It's a community and it's family, which is important to me outside of here, too. I think I always just kind of thought they were two separate things. They merge inevitably.

Cara: So were you playing around with that in advance because of the interview topic? Was that what that was?

Nina: I knew that you were going to ask a bit about values in the classroom. And so then I just started thinking like "Well, what do I value in the classroom and how do I see that come to life?" And, you know, I saw it today when we're out in the middle of the woods looking for bugs and I was thinking about reflecting on why was this important for me to say yes to the child that we were going to go into the woods instead of going to the playground for recess, like we do every day, and just really thinking about what drives me to do that? And so, yeah, it was definitely because of this, but it's been like a weeklong of reflecting and thinking about it. Nice. I know.

Nice. I know. Indeed.

YOU DO

- You've been given a menu of centering activities in this chapter that help you name and affirm your core values. Find a friend and/or colleague and create your own menu of activities that speak to you.
- Modify and adapt widely. Perhaps you don't want to write a poem but instead want to create a collage that answers similar prompts. Perhaps you want to list your values, then share a Recollection around a child who is challenging you, and then ask your friend to problem-solve with you.
- Reflect. What did you learn about yourself from these exercises?
- What from this exercise are you bringing back to the field tomorrow?
- Now go, try something out tomorrow. Enjoy and teach well.

REFERENCE LIST OF CHILDREN'S BOOKS

*I*magine you are in a classroom. Picture these books laid out on a table. Browse. Take the What We Read chart described in chapter 6. Notice, as recommended there, what is present in the collection. What is absent? What more should be supplemented? What do you like and dislike? Take these as a start and grow your libraries with ethics in mind. Categories match book chapters, but many of these books serve as mentor texts across these categories. So read and play!

CHAPTER 1

Windows and Welcomes

- *A roomy welcome into the classroom to helps students consider who they are and what they bring*

  Daydreamers by Tom Feelings and Eloise Greenfield (New York: Puffin Pied Piper, 1993)

The Day You Begin by Jacqueline Woodson and Rafael López
   (New York: Nancy Paulsen Books, 2018)
Madlenka by Peter Sís (New York: Frances Foster Books, 2000)
Windows by Julia Denos and E. B. Goodale (Somerville, MA:
   Candlewick Press, 2017)
The Year We Learned to Fly by Jacqueline Woodson and Rafael
   López (New York: Nancy Paulsen Books, 2022)

CHAPTER 2

How the World Came to Be

- *Folktales and fictions that offer an origin story about how a
person, place, or thing came to be*

Beautiful Blackbird by Ashley Bryan (New York: Atheneum Books
   for Young Readers, 2003)
A Big Bed for Little Snow by Grace Lin (New York: Little, Brown,
   2019)
A Big Mooncake for Little Star by Grace Lin (New York: Little,
   Brown, 2018)
*Braiding Sweetgrass for Young Adults: Indigenous Wisdom, Scientific
   Knowledge, and the Teachings of Plants* by Robin Wall Kim-
   merer (Minneapolis, MN: Milkweed Editions, 2015)
Coyote Tales by Thomas King (Toronto: Groundwood Books/
   House of Anansi Press, 2017)
Creation Gerald McDermott (New York: Dutton Children's
   Books, 2003)
*Jumping Mouse: A Native American Legend of Friendship and Sacri-
   fice* by Misty Schroe (Salem, MA: Page Street Kids, 2019)
Keepunumuk: Weeâchumun's Thanksgiving Story by Danielle Green-
   deer, Anthony Perry, and Alexis Bunten (Watertown, MA:
   Charlesbridge, 2022)
*Kuhkomossonuk akonutomuwinokot: Stories Our Grandmothers
   Told Us* edited by Wayne A. Newell and Robert M. Leavitt
   (Robbinston, ME: Resolute Bear Press, 2020)

Raccoon's Last Race: A Traditional Abenaki Story by Joseph Bruchac
and James Bruchac (New York: Dial Books for Young Readers,
2004)

The Seven Chinese Sisters by Kathy Tucker and Grace Lin (Morton
Grove, IL: A. Whitman, 2003)

Sunny by Celia Krampien (New York: Roaring Brook Press, 2020)

Trickster: Native American Tales: A Graphic Collection edited by
Matt Dembicki (Golden, CO: Fulcrum, 2010)

Where the Mountain Meets the Moon by Grace Lin (New York:
Little, Brown, 2009)

The Wolf, the Duck & The Mouse by Mac Barnett and Jon Klassen
(Somerville, MA: Candlewick Press, 2017)

CHAPTER 3

Picturing the Child

• *Who is the child, and how are they pictured in words and images? How does this change across communities and time?*

A Bad Case of Stripes by David Shannon (New York: Scholastic,
2004)

Bee-Bim-Bop! by Linda Sue Park and Ho Baek Lee (Orlando:
Harcourt School Publishers, 2007)

A Birthday for Frances by Russell Hoban and Lillian Hoban
(New York: HarperCollins, 1995)

Do Like Kyla by Angela Johnson and James Ransome (New York:
Orchard Books, 1993)

From the Desk of Zoe Washington by Janae Marks (New York:
Katherine Tegen Books, 2020)

Julián at the Wedding by Jessica Love (Somerville, MA: Candlewick
Press, 2020)

Julián Is a Mermaid by Jessica Love (Somerville, MA: Candlewick
Press, 2018)

Junie B. Jones and the Stupid Smelly Bus by Barbara Park (New York:
Random House, 1992)

Knuffle Bunny: A Cautionary Tale by Mo Willems (New York: Hyperion Books for Children, 2004)

Knuffle Bunny Too: A Case of Mistaken Identity by Mo Willems (New York: Hyperion Books for Children, 2007)

Knuffle Bunny Free: An Unexpected Diversion by Mo Willems (New York: Balzer + Bray, 2010)

Mommy's Khimar by Jamilah Thompkins-Bigelow and Ebony Glenn (New York: Salaam Reads, 2018)

My Papi Has a Motorcycle by Isabel Quintero and Zeke Peña (New York: Scholastic, 2020)

New Kid by Jerry Craft and Jim Callahan (New York: Harper, 2019)

No, David! by David Shannon (New York: Scholastic, 1998)

Olivia by Ian Falconer (New York: Atheneum Books for Young Readers, 2004)

Outside over There by Maurice Sendak (London: Picture Lions, 1993)

Pecan Pie Baby by Jacqueline Woodson and Sophie Blackall (New York,: Puffin Books, 2013)

Please, Baby, Please by Spike Lee, Tonya Lewis Lee, and Kadir Nelson (New York: Simon & Schuster, 2006)

Ramona the Pest by Beverly Cleary (Basingstoke: Macmillan Education, 1986)

Sky-High Guy by Nina Crews (New York: Henry Holt, 2010)

Tía Isa Wants a Car by Meg Media and Claudio Muñoz (Somerville, MA: Candlewick Press, 2016)

Wave by Suzy Lee (San Francisco: Chronicle Books, 2008)

When Aidan Became a Brother by Kyle Lukoff and Kaylani Juanita (New York: Lee & Low Books, 2019)

CHAPTER 4

Reading the Word, Reading the World

- *A nuanced and multifaceted take on a word or concept*

Everybody Needs a Rock by Byrd Baylor and Peter Parnall (New York: Macmillan, 1986)

If You're Not from the Prairie . . . by Dave Bouchard and Henry Ripplinger (New York: Aladdin Paperbacks, 1998)

I Like It When . . . by Mary Murphy (San Diego: Red Wagon Books, 2002)

Lines by Suzy Lee (San Francisco: Chronicle Books, 2017)

Love by Matt de la Peña and Loren Long (New York: G.P. Putnam's Sons, 2018)

Pots: A Playfully Flavorful Picture Book! by Ah-Keisha McCans and Et Green (Philadelphia: Whole Body Literacy & Education, 2022)

The Search for Delicious by Natalie Babbitt (New York: Farrar, Straus and Giroux, 1999)

Some Snow Is by Ellen Yeomans and Andrea Offermann (New York: Putnam, 2019)

The Sound of Silence by Katrina Goldsaito and Julia Kuo (New York: Little, Brown, 2016)

Ten Ways to Hear Snow by Cathy Camper and Kenard Pak (New York: Kokila, 2020)

When You Reach Me by Rebecca Stead (New York: Yearling, 2019)

CHAPTER 5

Paying Attention, Listening in New Ways

• *The power of listening carefully to travel to new worlds*

Drawn Together by Minh Lê and Dan Santat (New York: Little, Brown, 2018)

Dreamers by Yuyi Morales (New York: Neal Porter Books, 2018)

Once upon a Book by Grace Lin and Kate Messner (New York: Little, Brown, 2022)

On My Way to Buy Eggs by Zhiyuan Chen (New York: Scholastic, 2001)

The Other Way to Listen by Byrd Baylor and Peter Parnall (Boston: National Braille Press, 2014)

The Rabbit Listened by Cori Doerrfeld (New York: Dial Books for Young Readers, 2018)

"Slowly, Slowly, Slowly," Said the Sloth by Eric Carle (New York: Puffin Books, 2007)

Whose Tracks Are These: A Clue Book of Familiar Forest Animals by Jim Nail and Hyla Skudder (Lanham, MD: Roberts Rinehart, 1994)

CHAPTER 6

Ambiguity

- *Puzzling, unresolved messages or characters who unsettle inviting discussion*

Adrian Simcox Does NOT Have a Horse by Marcy Campbell and Corinna Luyken (New York: Dial Books for Young Readers, 2018)

Each Kindness by Jacqueline Woodson and E.B. Lewis (New York: Nancy Paulsen Books, 2012)

Frederick by Leo Lionni (New York: Knopf, 2012)

The Giving Tree by Shel Silverstein (New York: HarperCollins Children's Books, 1992)

Harriet the Spy by Louise Fitzhugh (New York: Ishi Press International, 2020)

How Chipmunk Got His Stripes: A Tale of Bragging and Teasing by James Bruchac and Joseph Bruchac (New York: Dial Books for Young Readers, 2001)

Tuck Everlasting by Natalie Babbitt (New York: Farrar, Straus, Giroux, 2000)

Multiple Perspectives

- *Multiple perspectives alongside each other*

Blue Sky White Stars by Sarvinder Naberhaus and Kadir Nelson (New York: Dial Books for Young Readers, 2017)

Goldilocks and Just One Bear by Leigh Hodgkinson (Somerville, MA: Nosy Crow, 2012)

Max and the Tag-Along Moon by Floyd Cooper (New York: Philomel Books, 2013)

Over and Under the Snow by Kate Messner and Christopher Silas Neal (San Francisco: Chronicle Books, 2011)

Round Trip by Ann Jonas (New York: Mulberry Books, 1990)

Seven Blind Mice by Ed Young (New York: Puffin Books, 2008)

CHAPTER 7

Genealogies

• *In addition to the "how the world came to be" books listed for chapter 2, these model how a particular child's or family's world came to be, or their ancestral origins. This might be paired with the earlier collection or offered later.*

Because by Mo Willems and Amber Ren (New York: Hyperion Books for Children, 2019)

Islandborn by Junot Diaz and Leo Espinosa (New York: Dial Books for Young Readers, 2018)

The Keeping Quilt by Patricia Palacco (New York: Simon & Schuster Books for Young Readers, 1988)

Momma, Where Are You From? by Marie Bradby and Chris K. Soentpiet (New York: Orchard Books, 2000)

The Rope: A Story from the Great Migration by Jacqueline Woodson and James Ransome (New York: Nancy Paulsen Books, 2013)

Show Way by Jacqueline Woodson and Hudson Talbott (New York: G. P. Putnam's Sons, 2005)

The 1619 Project: Born on the Water by Nikole Hannah-Jones and Renée Watson (New York: Kokila, 2021)

Stamped: Racism, Antiracism, and You by Ibram X. Kendi and Jason Reynolds (New York: Little, Brown, 2020)

Tumble by Celia C. Pérez (New York: Kokila, 2022)

The Undefeated by Kwame Alexander and Kadir Nelson (Boston: Houghton Mifflin Harcourt, 2018)

Where Are You From? by Yamile Saied Mendez and Jaimie Kim (New York: HarperCollins, 2019)

The Company We Keep

- *Characters are enriched when they join with others.*

Beautiful Yetta's Hanukkah Kitten by Daniel Manus Pinkwater and Jill Pinkwater (New York: Feiwel and Friends, 2014)

Flight of the Puffin by Ann Braden (New York: Nancy Paulsen Books, 2021)

Full, Full, Full of Love by Trish Cooke and Paul Howard (London: Walker Books, 2020)

Harbor Me by Jacqueline Woodson (New York: Nancy Paulsen Books, 2018)

I Walk with Vanessa: A Story About a Simple Act of Kindness by Kerascoët (New York: Schwartz & Wade Books, 2018)

Liar & Spy by Rebecca Stead (New York: A Yearling Book, 2013)

So Much! by Trish Cooke and Helen Oxenbury (Somerville, MA: Candlewick Press, 2008)

Who Are Your People? by Bakari Sellers and Reggie Brown (New York: Quill Tree Books, 2021)

CHAPTER 8

Reclaiming and Reauthoring

- *Declarations of self and celebration and/or building and re-building worlds. Many of these can be exchanged with those in chapter 1.*

The Big Orange Splot by Daniel Manus Pinkwater (New York: Scholastic, 1977)

The Book of Mistakes by Corinna Luyken (New York: Dial Books for Young Readers, 2017)

Fort-Building Time by Megan Wagner Lloyd and Abigail Halpin (New York: Alfred A. Knopf, 2017)

Goldilocks and the Three Dinosaurs by Mo Willems (New York: Balzer + Bray, 2012)

If I Built a School by Chris Van Dusen (New York: Dial Books for Young Readers, 2019)

I'm in Charge of Celebrations by Byrd Baylor and Bill Parnall (New York: Aladdin Paperbacks, 1995)

Interrupting Chicken by David Ezra Stein (London: Walker, 2012)

Life Doesn't Frighten Me by Maya Angelou, Jean-Michel Basquiat, and Sara Jane Boyers (New York: Abrams Books for Young Readers, 2017)

The List of Things That Will Not Change by Rebecca Stead (New York: Wendy Lamb Books, 2020)

The Neighborhood Mother Goose by Nina Crews (New York: Greenwillow Books, 2004)

The Neighborhood Sing-Along by Nina Crews (New York: Greenwillow Books, 2011)

You're Here for a Reason by Nancy Tillman (New York: Feiwel and Friends, 2015)

Notes

INTRODUCTION

1. Unless stated otherwise, first names only indicate pseudonyms. Full names are used with permission.

2. Doris A. Santoro, *Demoralized: Why Teachers Leave the Profession They Love and How They Can Stay* (Cambridge, MA: Harvard Education Press, 2018), 190.

3. For a summary and analysis of these, see Sheri Leafgren, *Reuben's Fall: A Rhizomatic Analysis of Disobedience in Kindergarten* (Walnut Creek, CA: Left Coast Press, Inc., 2009).

4. Doug Lemov, *Teach Like a Champion: 49 Techniques That Put Students on the Path to College* (San Francisco: Jossey-Bass, 2010); Mike Anderson, *The First Six Weeks of School* (Turner Falls, MA: Center for Responsive Schools Inc., 2015).

5. Grace Enriquez, ed., *Literacies, Learning, and the Body: Putting Theory and Research into Pedagogical Practice* (New York: Routledge, 2016).

6. Michel Foucault, *The Essential Works of Michel Foucault, 1954–1984*, trans. Paul Rabinow and James D. Faubion (New York: New Press, 1997).

7. John Dewey, *Democracy and Education: An Introduction to the Philosophy of Education* (New York: Free Press, 1916); Paulo Freire, *Pedagogy of the Oppressed*, 30th anniversary ed. (New York: Continuum, 2000); Cara E. Furman and Cecelia Traugh, *Descriptive Inquiry in Teacher Practice: Cultivating Practical Wisdom to Create Democratic Schools* (New York: Teachers College Press, 2021); David T. Hansen, *The Call to Teach* (New York: Teachers College Press, 1995); David T. Hansen, *Exploring the Moral Heart of Teaching: Toward a Teacher's Creed*

(New York: Teachers College Press, 2001); David T. Hansen, *Reimagining the Call to Teach: A Witness to Teachers and Teaching* (New York: Teachers College Press, 2021); Chris Higgins, *The Good Life of Teaching an Ethics of Professional Practice* (Malden, MA: Wiley-Blackwell, 2011); bell hooks, *Teaching to Transgress: Education as the Practice of Freedom* (New York: Routledge, 1994); Meira Levinson and Jacob Fay, eds., *Dilemmas of Educational Ethics: Cases and Commentaries* (Cambridge, MA: Harvard Education Press, 2016); Deborah Meier, *In Schools We Trust: Creating Communities of Learning in an Era of Testing and Standardization* (Boston: Beacon Press, 2002); Santoro, *Demoralized.*

8. Cara Furman and Shannon Larsen, "Interruptions as Collaborative Grappling with Time," *Journal of Curriculum and Pedagogy* 20, no. 2 (2021): 1–20, https://doi.org/10.1080/15505170.2021.1967228.

9. Leafgren, *Reuben's Fall.*

10. Aristotle, *Nicomachean Ethics*, trans. Terence Irwin, 2nd ed. (Indianapolis, IN: Hackett, 1999).

11. Megan Laverty, "Philosophy of Education: Overcoming the Theory-Practice Divide," *Paideusis* 15, no. 1 (2006): 31–44.

12. James Baldwin, "A Talk to Teachers," *Saturday Review*, December 21, 1963, https://www.spps.org/cms/lib010/MN01910242/Centricity/Domain/125/baldwin_atalktoteachers_1_2.pdf.

13. Plato, "Apology," in *Complete Works,* ed. John M. Cooper and D. S. Hutchinson (Indianapolis, IN: Hackett, 1997), LI.21d.

14. Barry Schwartz and Kenneth Sharpe, *Practical Wisdom: The Right Way to Do the Right Thing* (New York: Riverhead Books, 2010).

15. Michel Foucault, *Discipline and Punish: The Birth of the Prison,* 2nd Vintage Books ed. (New York: Vintage Books, 1995); Michel Foucault, *The History of Sexuality*, Vintage Books ed. (New York: Vintage Books, 1990).

16. Mariame Kaba, *We Do This 'til We Free Us: Abolitionist Organizing and Transforming Justice,* ed. Tamara K. Nopper (Chicago: Haymarket Books, 2021); Robin D. G. Kelley, *Freedom Dreams: The Black Radical Imagination* (Boston: Beacon Press, 2002).

17. Eddie S. Glaude, *In a Shade of Blue: Pragmatism and the Politics of Black America* (Chicago: University of Chicago Press, 2008).

18. Pierre Hadot, *Philosophy as a Way of Life: Spiritual Exercises from Socrates to Foucault*, trans. Arnold I. Davidson (Malden, MA: Blackwell, 1995).

19. Freire, *Pedagogy of the Oppressed*; hooks, *Teaching to Transgress*; Vivian Gussin Paley, *You Can't Say You Can't Play* (Cambridge, MA: Harvard University Press, 1992); Paley, *The Girl with the Brown Crayon* (Cambridge, MA: Harvard University Press, 1998).

20. Laverty, "Philosophy of Education," 33.

21. Hansen, *The Call to Teach*; Hansen, *Exploring the Moral Heart of Teaching*; Hansen, *Reimaging the Call to Teach*; Meira Levinson, "Moral Injury and the Ethics of Educational Injustice," *Harvard Educational Review* 85, no. 2 (2015): 203–228; Santoro, *Demoralized*.

22. Nicholas C. Burbules and Kathleen Knight Abowitz, "A Situated Philosophy of Education," *Philosophy and Education* 24, no. 2 (2008): 268–276; René Vincente Arcilla, "Why Aren't Philosophers and Educators Speaking to Each Other?," *Educational Theory* 52, no. 1 (2002): 1–11; Kathleen Knight Abowitz, "Responsibility, Not Relevance," *Philosophical Studies in Education* 43 (2012): 20–24; Laverty, "Philosophy of Education"; Howard Robert Woodhouse, *Critical Reflections on Teacher Education: Why Future Teachers Need Educational Philosophy* (New York: Routledge, 2023); Furman and Traugh, *Descriptive Inquiry in Teacher Practice*; Hansen, *The Call to Teach, Exploring the Moral Heart of Teaching, Reimaging the Call to Teach*; Santoro, *Demoralized*.

23. Santoro, *Demoralized*.

24. Woodhouse, *Critical Reflections on Teacher Education*.

25. Django Paris and H. Samy Alim, eds., *Culturally Sustaining Pedagogies: Teaching and Learning for Justice in a Changing World* (New York: Teachers College Press, 2017); Django Paris, "Culturally Sustaining Pedagogy: A Needed Change in Stance, Terminology, and Practice," *Educational Researcher* 41, no. 3 (2012): 93–97; Django Paris and H. Samy Alim, "What Are We Seeking to Sustain Through Culturally Sustaining Pedagogy? A Loving Critique Forward," *Harvard Educational Review* 84, no. 1 (2014): 85–100.

26. Miriam Beloglovsky and Lisa Daly, *Early Learning Theories Made Visible* (St. Paul, MN: Redleaf Press, 2015); David Elkind, *Giants in the Nursery: A Biographical History of Developmentally Appropriate Practice* (St. Paul, MN: Redleaf Press, 2015); Lissanna M. Follari, *Foundations and Best Practices in Early Childhood Education: History, Theories, and Approaches to Learning*, 2nd ed. (Boston: Pearson, 2011); Carol Garhart Mooney, *Theories of Childhood: An Introduction to Dewey, Montessori, Erickson, Piaget and Vygotsky* (St. Paul, MN:

Redleaf Press, 2000); Sandra Smidt, *Introducing Vygotsky: A Guide for Practitioners and Students in Early Years Education* (London: Routledge, 2009).

27. Steven M. Cahn, *Classic and Contemporary Readings in the Philosophy of Education*, 2nd ed. (New York: Oxford University Press, 2012).

28. Elkind, *Giants in the Nursery*.

29. Beloglovsky and Daly, *Early Learning Theories Made Visible*; Mooney, *Theories of Childhood*; Sandra Smidt, *Introducing Vygotsky*; Woodhouse, *Critical Reflections on Teacher Education*.

30. Laverty, "Philosophy of Education."

31. Philip Kitcher, *The Main Enterprise of the World: Rethinking Education* (New York: Oxford University Press, 2022).

32. Arcilla, "Why Aren't Philosophers and Educators Speaking to Each Other?"

33. Burbules and Knight Abowitz, "A Situated Philosophy of Education"; Cara Furman, "'Me and Socrates, We Are Tight Friends': Co-Constructing a Polis of Teachers and Philosophers of Education," *ACCESS: Contemporary Issues in Education* 41, no. 1 (2021): 36–51, https://doi.org/10.46786/ac21.8287.

34. Michail Bakhtin and Michail, *The Dialogic Imagination: Four Essays*, trans. Michael Holquist and Caryl Emerson (Austin: University of Texas Press, 2011), 358.

35. Cara Furman and Tomas Rocha, eds., *Teachers and Philosophy: Essays From a Contact Zone* (Albany: State University of New York Press, in press).

36. Furman, "Me and Socrates, We Are Tight Friends."

37. Patricia F. Carini and Margaret Himley, *Jenny's Story: Taking the Long View of the Child: Prospect's Philosophy in Action* (New York: Teachers College Press, 2010); Furman and Traugh, *Descriptive Inquiry in Teacher Practice*; Margaret Himley et al., eds., *Prospect's Descriptive Processes: The Child, the Art of Teaching and the Classroom and School*, rev. ed. (North Bennington, VT: The Prospect Center, 2002); Margaret Himley and Patricia F. Carini, eds., *From Another Angle: Children's Strengths and School Standards: The Prospect Center's Descriptive Review of the Child* (New York: Teachers College Press, 2000).

38. Aristotle, *Nicomachean Ethics*; Furman and Traugh, *Descriptive Inquiry in Teacher Practice*; Schwartz and Sharpe, *Practical Wisdom*.

39. F. A. J. Korthagen, *Linking Practice and Theory: The Pedagogy of Realistic Teacher Education* (Mahwah, NJ: L. Erlbaum Associates, 2001).

40. John Dewey, *Moral Principles in Education* (Carbondale: Southern Illinois University Press, 1975); Hansen, *Exploring the Moral Heart of Teaching*; Meier, *In Schools We Trust*.

41. Leafgren, *Reuben's Fall*.

42. Hannah Arendt, *Eichmann in Jerusalem: A Report on the Banality of Evil* (New York: Penguin Books, 2006); Jacques Taminiaux, *The Thracian Maid and the Professional Thinker: Arendt and Heidegger*, trans. Michael Gendre (Albany: State University of New York Press, 1997).

43. Paulo Freire, *Pedagogy of Freedom: Ethics, Democracy, and Civic Courage* (Lanham, MD: Rowman & Littlefield Publishers, 2000), http://public.eblib.com/choice/publicfullrecord.aspx?p=1352132.

44. Carla Shalaby, *Troublemakers: Lessons in Freedom from Young Children at School* (New York: The New Press, 2017), 172.

45. Carol Gilligan, *In a Different Voice: Psychological Theory and Women's Development* (Cambridge, MA: Harvard University Press, 2003); Vanessa Siddle Walker and John R. Snarey, eds., *Race-Ing Moral Formation: African American Perspectives on Care and Justice* (New York: Teachers College Press, 2004).

46. Nel Noddings, *Caring: A Feminine Approach to Ethics & Moral Education*, 2nd ed. (Berkeley: University of California Press, 2003).

47. Himley and Carini, eds., *From Another Angle*, 56.

48. Shalaby, *Troublemakers*, 172.

49. Shalaby, *Troublemakers*, 172.

50. Paris and Alim, *Culturally Sustaining Pedagogies*.

51. Mooney, *Theories of Childhood*.

52. Maria Montessori, *The Montessori Method* (Mineola, NY: Dover Publications, 2002).

53. L. S. Vygotsky, *Thought and Language*, rev. ed., trans. Eugenia Hanfmann, Gertruda Vakar, and Alex Kozulin (Cambridge, MA: MIT Press, 2012).

54. Ron Berger, *An Ethic of Excellence: Building a Culture of Craftsmanship with Students* (Portsmouth, NH: Heinemann, 2003); Montessori, *The Montessori Method*.

55. Carol Copple, Sue Bredekamp, and National Association for the Education of Young Children, eds., *Developmentally Appropriate Practice in Early Childhood Programs Serving Children from Birth Through Age 8*, 3rd ed. (Washington, DC: National Association for the Education of Young Children, 2009).

56. Dewey, *Democracy and Education.*

57. James Alexander McLellan and John Dewey, *The Psychology of Number and Its Applications to Methods of Teaching Arithmetic* (Charleston, SC: BiblioBazaar, 2009).

58. Eleanor Duckworth, *"The Having of Wonderful Ideas" and Other Essays on Teaching and Learning,* 3rd ed. (New York: Teachers College Press, 2006).

59. Patricia F. Carini, *Starting Strong: A Different Look at Children, Schools, and Standards* (New York: Teachers College Press, 2001); hooks, *Teaching to Transgress*; María Lugones, *Pilgrimages/Peregrinajes: Theorizing Coalition Against Multiple Oppressions* (Lanham, MD: Rowman & Littlefield, 2003).

60. Baldwin, "A Talk to Teachers."

61. *Meno* in Plato, *Complete Works,* LI.80a–d.

62. Dewey, *Democracy and Education.*

63. Baldwin, "A Talk to Teachers."

64. Paul Tough, *How Children Succeed: Grit, Curiosity, and the Hidden Power of Character* (New York: Mariner Books, 2013).

65. Kaisu Mälkki and Larry Green, "Ground, Warmth, and Light: Facilitating Conditions for Reflection and Transformative Dialogue," *Journal of Educational Issues* 2, no. 2 (2016): 169–183.

66. Carolyn P. Edwards, Lella Gandini, and George E. Forman, eds., *The Hundred Languages of Children: The Reggio Emilia Approach—Advanced Reflections,* 2nd ed. (Greenwich, CT: Ablex Publishing, 1998).

67. Cara Furman, "Reflective Teacher Narratives: The Merging of Practical Wisdom, Narrative, and Teaching" (PhD diss., Teachers College, Columbia University, 2014).

68. For a notable exception of students and teachers coauthoring a book and a curriculum, see Eleanor Duckworth, *Teacher to Teacher: Learning from Each Other* (New York: Teachers College Press, 1997).

69. John Dewey, *The Sources of Science* (New York: The Kappa Delta Phi Lecture Series, 1929), 10.

70. Janet L. Miller, *Sounds of Silence Breaking: Women, Autobiography, Curriculum,* vol. 1 (New York: P. Lang, 2005).

71. Thank you to the Elementary Teachers Network and the New York City Writing Project with guidance from Elaine Avidon for introducing me to the amazing What We Did chart on which teachers record activities from a professional development session that they would later use. See chapter 1 for more on this chart and a sample.

72. Tom Little and Katherine Ellison, *Loving Learning: How Progressive Education Can Save America's Schools* (New York: W. W. Norton, 2015).

CHAPTER 1

1. Ruth Stiles Gannett and Ruth Chrisman Gannett, *My Father's Dragon* (New York: Random House, 2014).

2. Doris A. Santoro, *Demoralized: Why Teachers Leave the Profession They Love and How They Can Stay* (Cambridge, MA: Harvard Education Press, 2018); Sarah M. Stitzlein and Amy Rector-Aranda, "The Role of 'Small Publics' in Teacher Dissent," *Educational Theory* 66, no. 1–2 (2016): 165–180.

3. Santoro, *Demoralized*; Stitzlein and Rector-Aranda, "The Role of 'Small Publics" in Teacher Dissent."

4. Santoro, *Demoralized*.

5. Pierre Hadot, *Philosophy as a Way of Life: Spiritual Exercises from Socrates to Foucault*, trans. Arnold I. Davidson (Malden, MA: Blackwell, 1995).

6. Plato, John M. Cooper, and D. S. Hutchinson, "Alcibiades," in *Complete Works* (Indianapolis, IN: Hackett, 1997), 557–595, Li: 124b.

7. Plato, Cooper, and Hutchinson, "Alcibiades," Li: 129a.

8. Michel Foucault, *The Essential Works of Michel Foucault, 1954–1984*, trans. Paul Rabinow and James D. Faubion (New York: New Press, 1997).

9. David T. Hansen, *Exploring the Moral Heart of Teaching: Toward a Teacher's Creed* (New York: Teachers College Press, 2001); F. A. J. Korthagen, *Linking Practice and Theory: The Pedagogy of Realistic Teacher Education* (Mahwah, NJ: L. Erlbaum Associates, 2001); Meira Levinson, "Moral Injury and the Ethics of Educational Injustice," *Harvard Educational Review* 85, no. 2 (2015): 203–228; Deborah Meier, *In Schools We Trust: Creating Communities of Learning in an Era of Testing and Standardization* (Boston: Beacon Press, 2002).

10. Hansen, *Exploring the Moral Heart of Teaching*, 87.

11. Julie Diamond, *Welcome to the Aquarium: A Year in the Lives of Children* (New York: New Press, 2008), 9.

12. Later in the semester, I sometimes ask students what seating arrangement would be best for a particular activity. Some groups love desks set up individually, and others prefer desks combined to make table groups.

13. Thank you to Tina Cella, who suggested this activity when I was a first-year teacher to build community and open up the block area.

14. Jacqueline Woodson and Rafael López, *The Year We Learned to Fly* (New York: Nancy Paulsen Books, 2022). Another favorite is Jacqueline Woodson and Rafael López, *The Day You Begin* (New York: Nancy Paulsen Books, 2018).

15. Students choose their own text and read independently.

16. This series of prompts I've derived from practicing yoga over many years. I also often begin with this "body practice" from somatic and antiracist counselor Resmaa Menakem, *My Grandmother's Hands: Racialized Trauma and the Pathway to Mending Our Hearts and Bodies* (Las Vegas: Central Recovery Press, 2017), 30.

17. Robin Wall Kimmerer, *Braiding Sweetgrass: Indigenous Wisdom, Scientific Knowledge, and the Teachings of Plants* (Minneapolis, MN: Milkweed Editions, 2015), 115.

18. John Dewey, *Democracy and Education: An Introduction to the Philosophy of Education* (New York: Free Press, 1916).

19. Mike Anderson, *The First Six Weeks of School* (Turner Falls, MA: Center for Responsive Schools, 2015).

20. Guidance Counselor Tina Cella introduced me to this activity to build community my first week in the classroom.

21. Gholdy Muhammad, *Cultivating Genius: An Equity Framework for Culturally and Historically Responsive Literacy* (New York: Scholastic, 2020), 71.

22. M. M. Bakhtin, *Speech Genres and Other Late Essays*, trans. Michael Holquist and Caryl Emerson (Austin: University of Texas Press, 1986), 358.

23. Elisabeth S. Hirsch, ed., *The Block Book*, 3rd ed. (Washington, DC: National Association for the Education of Young Children, 1996).

24. Cara E. Furman and Cecelia Traugh, *Descriptive Inquiry in Teacher Practice: Cultivating Practical Wisdom to Create Democratic Schools* (New York: Teachers College Press, 2021).

25. L. S. Vygotsky, *Thought and Language*, trans. Eugenia Hanfmann, Gertruda Vakar, and Alex Kozulin, rev. ed. (Cambridge, MA: MIT Press, 2012).

26. Carolyn P. Edwards, Lella Gandini, and George E. Forman, eds., *The Hundred Languages of Children: The Reggio Emilia Approach to Early Childhood Education* (Norwood, NJ: Ablex, 1993).

27. Hirsch, *The Block Book*.

28. Jeff Frank, "Teaching Is Oppositional: On the Importance of Supporting Experimental Teaching During Student Teaching," *Studies in Philosophy and Education* 37, no. 5 (2018): 499–512.

29. Paulo Freire, *Pedagogy of the Oppressed*, 30th anniversary ed. (New York: Continuum, 2000).

30. Freire, *Pedagogy of the Oppressed*; bell hooks, *Teaching to Transgress: Education as the Practice of Freedom* (New York: Routledge, 1994).

CHAPTER 2

1. Laia Bové, "Root to Rise: What Does This Common Yoga Phrase Mean?," *Yogajala* (blog), 2023, https://yogajala.com/root-to-rise/.

2. For a compelling curriculum on rooting in one's ancestors to engage with antiracist and justice-oriented practice, see https://www.virginiadearaniconsulting.com. My deep gratitude to Virginia Dearani for all our discussions about the role of ancestral past in teaching and her research and work.

3. For more on this process, see Björn Krondorfer, *Remembrance and Reconciliation: Encounters Between Young Jews and Germans* (New Haven, CT: Yale University Press, 1995) and my account in Cara E. Furman, "Welcoming Entanglements with Ghosts: Re-Turning, Re-Membering, and Facing the Incalculable in Teacher Education," *Contemporary Issues in Early Childhood* 23, no. 3 (September 2022): 253–264, https://doi.org/10.1177/14639491221117210.

4. Richard Hugo, *The Triggering Town: Lectures and Essays on Poetry and Writing* (New York: W. W. Norton, 1992).

5. We had been reading Faith Ringgold, *My Dream of Martin Luther King* (New York: Dragonfly Books, 1995).

6. Debbie Sonu et al., "Sick at School: Teachers' Memories and the Affective Challenges That Bodies Present to Constructions of Childhood Innocence, Normalcy, and Ignorance," *Review of Education, Pedagogy, and Cultural Studies* 44, no. 2 (2022): 147–165, https://doi.org/10.1080/10714413.2022.2031693.

7. Denise Taliaferro Baszile, "Another Lesson Before Dying: Toward a Pedagogy of Black Self-Love," in *Black Women's Liberatory Pedagogies*, ed. Olivia N. Perlow et al. (Cham: Springer International, 2018), 267, https://doi.org/10.1007/978-3-319-65789-9_15.

8. Karin Murris, *The Posthuman Child: Educational Transformation Through Philosophy with Picturebooks* (London: Routledge, 2016).

9. Furman, "Welcoming Entanglements with Ghosts."

10. Cara E. Furman, "Conversations About Death That Are Provoked by Literature," *Bank Street Occasional Papers Series* (blog), 2020, https://educate.bankstreet.edu/occasional-paper-series/vol2020/iss44/13.

11. David A. Sousa, *How the Brain Learns Mathematics* (Thousand Oaks, CA: Corwin Press, 2008).

12. Resmaa Menakem, *My Grandmother's Hands: Racialized Trauma and the Pathway to Mending Our Hearts and Bodies* (Las Vegas: Central Recovery Press, 2017).

13. Menakem, *My Grandmother's Hands*; María Lugones, *Pilgrimages/Peregrinajes: Theorizing Coalition Against Multiple Oppressions* (Lanham, MD: Rowman & Littlefield, 2003).

14. Mary Midgley, "Rings and Books," *The Raven: A Magazine of Philosophy* (blog), 2022, https://ravenmagazine.org/magazine/rings-books/.

15. Lugones, *Pilgrimages*.

16. Baszile, "Another Lesson Before Dying"; Lugones, *Pilgrimages*.

17. Keeanga-Yamahtta Taylor, ed., *How We Get Free: Black Feminism and the Combahee River Collective* (Chicago: Haymarket Books, 2017), 22–23.

18. Hugo, *Triggering Town*, 15, 12.

19. Furman, "Welcoming Entanglements with Ghosts." Links between personal educational history and ethos occur multiple times in Jarvis R. Givens, *Fugitive Pedagogy: Carter G. Woodson and the Art of Black Teaching* (Cambridge, MA: Harvard University Press, 2022).

20. Paulo Freire, *Pedagogy of Freedom: Ethics, Democracy, and Civic Courage* (Lanham, MD: Rowman & Littlefield, 2000), 47.

21. Cara Furman, "Meditating with Carini: Cultivation of Attention with Care to Shape the Teacher," *Schools* 19, no. 2 (2022): 342–352, https://doi.org/10.1086/722015.

22. Furman, "Welcoming Entanglements with Ghosts"; Cara Furman, "Eavesdropping Books as Testimony: Witnessing Secondhand Crimes Against Humanity with Young Children," *Education Theory* 72, no. 5 (October 2022): 595–626, https://doi.org/10.1111/edth.12547.

23. bell hooks, *Teaching to Transgress: Education as the Practice of Freedom* (New York: Routledge, 1994), 71.

24. Elizabeth Alexander, "The Trayvon Generation," *The New Yorker*, June 22, 2020, https://www.newyorker.com/magazine/2020/06/22/the-trayvon-generation; W. E. B. Du Bois, *The Souls of Black Folk* (North Charleston, SC: CreateSpace Independent Publishing Platform, 2014); Ernest J. Gaines, *A Lesson Before Dying* (New York:

Vintage Books, 1994); Ruth Wilson Gilmore, *Abolition Geography: Essays Towards Liberation* (New York: Verso Books, 2023); Denisha Jones, Jesse Hagopian, and Opal Tometi, eds., *Black Lives Matter at School: An Uprising for Educational Justice* (Chicago: Haymarket Books, 2020); Saidiya V. Hartman, *Scenes of Subjection: Terror, Slavery, and Self-Making in Nineteenth-Century America* (New York: Oxford University Press, 1997); Menakem, *My Grandmother's Hands*; Isabel Wilkerson, *Caste: The Origins of Our Discontents* (New York: Random House, 2020); Jesmyn Ward, ed., *The Fire This Time: A New Generation Speaks About Race* (New York: Scribner, 2016).

25. Gilmore, *Abolition Geography*; Saidiya V. Hartman, *Scenes of Subjection: Terror, Slavery, and Self-Making in Nineteenth-Century America* (New York: Oxford University Press, 1997).

26. Cynthia Ballenger, *Teaching Other People's Children: Literacy and Learning in a Bilingual Classroom* (New York: Teachers College Press, 1999); Cynthia Ballenger, *Puzzling Moments, Teachable Moments: Practicing Teacher Research in Urban Classrooms* (New York: Teachers College Press, 2009).

27. Furman, "Conversations About Death."

28. Furman, "Welcoming Entanglements with Ghosts."

29. Furman, "Welcoming Entanglements with Ghosts," 11.

30. Misty Schroe, *Jumping Mouse: A Native American Legend of Friendship and Sacrifice* (Salem, MA: Page Street Kids, 2019).

31. Stephanie Jones and Lane W. Clarke, "Disconnections: Pushing Readers Beyond Connections and Toward the Critical," *Pedagogies: An International Journal* 2, no. 2 (2007): 95–115.

32. Elizabeth Dutro, *The Vulnerable Heart of Literacy: Centering Trauma as Powerful Pedagogy* (New York: Teachers College Press, 2019).

33. Kathy Tucker and Grace Lin, *The Seven Chinese Sisters* (Morton Grove, IL: A. Whitman, 2003).

34. Stephanie Jones, *Girls, Social Class, and Literacy: What Teachers Can Do to Make a Difference* (Portsmouth, NH: Heinemann, 2006).

35. Patricia F. Carini and Margaret Himley, "Conviction: The Teacher I Want to Be," in *Jenny's Story: Taking the Long View of the Child: Prospect's Philosophy in Action* (New York: Teachers College Press, 2010): 122.

36. Julia Denos and E. B. Goodale, *Windows* (Somerville, MA: Candlewick Press, 2017).

37. hooks, *Teaching to Transgress*, 21.

38. Dutro, *Vulnerable Heart of Literacy*.

39. Here I provide a link to Lyon's poem.
40. Here I link my own poem.
41. hooks, *Teaching to Transgress.*
42. hooks, *Teaching to Transgress*, 61.
43. hooks, *Teaching to Transgress*, 186.
44. Timothy J. Lensmire, *When Children Write: Critical Re-Visions of the Writing Workshop* (New York: Teachers College Press, 1994); Cara Elizabeth Furman, "Ways of Knowing: Implications of Writing Curriculum in an Early Childhood Classroom," *Curriculum Inquiry* 47, no. 3 (2017): 246–262.
45. Brené Brown, *Daring Greatly: How the Courage to Be Vulnerable Transforms the Way We Live, Love, Parent, and Lead*, 2015, http://jeffco.axis360.baker-taylor.com/Title?itemid=0010971012.
46. Jones, *Girls, Social Class, and Literacy.*
47. Nikole Hannah-Jones, Renée Watson, and Nikkolas Smith, *Born on the Water* (New York: Kokila, 2021).
48. John Dewey, *Experience and Education* (New York: Simon & Schuster, 1997).
49. hooks, *Teaching to Transgress.*
50. John Dewey, *Human Nature and Conduct an Introduction to Social Psychology* (New York: Cosimo, 2007).
51. Lugones, *Pilgrimages*; Walter Mignolo, "I Am Where I Think: Remapping the Order of Knowing," in *The Creolization of Theory*, ed. Françoise Lionnet and Shu-mei Shih (Durham, NC: Duke University Press, 2011); Menakem, *My Grandmother's Hands.*
52. Robin J. DiAngelo, *White Fragility: Why It's So Hard for White People to Talk About Racism* (Boston: Beacon Press, 2018); Menakem, *My Grandmother's Hands.*
53. hooks, *Teaching to Transgress*, 43.

CHAPTER 3

1. Jon Scieszka and Lane Smith, eds., *The True Story of the 3 Little Pigs* (New York: Puffin Books, 1996).
2. Mariana Souto-Manning and Jessica Martell, *Reading, Writing, and Talk: Inclusive Teaching Strategies for Diverse Learners, K–2* (New York: Teachers College Press, 2016).
3. Louise M. Rosenblatt, *The Reader, the Text, the Poem: The Transactional Theory of the Literary Work* (Carbondale: Southern Illinois University Press, 1994).

4. Django Paris and H. Samy Alim, eds., *Culturally Sustaining Pedagogies: Teaching and Learning for Justice in a Changing World* (New York: Teachers College Press, 2017).
5. Maria Tatar, ed., *The Classic Fairy Tales: Texts, Criticism* (New York: W. W. Norton, 1999).
6. Reprinted from Cara Furman, "Learning from Fairy Tales in the New Teacher Diaries," *United Federation of Teachers New Teacher Diaries*, 2008.
7. Thomas Kuhn, *The Structure of Scientific Revolution* (Chicago: University of Chicago Press, 1996), cited in Ruth Wilson Gilmore, *Abolition Geography: Essays Towards Liberation* (London: Verso Books, 2023), 110.
8. Gilmore, *Abolition Geography*, 110.
9. Karin Murris, *The Posthuman Child: Educational Transformation Through Philosophy with Picturebooks* (London: Routledge, 2016).
10. Cara E. Furman, "Eavesdropping Books as Testimony: Witnessing Secondhand Crimes Against Humanity with Young Children," *Educational Theory* 72, no. 5 (October 2022): 595–616, https://doi.org/10.1111/edth.12547.
11. Martha C. Nussbaum, *Love's Knowledge: Essays on Philosophy and Literature* (New York: Oxford University Press, 1992).
12. Bruno Bettelheim, *The Uses of Enchantment: The Meaning and Importance of Fairy Tales* (New York: Vintage Books, 1989); Nicholas C. Burbules, "Tootle: A Parable of Schooling and Destiny," *Harvard Educational Review* 56, no. 3 (1986): 239–257; Patricia M. Cooper, "Teaching Young Children Self-Regulation Through Children's Books," *Early Childhood Education Journal* 34, no. 5 (2007): 315–322, https://doi.org/10.1007/s10643-006-0076-0; Bruce Handy, *Wild Things: The Joy of Reading Children's Literature as an Adult* (New York: Simon & Schuster, 2017); Seth Lerer, *Children's Literature: A Reader's History, from Aesop to Harry Potter* (Chicago: University of Chicago Press, 2009); Lisa Sainsbury, *Ethics in British Children's Literature: Unexamined Life* (London: Bloomsbury Academic, 2015).
13. Bettelheim, *Uses of Enchantment*; Burbules, "Tootles"; Cooper, "Teaching Young Children Self-Regulation."
14. Bettelheim, *Uses of Enchantment*.
15. Kate Manne, *Down Girl: The Logic of Misogyny* (New York: Oxford University Press, 2018): 300.
16. Jerome S. Bruner, *Actual Minds, Possible Worlds* (Cambridge, MA: Harvard University Press, 1986); Robert Coles, *The Call of Stories:*

Teaching and the Moral Imagination (Boston: Houghton Mifflin, 1989); Marshall W. Gregory, *Shaped by Stories: The Ethical Power of Narratives* (Notre Dame, IN: University of Notre Dame Press, 2009).

17. Karen Coats, *Looking Glasses and Neverlands: Lacan, Desire, and Subjectivity in Children's Literature* (Iowa City: University of Iowa Press, 2004); Maria Tatar, *Enchanted Hunters: The Power of Stories in Childhood* (New York: W. W. Norton, 2009); Ellen Handler Spitz, "Ethos in Steig's and Sendak's Picture Books: The Connected and the Lonely Child," *Journal of Aesthetic Education* 43, no. 2 (2009): 64–76.

18. Margaret Wise Brown and Clement Hurd, *The Runaway Bunny*, rev. ed. (New York: Harper, 2017).

19. Amy Gary, *In the Great Green Room: The Brilliant and Bold Life of Margaret Wise Brown* (New York: Flatiron Books, 2017); Handy, *Wild Things*.

20. Julie Beck, "Romantic Comedies: When Stalking Has a Happy Ending," *The Atlantic*, 2016, https://www.theatlantic.com/health/archive/2016/02/romantic-comedies-where-stalking-meets-love/460179/.

21. Hans-Georg Gadamer, *Truth and Method*, trans. Joel Weinsheimer and Donald G. Marshall, 2nd rev. ed. (London; New York: Continuum, 2004).

22. Gadamer, *Truth and Method*, 300–305.

23. Karen Hale Hankins, *Teaching Through the Storm: A Journal of Hope* (New York: Teachers College Press, 2003), 9.

24. Gratitude to philosopher of education Cristina Cammarano for helping me phrase definitions of *hermeneutics* and *exegesis*.

25. Spitz, "Ethos in Steig's and Sendak's Picture Books."

26. Beth Alberty, "Pat Carini and the Prospect Archive of Children's Work," *Schools* 19, no. 2 (2022): 240–266, https://doi.org/10.1086/722009; Patricia F. Carini, "Dear Sister Bess: An Essay on Standards, Judgement and Writing," *Assessing Writing* 1, no. 1 (1994): 29–65; Cara Furman, "Responding to the Writer in Student Writing: Engaging in a Descriptive Review of Written Work," *Schools* 16, no. 2 (2019): 175–195, https://doi.org/10.1086/705643; Margaret Himley et al., eds., *Prospect's Descriptive Processes: The Child, the Art of Teaching and the Classroom and School*, rev. ed. (North Bennington, VT: The Prospect Center, 2002); Margaret Himley and Patricia F. Carini, eds., *From Another Angle: Children's Strengths and School Standards: The Prospect Center's Descriptive Review of the Child* (New York: Teachers College Press, 2000).

27. Alberty, "Pat Carini and the Prospect Archive of Children's Work."

28. Patricia F. Carini, *Starting Strong: A Different Look at Children, Schools, and Standards* (New York: Teachers College Press, 2001).

29. Kathe Jervis, "'The Stories We Tell Ourselves Shape Our Identities': Journals in a Plague Year," *Schools* 20, no. 1 (2023): 25–51, https://doi .org/10.1086/724405.

30. Gaia Cornwall, *Jabari Jumps* (Somerville, MA: Candlewick Press, 2017); Nina Crews, *Sky-High Guy* (New York: Henry Holt, 2010).

31. Katie Wood Ray, *Wondrous Words: Writers and Writing in the Elementary Classroom* (Urbana, IL: National Council of Teachers of English, 1999), 84.

32. In literacy classes, I do a similar activity with images of children reading and writing through time.

33. Furman, "Responding to the Writer in Student Writing."

34. Carrie Mae Weems, *The Kitchen Table Series*, 1990, https:// carriemaeweems.net/galleries/kitchen-table.html; Mary Cassatt, *Young Mother Sewing*, 1900, https://www.metmuseum.org/art /collection/search/10425; Wayne F. Miller, *Father and Son at Lake Michigan*, 1947, https://www.sfmoma.org/artwork/2001.191/.

35. Bill Watterson, *Calvin and Hobbes*, trans. Nicoletta Pardi (Modena: Comix, 2015); H. K. Parra, "Famed Baby Photographer Anne Geddes Has Fallen on Hard Times," *Babygaga* (blog), 2020, https://www .babygaga.com/famed-baby-photographer-anne-geddes-has-fallen-on -hard-times/; *Shirley Posing with Glass of Milk*, 1933, Hulton Archive, https://news.yahoo.com/29-ridiculously-adorable-pictures-shirley -150000626.html; David Shannon, *No, David!* (New York: Blue Sky Press, 1998).

36. Filippo Lippi, *Madonna and Child with Two Angels*, 1460–1465, https://www.uffizi.it/en/artworks/lippi-madonna-and-child-with -two-angels; Kadir Nelson, *A Day at The Beach*, 2016, https://store .kadirnelson.com/product/adayatthebeach/95.

37. Gilmore, *Abolition Geography*.

38. Manne, *Down Girl*.

39. For a full account, see Paley's fantastic opus. Three of my favorites are Vivian Gussin Paley, *The Boy Who Would Be a Helicopter* (Cambridge, MA: Harvard University Press, 1990); Vivian Gussin Paley, *The Girl with the Brown Crayon* (Cambridge, MA: Harvard University Press, 1998); and Vivian Gussin Paley, *You Can't Say You Can't Play* (Cambridge, MA: Harvard University Press, 1992).

40. Grace Lin, *A Big Bed for Little Snow* (New York: Little, Brown, 2019); Maurice Sendak, *Where the Wild Things Are*, 50th anniversary ed. (New York: HarperCollins, 2013).

41. Cooper, "Teaching Young Children Self-Regulation."

42. Katelyn Beedy, *Barrie Wade, Little Monster*, 1st U.S. ed. (New York: Lothrop, Lee & Shepard Books, 1990).

43. Cooper, "Teaching Young Children Self-Regulation."

44. Ian Falconer, *Olivia* (New York: Atheneum Books for Young Readers, 2004); Lee, *Please Baby, Please*; Shannon, *No, David!*

45. Gadamer, *Truth and Method*, 129

46. Gilmore, *Abolition Geography*, 109.

47. Pamela Druckerman, *Bringing Up Bébé: One American Mother Discovers the Wisdom of French Parenting* (New York: Penguin Books, 2014); Greg Lukianoff and Jonathan Haidt, *The Coddling of the American Mind: How Good Intentions and Bad Ideas Are Setting Up a Generation for Failure* (New York: Penguin Press, 2018); Lenore Skenazy, *Free-Range Kids: How to Raise Safe, Self-Reliant Children (Without Going Nuts with Worry)* (San Francisco: Jossey-Bass, 2010).

48. L. S. Vygotsky, *Thought and Language*, trans. Eugenia Hanfmann, Gertruda Vakar, and Alex Kozulin, rev. ed. (Cambridge, MA: MIT Press, 2012).

49. David Elkind, *Giants in the Nursery: A Biographical History of Developmentally Appropriate Practice* (St. Paul, MN: Redleaf Press, 2015).

50. Shout-out to the amazing professor Mellisa Clawson.

51. Vygotsky, *Thought and Language*.

52. For more on introducing this process in a range of courses, see Furman, "Responding to the Writer in Student Writing"; Cara Furman, "'To Think What We Are Doing': A Challenge of Our Time for the School of Education," *Curriculum and Teaching Dialogue* 19, no. 1–2 (2017): 103–116.

53. Gilmore, *Abolition Geography*, 98.

54. Emily Oster, *Cribsheet: A Data-Driven Guide to Better, More Relaxed Parenting, from Birth to Preschool* (New York: Penguin Press, 2019).

55. Oster, *Cribsheet*, 100.

56. Robert McCloskey, *Make Way for Ducklings* (New York: Viking Press, 1999).

57. See chapter 7 for a description of this activity.

58. Janna Chan, "3 Common Misconceptions About High-Quality Instructional Materials," *Edreports* (blog), 2022, https://www.edreports

.org/resources/article/3-common-misconceptions-about-high-quality-instructional-materials. Gratitude to Shannon Larsen, who first introduced me to this new distinction between fidelity and integrity.

59. Cornelius Minor, *We Got This: Equity, Access, and the Quest to Be Who Our Students Need Us to Be* (Portsmouth, NH: Heinemann, 2019).

CHAPTER 4

The phrase used in this chapter's subtitle, "Reading the World, Reading the Word," comes from Freire, *Pedagogy of the Oppressed*, and bell hooks's rephrasing in bell hooks, *Teaching to Transgress: Education as the Practice of Freedom* (New York: Routledge, 1994).

1. Freire, *Pedagogy of the Oppressed*, 76,
2. Arlie Russel Hochschild, *The Managed Heart: Commercialization of Human Feeling*, rev. ed. (Berkeley: University of California Press, 2012); Sarah Jaffe, *Work Won't Love You Back: How Devotion to Our Jobs Keeps Us Exploited, Exhausted, and Alone* (New York: Bold Type Books, 2022).
3. Jaffe, *Work Won't Love You Back*.
4. Cara Furman, "'How I Became a Better Teacher': Expanding Assessment Practices Rooted in Ethical Ideals," *The New Educator*, October 4, 2022, 1–19, https://doi.org/10.1080/1547688X.2022.2126053; Doris A. Santoro, *Demoralized: Why Teachers Leave the Profession They Love and How They Can Stay* (Cambridge, MA: Harvard Education Press, 2018); David T. Hansen and Yibing Quek, "The Call to Teach and the Ethics of Care: A Dynamic Educational Crossroads," *Journal of Curriculum Studies* 55, no. 1 (2023): 8–20, https://doi.org/10.1080/00220272.2022.2143243; Yibing Quek, "An Interpretation of the 2019 Chicago Teachers' Strike Through the Ethics of Care," *Studies in Philosophy and Education* 40, no. 6 (2021): 609–627, https://doi.org/10.1007/s11217-021-09779-4; Wanda Watson, "We Got Soul: Exploring Contemporary Black Women Educators' Praxis of Politicized Care," *Equity & Excellence in Education* 51, no. 3–4 (2018): 362–377, https://doi.org/10.1080/10665684.2019.1571464.
5. Cara Furman, "Seeing Us as Unbroken: Learning with Others to Gaze with Love," *Philosophy of Education* 78, no. 1 (2022): 14–19.
6. Sally Haslanger, "What Are We Talking About? The Semantics and Politics of Social Kinds," *Hypatia* 20, no. 4 (2005): 10–26.
7. For this approach, see Doug Lemov, *Teach Like a Champion: 49 Techniques That Put Students on the Path to College* (San Francisco:

Jossey-Bass, 2010). For critiques, see Grace Enriquez, ed., *Literacies, Learning, and the Body: Putting Theory and Research into Pedagogical Practice* (New York: Routledge, 2016); and Sheri Leafgren, *Reuben's Fall: A Rhizomatic Analysis of Disobedience in Kindergarten* (Walnut Creek, CA: Left Coast Press, Inc., 2009).

8. Deborah Meier, "Explaining KIPP's 'SLANT,'" *Assessment* (blog), 2013, https://www.edweek.org/teaching-learning/opinion-explaining -kipps-slant/2013/04.

9. Enriquez, *Literacies, Learning, and the Body*; Michael Anthony Rose, *The Mind at Work: Valuing the Intelligence of the American Worker* (New York: Penguin Books, 2005).

10. Enriquez, *Literacies, Learning, and the Body*.

11. Paulo Freire, *Pedagogy of Freedom: Ethics, Democracy, and Civic Courage* (Lanham, MD: Rowman & Littlefield Publishers, 2000).

12. See also Gloria Boutte and Nathaniel Bryan, "When Will Black Children Be Well? Interrupting Anti-Black Violence in Early Childhood Classrooms and Schools," *Contemporary Issues in Early Childhood* (2019): 1–12; Leafgren, *Reuben's Fall*; Bettina L. Love, *We Want to Do More Than Survive: Abolitionist Teaching and the Pursuit of Educational Freedom* (Boston: Beacon Press, 2019); Carla Shalaby, *Troublemakers: Lessons in Freedom from Young Children at School* (New York: The New Press, 2017).

13. Furman, "Seeing Us as Unbroken.

14. Shalaby, *Troublemakers*, 173.

15. Shalaby, *Troublemakers*, 173.

16. Leafgren, *Reuben's Fall*.

17. Freire, *Pedagogy of the Oppressed*; Haslanger, "What Are We Talking About?"; hooks, *Teaching to Transgress*.

18. hooks, *Teaching to Transgress*, 167.

19. Hannah Arendt, "Thinking and Moral Considerations: A Lecture," *School Research* 51, no. 1/2 (1984): 21.

20. Arendt, "Thinking and Moral Considerations," 21.

21. Myisha V. Cherry, *The Case for Rage: Why Anger Is Essential to Anti-Racist Struggle* (New York: Oxford University Press, 2021), 90.

22. Arendt, "Thinking and Moral Considerations," 21.

23. Freire, *Pedagogy of the Oppressed*.

24. Haslanger, "What Are We Talking About?"

25. In other semesters, the word was *play*.

26. Cherry, *The Case for Rage*, 90.

27. Patricia F. Carini and Margaret Himley, *Jenny's Story: Taking the Long View of the Child; Prospect's Philosophy in Action* (New York: Teachers College Press, 2010), 36.
28. Gratitude to Kristen Case for leading this iteration of the group and Jonathan Cohen for bringing me into it.
29. Check out Suzy Lee, *Lines* (San Francisco: Chronicle Books, 2017).
30. hooks, *Teaching to Transgress*, 223; Lee, *Lines*, 224.
31. Lee, *Lines*, 225.
32. Robin Wall Kimmerer, *Braiding Sweetgrass: Indigenous Wisdom, Scientific Knowledge and the Teachings of Plants* (Minneapolis, MN: Milkweed Editions, 2015).
33. Deborah Meier, "The Dangers Facing Us," *Assessment* (blog), 2007, https://www.edweek.org/teaching-learning/opinion-the-dangers -facing-us/2007/09.
34. Thank you to Krystal Dillard Akins for creating this prompt with me.
35. Haslanger, "What Are We Talking About?"
36. Haslanger, "What Are We Talking About?," 16.
37. Stanley Cavell, *Must We Mean What We Say?: A Book of Essays*, 2nd ed. (Cambridge: Cambridge University Press, 2015), https://doi .org/10.1017/CBO9781316286616; Stanley Cavell, *In Quest of the Ordinary: Lines of Skepticism and Romanticism* (Chicago: University of Chicago Press, 1994).
38. Cherry, *The Case for Rage*.
39. Haslanger, "What Are We Talking About?," 12.
40. Kate Manne, *Down Girl: The Logic of Misogyny* (New York: Oxford University Press, 2018).
41. hooks, *Teaching to Transgress*, 167–175.
42. hooks, *Teaching to Transgress*, 167.
43. Haslanger, "What Are We Talking About?," 12.
44. Cherry, *The Case for Rage*.
45. Shalaby, *Troublemakers*, 173.
46. "Alexa Buono, PhD," 2020, https://www.alexiabuono.com.
47. Cara E. Furman and Cecelia Traugh, *Descriptive Inquiry in Teacher Practice: Cultivating Practical Wisdom to Create Democratic Schools* (New York: Teachers College Press, 2021), 34.
48. Haslanger, "What Are We Talking About?," 16.
49. Cherry, *The Case for Rage*; Maleka Donaldson, *From Oops to Aha: Portraits of Learning from Mistakes in Kindergarten* (Lanham, MD: Rowman & Littlefield, 2021); Shalaby, *Troublemakers*.

50. Vivian Gussin Paley, *Kindness of Children* (Cambridge, MA: Harvard University Press, 2000).

51. Sara Lawrence-Lightfoot, *Respect: An Exploration* (Reading, MA: Perseus Books, 2000).

52. Mary Murphy, *I Like It When . . . /Me Gusta Cuando* (Orlando: Harcourt, 2008).

53. Shalaby, *Troublemakers*.

54. Furman and Traugh, *Descriptive Inquiry in Teacher Practice*, 34.

55. Haslanger, "What Are We Talking About?," 17.

56. Haslanger, "What Are We Talking About?," 17.

57. Ruth Charney, *Teaching Children to Care: Classroom Management for Ethical and Academic Growth, K–8*, rev. ed. (Greenfield, MA: Northeast Foundation for Children, 2002).

58. Nel Noddings, *Caring: A Feminine Approach to Ethics & Moral Education*, 2nd ed. (Berkeley: University of California Press, 2003).

59. Haslanger, "What Are We Talking About?"

60. hooks, *Teaching to Transgress*, 186; Mary Midgley, "Rings and Books," *The Raven: A Magazine of Philosophy* (blog), 2022, https://ravenmagazine.org/magazine/rings-books/.

61. hooks, *Teaching to Transgress*.

62. Cara Furman and Derek Gottlieb, "On Language and Languaging," 2023, https://podcasts.apple.com/us/podcast/18-on-language-and-languaging/id1668433164?i=1000618090612.

CHAPTER 5

1. María Lugones, *Pilgrimages/Peregrinajes: Theorizing Coalition Against Multiple Oppressions* (Lanham, MD: Rowman & Littlefield, 2003). Gratitude to Cristina Cammarano for bring this text into my life and the Philosophy Fellowship for studying it with me.

2. Lugones, *Pilgrimages*, 26.

3. Lugones, *Pilgrimages*, 26.

4. Lugones, *Pilgrimages*.

5. Rachel Wahl, "Dispelling the Burden of Agency: Receptive Learning During Political Crisis," *Educational Theory* 68, no. 4–5 (2019): 403–426.

6. Plato, John M. Cooper, and D. S. Hutchinson, "Alcibiades," in *Complete Works* (Indianapolis, IN: Hackett Pub, 1997), 557–595, Li: 104b.

7. Wayne C. Booth, *The Company We Keep: An Ethics of Fiction* (Berkeley: University of California Press, 1988); Jane Isenberg, *Going by*

the Book: *The Role of Popular Classroom Chronicles in the Professional Development of Teachers* (Westport, CT: Bergin & Garvey, 1994); Azar Nafisi, *Reading Lolita in Tehran: A Memoir in Books* (New York: Random House Trade Paperbacks, 2008).

8. bell hooks, *Teaching to Transgress: Education as the Practice of Freedom* (New York: Routledge, 1994), 17.

9. Robin Wall Kimmerer, *Braiding Sweetgrass: Indigenous Wisdom, Scientific Knowledge, and the Teachings of Plants* (Minneapolis, MN: Milkweed Editions, 2015).

10. Kimmerer, *Braiding Sweetgrass*, 116.

11. Kathryn T. Gines et al., "Teaching and Learning Philosophical 'Special' Topics: Black Feminism and Intersectionality," in *Black Women's Liberatory Pedagogies*, ed. Olivia N. Perlow et al. (Cham: Springer International Publishing, 2018), 153.

12. Patricia F. Carini and Margaret Himley, *Jenny's Story: Taking the Long View of the Child: Prospect's Philosophy in Action* (New York: Teachers College Press, 2010); Kevin Hood Gary, *Why Boredom Matters: Education, Leisure, and the Quest for a Meaningful Life* (Cambridge: Cambridge University Press, 2022).

13. Lugones, *Pilgrimages*, 90.

14. Cara E. Furman and Cecelia Traugh, *Descriptive Inquiry in Teacher Practice: Cultivating Practical Wisdom to Create Democratic Schools* (New York: Teachers College Press, 2021).

15. Karen Barad, *Meeting the Universe Halfway: Quantum Physics and the Entanglement of Matter and Meaning* (Durham, NC: Duke University Press, 2007). I am grateful for the reading groups organized by Karin Murris in which this form of reading is practiced each week. For published models of diffracted reading, see Karen Barad, "What Flashes Up: Theological-Political-Scientific Fragments," in *Entangled Worlds: Religion, Science, and New Materialisms*, ed. Catherine Keller and Mary-Jane Rubenstein (New York: Fordham University Press, 2017), 21–88, https://doi.org/10.5422/fordham/9780823276219.001.0001; Cara Furman, "Meditating with Carini: Cultivation of Attention with Care to Shape the Teacher," *Schools* 19, no. 2 (2022): 342–352, https://doi.org/10.1086/722015; Karin Murris and Vivienne Bozalek, "Diffraction and Response-Able Reading of Texts: The Relational Ontologies of Barad and Deleuze," *International Journal of Qualitative Studies in Education* 32, no. 7 (2019): 872–886, https://doi.org/10.1080/09518398.2019.1609122.

16. Margaret Himley et al., eds., *Prospect's Descriptive Processes: The Child, the Art of Teaching and the Classroom and School*, rev. ed. (North Bennington, VT: The Prospect Center, 2002).

17. Ernest G. Schachtel, *Metamorphosis: On the Conflict of Human Development and the Psychology of Creativity* (Hillsdale, NJ: Analytic Press, 2001), chapter 10.

18. Of note, I had observed students at this point move in class and modify when the physical demands seem inappropriate.

19. Karen Barad, *Meeting the Universe Halfway*.

20. Lugones, *Pilgrimages*, 78.

21. John Locke, *Some Thoughts Concerning Education* (Mineola, NY: Dover Philosophical Classics, 2007), 55–58.

22. Plato et al., *Complete Works*.

23. Vivian Gussin Paley, *The Boy Who Would Be a Helicopter* (Cambridge, MA: Harvard University Press, 1990).

24. Stefano Harney and Fred Moten, *The Undercommons: Fugitive Planning & Black Study* (Wivenhoe, NY: Minor Compositions, 2013), 120.

25. Carol Garhart Mooney, *Theories of Childhood: An Introduction to Dewey, Montessori, Erickson, Piaget and Vygotsky* (St. Paul: Redleaf Press, 2000); Andrew Boryga, "Phonics Is Critical—but True Literacy Requires More," *Edutopia* (blog), 2023, https://www.edutopia.org/article/to-improve-literacy-focus-on-broad-range-of-skills/.

26. John Dewey, *Moral Principles in Education* (Carbondale: Southern Illinois University Press, 1975).

27. Katie Wood Ray and Lisa B. Cleaveland, *A Teacher's Guide to Getting Started with Beginning Writers: Grades K–2* (Portsmouth, NH: Heinemann, 2018); Katie Wood Ray and Matt Glover, *Already Ready: Nurturing Writers in Preschool and Kindergarten* (Portsmouth, NH: Heinemann, 2008); Katie Wood Ray and Lisa B. Cleaveland, *About the Authors: Writing Workshop with Our Youngest Writers* (Portsmouth, NH: Heinemann, 2004).

28. Jan Miller Burkins and Kari Yates, *Shifting the Balance: 6 Ways to Bring the Science of Reading into the Balanced Literacy Classroom* (Portsmouth, NH: Stenhouse Publishers, 2021); Heidi Anne E. Mesmer, *Letter Lessons and First Words: Phonics Foundations That Work, PreK–2* (Portsmouth, NH: Heinemann, 2019).

29. Mike Anderson, *The First Six Weeks of School* (Turner Falls, MA: Center for Responsive Schools, 2015); Ruth Charney, *Teaching Children to Care: Classroom Management for Ethical and Academic*

Growth, K–8, rev. ed. (Greenfield, MA: Northeast Foundation for Children, 2002).

30. Boryga, "Phonics Is Critical."
31. Paul Tough, *How Children Succeed: Grit, Curiosity, and the Hidden Power of Character* (New York: Mariner Books, 2013).
32. Paul LeMahieu, "What We Need in Education Is More Integrity (and Less Fidelity) of Implementation," *Carnegie Commons Blog*, 2011, https://www.carnegiefoundation.org/blog/what-we-need-in-education -is-more-integrity-and-less-fidelity-of-implementation/.
33. Paulo Freire, *Pedagogy of Freedom: Ethics, Democracy, and Civic Courage* (Lanham, MD: Rowman & Littlefield, 2000), 108.
34. Aristotle, *Nicomachean Ethics*, trans. Terence Irwin, 2nd ed. (Indianapolis, IN: Hackett, 1999).
35. Adapted from Cara Furman, "Dwelling Between Philosophy and Education: Fruits, Challenges, and 6 Tips!," *Medium* (blog), 2022, https://medium.com/@cara.furman/dwelling-between-philosophy -and-education-fruits-challenges-and-8fc57cdf7e1e.

CHAPTER 6

1. Mariame Kaba, *We Do This 'til We Free Us: Abolitionist Organizing and Transforming Justice*, ed. Tamara K. Nopper (Chicago: Haymarket Books, 2021).
2. Ruth Charney, *Teaching Children to Care: Classroom Management for Ethical and Academic Growth, K–8*, rev. ed. (Greenfield, MA: Northeast Foundation for Children, 2002).
3. Kate Manne, *Down Girl: The Logic of Misogyny* (New York: Oxford University Press, 2018), 226.
4. Kaba, *We Do This 'til We Free Us*.
5. Manne, *Down Girl*, 201.
6. Karen Gallas, *"Sometimes I Can Be Anything": Power, Gender, and Identity in a Primary Classroom* (New York: Teachers College Press, 1998).
7. Cara Furman and Shannon Larsen, "Interruptions as Collaborative Grappling with Time," *Journal of Curriculum and Pedagogy*, September 10, 2021, 1–20, https://doi.org/10.1080/15505170.2021.1967228.
8. Meira Levinson, "Moral Injury and the Ethics of Educational Injustice," *Harvard Educational Review* 85, no. 2 (2015): 203–228.
9. Michel Foucault, *The Essential Works of Michel Foucault, 1954–1984*, trans. Paul Rabinow and James D. Faubion (New York: New Press, 1997).

10. Cornelius Minor, *We Got This: Equity, Access, and the Quest to Be Who Our Students Need Us to Be* (Portsmouth, NH: Heinemann, 2019).
11. Meira Levinson and Jacob Fay, eds., *Dilemmas of Educational Ethics: Cases and Commentaries* (Cambridge, MA: Harvard Education Press, 2016); Meira Levinson and Jacob Fay, eds., *Democratic Discord in Schools: Cases and Commentaries in Educational Ethics* (Cambridge, MA: Harvard Education Press, 2019).
12. Cara E. Furman and Cecelia Traugh, *Descriptive Inquiry in Teacher Practice: Cultivating Practical Wisdom to Create Democratic Schools* (New York: Teachers College Press, 2021).
13. Paulo Freire, *Pedagogy of the Oppressed* (New York: Bloomsbury, 2000). For adaptations of culture circles with children, teachers, and college students, see Dana Frantz Bentley and Mariana Souto-Manning, *Pre-K Stories: Playing with Authorship and Integrating Curriculum in Early Childhood* (New York: Teachers College Press, 2019); Ira Shor, *When Students Have Power: Negotiating Authority in a Critical Pedagogy* (Chicago: University of Chicago Press, 1996); Mariana Souto-Manning, *Freire, Teaching, and Learning: Culture Circles Across Contexts* (New York: Peter Lang, 2010).
14. bell hooks, *Teaching to Transgress: Education as the Practice of Freedom* (New York: Routledge, 1994).
15. David T. Hansen, *Exploring the Moral Heart of Teaching: Toward a Teacher's Creed* (New York: Teachers College Press, 2001), 87.
16. Hansen, *Exploring the Moral Heart of Teaching*, 87.
17. Dana Franz Bentley, "'Your Job Is to Take Care of Us': Teaching Our Way Through the Boston Marathon Bombings," *Contemporary Issues in Early Childhood Education* 16, no. 3 (2015): 272–283.
18. Sigal R. Ben-Porath, *Cancel Wars: How Universities Can Foster Free Speech, Promote Inclusion, and Renew Democracy* (Chicago: University of Chicago Press, 2023).
19. Hansen, *Exploring the Moral Heart of Teaching*, 87.
20. Courtney B. Cazden, *Classroom Discourse: The Language of Teaching and Learning*, 2nd ed. (Portsmouth, NH: Heinemann, 2001) and more tips on student-led conversations in Dan Rothstein and Luz Santana, *Make Just One Change: Teach Students to Ask Their Own Questions* (Cambridge, MA: Harvard Education Press, 2011).
21. Cecilia M. Espinosa and Laura Ascenzi-Moreno, *Rooted in Strength: Using Translanguaging to Grow Multilingual Readers and Writers* (New York: Scholastic Inc., 2021).

22. Stephanie Jones and Lane W. Clarke, "Disconnections: Pushing Readers Beyond Connections and Toward the Critical," *Pedagogies: An International Journal* 2, no. 2 (2007): 95–115.

23. Rudine Sims Bishop, "Mirrors, Windows, and Sliding Glass Doors," *Perspectives: Choosing and Using Books for the Classroom* 6, no. 3 (1990); Chimamanda Ngozi Adichie, "The Danger of a Single Story," TED-Global, July 2009, https://www.ted.com/talks/chimamanda_ngozi _adichie_the_danger_of_a_single_story?language=en; Grace Lin, "The Windows and Mirrors of Your Child's Bookshelf," TEDx Talks, January 2016, https://www.youtube.com/watch?v=_wQ8wiV3FVo.

24. Gerald McDermott, *Coyote: A Trickster Tale from the American Southwest* (San Diego: Harcourt Brace, 1994). In all other references, I have dropped the subtitle because, as discussed, it is wrong.

25. For a useful checklist "to interrogate your classroom library," see Espinosa and Ascenzi-Moreno, *Rooted in Strength*, 49.

26. Judy Iseke-Barnes, "Unsettling Fictions: Disrupting Popular Discourses and Trickster Tales in Books for Children," *Journal of the Canadian Association for Curriculum Studies* 7, no. 1 (2009): 24–57.

27. Iseke-Barnes, "Unsettling Fictions," 27.

28. Janice Baines, Carmen Tisdale, and Susi Long, *We've Been Doing It Your Way Long Enough: Choosing the Culturally Relevant Classroom* (New York: Teachers College Press, 2018); Stephanie Jones, *Girls, Social Class, and Literacy: What Teachers Can Do to Make a Difference* (Portsmouth, NH: Heinemann, 2006); Mariana Souto-Manning, *Multicultural Teaching in the Early Childhood Classroom: Approaches, Strategies, and Tools, Preschool–2nd Grade* (New York: Teachers College Press, 2013).

29. Gerald McDermott, *Creation* (New York: Dutton Children's Books, 2003).

30. Iseke-Barnes, "Unsettling Fictions."

31. Vivian Gussin Paley, "On Listening to What the Children Say," *Harvard Educational Review* 56, no. 4 (1986): 124.

32. Cara E. Furman, "Interruptions: Cultivating Truth-Telling as Resistance with Pre-Service Teachers," *Studies in Philosophy and Education* 39, no. 1 (2020): 1–17, https://doi.org/10.1007/s11217 -019-09681-0; Cara Furman and Shannon Larsen, "Interruptions: Thinking-in-Action in Teacher Education," *Teachers College Record: The Voice of Scholarship in Education* 122, no. 4 (2020): 1–26, https:// doi.org/10.1177/016146812012200403.

33. Iseke-Barnes, "Unsettling Fictions"; Robin Wall Kimmerer, *Braiding Sweetgrass: Indigenous Wisdom, Scientific Knowledge and the Teachings of Plants* (Minneapolis, MN: Milkweed Editions, 2015).
34. Aristotle, *Nicomachean Ethics*, trans. Terence Irwin, 2nd ed. (Indianapolis, IN: Hackett, 1999).
35. Freire, *Teaching to Transgress*.

CHAPTER 7

1. Joanna Ho and Faith Pray, *One Day* (New York: Harper, 2023).
2. Katie Wood Ray and Matt Glover, *Already Ready: Nurturing Writers in Preschool and Kindergarten* (Portsmouth, NH: Heinemann, 2008); Katie Wood Ray and Lisa B. Cleaveland, *About the Authors: Writing Workshop with Our Youngest Writers* (Portsmouth, NH: Heinemann, 2004).
3. I was inspired to cut out images from an activity described in Stephanie Jones, *Girls, Social Class, and Literacy: What Teachers Can Do to Make a Difference* (Portsmouth, NH: Heinemann, 2006).
4. Michel Foucault, *The History of Sexuality* (New York: Vintage Books, 1990).
5. Daniel Mendelsohn, "But Enough About Me: What Does the Popularity of Memories Tell Us About Ourselves," *New Yorker*, January 25, 2010, https://www.newyorker.com/magazine/2010/01/25/but-enough-about-me-2.
6. Cara Furman, "Dwelling Between Philosophy and Education: Fruits, Challenges, and 6 Tips!," *Medium* (blog), 2022, https://medium.com/@cara.furman/dwelling-between-philosophy-and-education-fruits-challenges-and-8fc57cdf7e1e.
7. Brené Brown, *Daring Greatly: How the Courage to Be Vulnerable Transforms the Way We Live, Love, Parent, and Lead*, 2015, http://jeffco.axis360.baker-taylor.com/Title?itemid=0010971012; Robin J. DiAngelo, *White Fragility: Why It's So Hard for White People to Talk About Racism* (Boston: Beacon Press, 2018); Erin Gruwell and Freedom Writers Teachers, eds., *Teaching Hope: Stories from the Freedom Writer Teachers and Erin Gruwell* (New York: Broadway Books, 2009); Freedom Writers and Erin Gruwell, eds., *The Freedom Writers Diary: How a Teacher and 150 Teens Used Writing to Change Themselves and the World Around Them* (New York: Doubleday, 1999); Timothy J. Lensmire et al., "McIntosh as Synecdoche: How Teacher Education's Focus on White Privilege Undermines

Antiracism," *Harvard Educational Review* 83, no. 3 (2013): 410–431; Meira Levinson and Jacob Fay, eds., *Dilemmas of Educational Ethics: Cases and Commentaries* (Cambridge, MA: Harvard Education Press, 2016): 9–38; Tyler Austin Harper, "I Teach at an Elite College. Here's a Look Inside the Racial Gaming of Admissions," *New York Times*, 2023, https://www.nytimes.com/2023/06/29/opinion/college-admissions-affirmative-action.html.

8. Pierre Bourdieu, *The Logic of Practice* (Stanford, CA: Stanford University Press, 2008).

9. Bourdieu, *Logic of Practice*, 42.

10. Robbie McClintock, "My Canon," *The Reflective Commons* (blog), 2014.

11. David T. Hansen, *The Teacher and the World: A Study of Cosmopolitanism as Education* (New York: Routledge, 2011), 19

12. Hansen, *The Teacher and the World*, 19.

13. I borrow this phrase from Wayne C. Booth, *The Company We Keep: An Ethics of Fiction* (Berkeley: University of California Press, 1988).

14. Karen Barad, "What Flashes Up: Theological-Political-Scientific Fragments," in *Entangled Worlds: Religion, Science, and New Materialisms*, ed. Catherine Keller and Mary-Jane Rubenstein (New York: Fordham University Press, 2017), 21–88, https://doi.org/10.5422/fordham/9780823276219.001.0001.

15. Karen Barad, "Troubling Time/s and Ecologies of Nothingness: Re-Turning, Re-Membering, and Facing the Incalculable," *New Formations* 92, no. 92 (2017): 56–86, https://doi.org/10.3898/NEWF:92.05.2017.

16. Cara E. Furman, "Welcoming Entanglements with Ghosts: Re-Turning, Re-Membering, and Facing the Incalculable in Teacher Education," *Contemporary Issues in Early Childhood* 23, no. 3 (2022): 253–264, https://doi.org/10.1177/14639491221117210.

17. Gholdy Muhammad, *Cultivating Genius: An Equity Framework for Culturally and Historically Responsive Literacy* (New York: Scholastic, 2020), 101.

18. Alasdair C. MacIntyre, *After Virtue: A Study in Moral Theory*, 3rd ed. (Notre Dame, IN: University of Notre Dame Press, 2007), 221.

19. MacIntyre, *After Virtue*, 216.

20. Sally Haslanger, "What Are We Talking About? The Semantics and Politics of Social Kinds," *Hypatia* 20, no. 4 (2005): 10–26; Friedrich Nietzsche, Walter Arnold Kaufmann, and Friedrich Nietzsche, *On the Genealogy of Morals* (New York: Vintage Books, 2011).

21. Foucault, *History of Sexuality.*

22. Haslanger, "What Are We Talking About?"

23. Isabel Wilkerson, *Caste: The Origins of Our Discontents* (New York: Random House, 2020).

24. Robin Wall Kimmerer, *Braiding Sweetgrass: Indigenous Wisdom, Scientific Knowledge, and the Teachings of Plants* (Minneapolis, MN: Milkweed Editions, 2015), 41.

25. Spivak in bell hooks, *Teaching Community: A Pedagogy of Hope* (New York: Routledge, 2003), 7.

26. Walter Mignolo, "I Am Where I Think: Remapping the Order of Knowing," in *The Creolization of Theory*, ed. Françoise Lionnet and Shu-mei Shih (Durham, NC: Duke University Press, 2011), 171.

27. María Lugones, *Pilgrimages/Peregrinajes: Theorizing Coalition Against Multiple Oppressions* (Lanham, MD: Rowman & Littlefield, 2003).

28. Ruth Wilson Gilmore, *Abolition Geography: Essays Towards Liberation* (New York: Verso Books, 2023); bell hooks, *Teaching to Transgress: Education as the Practice of Freedom* (New York: Routledge, 1994); Lugones, *Pilgrimages*; Kimmerer, *Braiding Sweetgrass*; Mignolo, "I Am Where I Think."; Django Paris and H. Samy Alim, eds., *Culturally Sustaining Pedagogies: Teaching and Learning for Justice in a Changing World* (New York: Teachers College Press, 2017); Django Paris and H. Samy Alim, "What Are We Seeking to Sustain Through Culturally Sustaining Pedagogy? A Loving Critique Forward," *Harvard Educational Review* 84, no. 1 (2014): 85–100; Olivia N. Perlow et al., *Black Women's Liberatory Pedagogies: Resistance, Transformation, and Healing Within and Beyond the Academy* (London: Palgrave Macmillan, 2018).

29. Günter Grass, *Cat and Mouse* (San Diego: Harcourt Brace Jovanovich, 1991).

30. Denise Taliaferro Baszile, "Another Lesson Before Dying: Toward a Pedagogy of Black Self-Love," in *Black Women's Liberatory Pedagogies*, ed. Olivia N. Perlow et al. (Cham: Springer International Publishing, 2018), 272, https://doi.org/10.1007/978-3-319-65789-9_15.

31. Eddie S. Glaude, *In a Shade of Blue: Pragmatism and the Politics of Black America* (Chicago: University of Chicago Press, 2008).

32. Adrienne Rich, *On Lies, Secrets and Silence: Selected Prose, 1966–1978* (New York: Norton, 1995), 35.

33. Muhammad, *Cultivating Genius.*

34. Jarvis R. Givens, *Fugitive Pedagogy: Carter G. Woodson and the Art of Black Teaching* (Cambridge, MA: Harvard University Press, 2022).

35. Givens, *Fugitive Pedagogy*.

36. Carole K. Lee and Patti Ensel Bailie, "Nature-Based Education: Using Nature Trails as a Tool to Promote Inquiry-Based Science and Math Learning in Young Children," *Science Activities* 56, no. 4 (2019): 147–158, https://doi.org/10.1080/00368121.2020.1742641. For more on nature-based education, see David Sobel, ed., *Nature Preschools and Forest Kindergartens: The Handbook for Outdoor Learning* (St. Paul, MN: Redleaf Press, 2016).

37. In literacy classes, we often edit and expand the language over multiple days to turn the notes into a poem.

38. Kerascoët, *I Walk with Vanessa: A Story About a Simple Act of Kindness* (New York: Schwartz & Wade Books, 2018).

39. Mo Willems and Amber Ren, *Because* (New York: Hyperion Books for Children, 2019).

40. We also read a short piece titled "My Canon" by Robbie McClintock that is no longer available online.

41. Muhammad, *Cultivating Genius*.

42. Rich, *On Lies, Secrets and Silence*, 35.

43. Miriam Beloglovsky and Lisa Daly, *Early Learning Theories Made Visible* (St. Paul, MN: Redleaf Press, 2015); Steven M. Cahn, *Classic and Contemporary Readings in the Philosophy of Education*, 2nd ed. (New York: Oxford University Press, 2012); David Elkind, *Giants in the Nursery: A Biographical History of Developmentally Appropriate Practice* (St. Paul, MN: Redleaf Press, 2015).

44. Tom Little and Katherine Ellison, *Loving Learning: How Progressive Education Can Save America's Schools* (New York: W. W. Norton & Company, 2015).

45. Doreen Rappaport and Bryan Collier, *Martin's Big Words: The Life of Dr. Martin Luther King, Jr.*, 1st Jump at the Sun pbk. ed. (New York: Jump at the Sun / Hyperion Paperbacks for Children, 2007).

46. DiAngelo, *White Fragility*; Layla F. Saad, *Me and White Supremacy: Combat Racism, Change the World, and Become a Good Ancestor* (Naperville, IL: Sourcebooks, 2020).

47. Hansen, *The Teacher and the World*, 19.

48. Michel Foucault, *Fearless Speech*, trans. Joseph Pearson (Los Angeles: Semiotext(e), 2001).

49. Elizabeth Dutro, *The Vulnerable Heart of Literacy: Centering Trauma as Powerful Pedagogy* (New York: Teachers College Press, 2019).
50. hooks, *Teaching to Transgress*; Lugones, *Pilgrimages*.

CHAPTER 8

1. Lucy Calkins, ed., *Units of Study for Primary Writing* (Portsmouth, NH: FirstHand, 2003); Katie Wood Ray and Lisa B. Cleaveland, *About the Authors: Writing Workshop with Our Youngest Writers* (Portsmouth, NH: Heinemann, 2004); Katie Wood Ray and Lisa B. Cleaveland, *A Teacher's Guide to Getting Started with Beginning Writers: Grades K–2* (Portsmouth, NH: Heinemann, 2018).
2. John Dewey, *Experience and Education* (New York: Simon & Schuster, 1997).
3. Cecilia M. Espinosa and Laura Ascenzi-Moreno, *Rooted in Strength: Using Translanguaging to Grow Multilingual Readers and Writers* (New York: Scholastic Inc., 2021); Mariana Souto-Manning and Jessica Martell, *Reading, Writing, and Talk: Inclusive Teaching Strategies for Diverse Learners, K–2* (New York: Teachers College Press, 2016).
4. Katie Wood Ray, *Wondrous Words: Writers and Writing in the Elementary Classroom* (Urbana, IL: National Council of Teachers of English, 1999).
5. Carl Anderson, *A Teacher's Guide to Writing Conferences* (Portsmouth, NH: Heinemann, 2018); Jennifer Serravallo, *A Teacher's Guide to Reading Conferences* (Portsmouth, NH: Heinemann, 2018).
6. Gretchen Owocki, *Make Way for Literacy!: Teaching the Way Young Children Learn* (Portsmouth, NH: Heinemann, 2001); Kathy Egawa, "Harnessing the Power of Language: First Graders Literature Engagement with Owl Moon," *Language Arts* 67, no. 6 (1990): 582–588.
7. John Dewey, *Moral Principles in Education* (Carbondale: Southern Illinois University Press, 1975); Frank Smith, *The Book of Learning and Forgetting* (New York: Teachers College Press, 1998).
8. L. S. Vygotsky, *Thought and Language*, trans. Eugenia Hanfmann, Gertruda Vakar, and Alex Kozulin, rev. ed. (Cambridge, MA: MIT Press, 2012).
9. Jan Miller Burkins and Kari Yates, *Shifting the Balance: 6 Ways to Bring the Science of Reading into the Balanced Literacy Classroom* (Portsmouth, NH: Stenhouse Publishers, 2021).
10. Espinosa and Ascenzi-Moreno, *Rooted in Strength*.
11. For more, see Cara Furman, "The Dangerous Necessity of Assessment: A Teacher's Dilemma," *Horace* 24, no. 4 (2009): 22–24.

12. Burkins and Yeats, *Shifting the Balance*; Timothy Shanahan, "It Works" and Other Myths of the Science of Reading Era," *Shanahan on Literacy* (blog), March 4, 2023, https://www.shanahanonliteracy .com/blog/it-works-and-other-myths-of-the-science-of-reading-era; Maryanne Wolf, *Proust and the Squid: The Story and Science of the Reading Brain* (New York: Harper Perennial, 2010).

13. Heidi Anne E. Mesmer, *Letter Lessons and First Words: Phonics Foundations That Work, PreK–2* (Portsmouth, NH: Heinemann, 2019).

14. To build fluency, preservice teachers make phonics books for a focus child. They play with premade materials and assess whether a game is worth purchasing, worth making on their own, or not particularly helpful.

15. Paul LeMahieu, "What We Need in Education Is More Integrity (and Less Fidelity) of Implementation," *Carnegie Commons Blog*, 2011, https://www.carnegiefoundation.org/blog/what-we-need-in-education -is-more-integrity-and-less-fidelity-of-implementation/.

16. Emily Hanford, "Sold a Story: How Teaching Kids to Read Went So Wrong," American Public Media, n.d., https://features.apmreports .org/sold-a-story/.

17. Patricia F. Carini and Margaret Himley, *Jenny's Story: Taking the Long View of the Child: Prospect's Philosophy in Action* (New York: Teachers College Press, 2010), 165.

18. Doris A. Santoro, *Demoralized: Why Teachers Leave the Profession They Love and How They Can Stay* (Cambridge, MA: Harvard Education Press, 2018).

19. bell hooks, *Teaching Community: A Pedagogy of Hope* (New York: Routledge, 2003), 21.

20. bell hooks, *Teaching to Transgress: Education as the Practice of Freedom* (New York: Routledge, 1994).

21. Hannah Arendt, *Eichmann in Jerusalem: A Report on the Banality of Evil*, Penguin Classics (New York: Penguin Books, 2006).

22. Robin Wall Kimmerer, *Braiding Sweetgrass: Indigenous Wisdom, Scientific Knowledge and the Teachings of Plants* (Minneapolis, MN: Milkweed Editions, 2015), 34.

23. Kimmerer, *Braiding Sweetgrass*, 37.

24. Kimmerer, *Braiding Sweetgrass*, 37–38.

25. Kimmerer, *Braiding Sweetgrass*, 35.

26. Elizabeth Dutro, *The Vulnerable Heart of Literacy: Centering Trauma as Powerful Pedagogy* (New York: Teachers College Press, 2019).

27. Megan Laverty, "Philosophy of Education: Overcoming the Theory-Practice Divide," *Paideusis* 15, no. 1 (2006): 31–44.

28. F. A. J. Korthagen, *Linking Practice and Theory: The Pedagogy of Realistic Teacher Education* (Mahwah, NJ: L. Erlbaum Associates, 2001), 167.

29. NCTE/IRA, "Writing an 'I Am' Poem," Read Write Think (blog), 2004, https://www.readwritethink.org/sites/default/files/resources/lesson_images/lesson391/I-am-poem.pdf.

30. David T. Hansen, Megan Jane Laverty, and Rory Varrato, "Reimagining Research and Practice at the Crossroads of Philosophy, Teaching, and Teacher Education," *Teachers College Record: The Voice of Scholarship in Education* 122, no. 4 (April 2020): 1–28, https://doi.org/10.1177/016146812012200401.

31. Much gratitude to ECH 201 in fall 2016 for trying this out with me for the first time and doing work that was so marvelous, I knew there was no going back.

32. Patricia F. Carini, "A Letter to Parents and Teachers on Some Ways of Looking at and Reflecting on Children," in *From Another Angle: Children's Strengths and School Standards: The Prospect Center's Descriptive Review of the Child*, ed. Margaret Himley and Patricia F. Carini (New York: Teachers College Press, 2000), 56–64.

33. Korthagen, *Linking Practice and Theory*.

34. Hannah Arendt, *The Human Condition*, 2nd ed. (Chicago: University of Chicago Press, 1998).

35. Aristotle, *Nicomachean Ethics*, trans. Terence Irwin, 2nd ed. (Indianapolis: Hackett, 1999).

36. Cara E. Furman and Cecelia E. Traugh, "To Ask Questions of the Universe: Confronting Habitus for Racial Equity with Descriptive Inquiry," *Studies in Philosophy and Education*, March 1, 2022, https://doi.org/10.1007/s11217-022-09816-w.

37. Julia Fournier, "Conviction: The Teacher I Want to Be," in Patricia F. Carini and Margaret Himley, *Jenny's Story: Taking the Long View of the Child: Prospect's Philosophy in Action* (New York: Teachers College Press, 2010), 116.

38. Karen Gallas, *"Sometimes I Can Be Anything": Power, Gender, and Identity in a Primary Classroom* (New York: Teachers College Press, 1998).

39. Michael Fullan and Andy Hargreaves, *What's Worth Fighting For in Your School?* (New York: Teachers College Press, 1996), 21.

Acknowledgments

Thank you to all the young children and teachers whose wisdom has filled these pages and given me something to write about. A particular thank-you to those whom I interviewed who don't appear by name.

This book began in a class. While I feature many former students, I want to highlight four from that class: Katelyn Beedy, Sasha Hampton, Carlene Mosca, and Erin Silver. Their enthusiasm for the coursework made it clear that philosophy with teachers needed to be done and this book needed to be written.

Gratitude to my colleagues at the University of Maine at Farmington who have supported my research and my teaching. I teach my ethics because I have space to do this *and* colleagues to think with. I am also grateful to the Trustee Professorship at the University of Maine at Farmington, which awarded me time and space to research and write as well as funding for the podcast that accompanies this book. Many thought partners have deeply influenced this work along the way and are recognized throughout. At the risk of naming too many and therefore leaving out, I will offer just a few who have proved particularly consistent and influential on the scope of this particular project: Eric Brown, David Hansen, Cecelia Traugh, Ann Bartges, Stephanie

Burdick-Shepherd, Cristina Cammarano, Cecilia Espinosa, Joy Dangora Erickson, Shannon Larsen, Virginia Dearani, Jeff Frank, Doris Santoro, Wanda Watson, and Kathryn Will.

Thank you to the regulars of the Philosophy Fellowship. Our thinking together radically turned this book into something better.

Thank you also to a few consistent teacher-philosopher interlocutors: Jane Andrias, Krystal Dillard Akins, Joan Bradbury, Alexander Doan, Michelle Harring, Hillary Post, Regina Ritscher, and Bruce Turnquist.

Gratitude to my fantastic undergraduate research assistants who did all kinds of tasks large and small to make this readable and meaningful: Kiley Chambers, Emma Goltz, Hailey Hall, and Christina Lougee.

My capacity to be a scholar is entirely dependent on my faith that my children are well cared for when I am not with them. So much gratitude to Fran Gustman, Sandy Furman, Lexi Dube, Matti Rice, Kristen Bullard, Julie Shores, Maureen Vashon, and Kristen Gagnon. You do the best of work, truly.

Finally, Daniel Schwartz—thank you for supporting me in all ways large and small. You have given me space to travel into worlds as I write, and I am beyond grateful. Max and Ethan, you light up my life, and I admire and love you beyond words.

About the Author

Cara E. Furman is an associate professor of early childhood care and education at Hunter College and a former teacher at an urban public school. She has a master's in philosophy and education and a doctorate in philosophy, bringing together her two abiding commitments. Her coauthored book *Descriptive Inquiry in Teacher Practice: Cultivating Practical Wisdom to Create Democratic Schools* offers a philosophical framework and analysis for a longitudinal study of how the leaders of four urban public schools drew on Descriptive Inquiry to care for their ethical selves and foster practical wisdom. The forthcoming coedited collection *Teachers and Philosophy: Essays from a Contact Zone* explores what it means to think and write from the contact zone that is philosophy and practice. Furman publishes in a range of journals integrating qualitative data and philosophy to study teacher development. Furman is a frequent contributor to practitioner-oriented resources such as *Edutopia* and is the cohost of *Thinking in the Midst*, a podcast that thinks philosophically about contemporary issues. She is a long-term practitioner of Descriptive Inquiry and is the immediate past codirector of the Summer Institute on Descriptive Inquiry.

Index

accessibility, 3, 32
accompaniment, xi
acting, story performance in, 92–94, 108
activist-scholars and scholar-activists, 99
actors in story performance, 93, 94
Alberty, Beth, 89
Alcibiades, 30, 133–134
Algava, Alisa, 192, 197
Alim, Samy, 9
ameliorative approach, 115–116, 124–126, 129, 183
Andrias, Jane, 2
Anecdotal Recollections, 121–123, 127, 140, 192
aporia, 17, 48, 98
appropriation, cultural, 60
  in *Coyote,* 168–169, 172, 174, 175
Arendt, Hannah, 11, 147, 215, 224
  on frozen words, 109, 110, 111
Aristotle, xii, 13, 35, 154, 224
arrogant perception, 141–142
art
  harsh response of teacher to, 43, 44
  and image analysis, 88–92
Artist Who Painted a Blue Horse, The (Carle), 43
attending with care, 14–15
  in block activity, 45
  as core value, 104

in image analysis, 98
in interview on values, 45–46
listening in, 74–75, 127
making meaning in, 126
in reading philosophy, 151–152
in "Where I'm From" poems, 74–75
attention from teacher
  lack of, as hurtful, 133
  positive attributes noticed in, 164
  as positive experience, 61, 78, 106
  in world travel and pilgrimage, 131–133
audience
  of poetry, 69
  of story performance, 93, 94
authors, teachers as, 18–19
autism, 136–137
autonomy, 32, 207, 209, 226

Bailie, Patti, 189
Bakhtin, Mikhail, 11, 44
balance, 139
  and disequilibrium, 57, 77, 79, 139
  and emotional equilibrium, 139
  in meditation practice, 56, 62–65, 76
Baldwin, James, 5, 16, 17
Band-Aid story, 49–50
Barad, Karen, 136, 141, 185
Baszile, Denise Taliaferro, 59, 60, 188, 189

Because (Willems), 191
because stories, 191–192
Beedy, Katelyn, 47, 81, 95, 96
  on confidence in values, 217–218
  on Dewey, 149, 195
  equity concerns of, 49, 50
  on pride in participation, 151–152,
    154
  on reading philosophy, 148–149,
    195–196, 199–200
  values interview with, 40–44, 45,
    49, 225
behavior of children, management
    of, 123
  in children's stories, 94, 95–96
  punishment in, 156–157
  reflection on values in, 225–226
  rigid discipline in, 104–106, 153–154
  seating requirements in, 104–108
being love, 14–15, 106–107, 121
Bentley, Dana, 162, 163
best interests of students, 27, 100, 209
best practices, 13–14
Big Bed for Little Snow, A (Lin), 93
"Big Ideas" ritual, 162
birthing, as metaphor, 111–112
Blacks, 60, 112–113, 115
  and racial cruelty, 62
  self-love, 60, 188
  women, 60, 119
block activity, 36–40, 44–45, 51
  community building in, 36, 38, 47
  experiential learning in, 47
  as interruption, 48
  scaffolding in, 46
  trust and comfort in, 48
body
  care in, 117
  words in, 110–113
body awareness
  balance in, 56, 62–65, 76, 139
  in calming activities, 34
book bans, 167
Born on the Water (Hannah-Jones,
    Watson, & Smith), 75
Bourdieu, Pierre, 183

*Boy Who Would Be a Helicopter,
    The* (Paley), 146, 147, 148
"brain buttons," 104–108, 109, 129
brain research, 59
"brick brain," label of, 129–130, 152
Brown, Margaret Wise, 87
Bruner, Jerome, 15, 97, 150
"bubble gum" brain, label of, 129–130
building from the learner, 15
  in culture circles, 173–174
  in image analysis, 97–98
  in philosophy reading, 150
  in Recollections on care, 127
  scaffolds in. *See* scaffolding
  in values journal, 46–47
  in "Where I'm From" poems, 75
bullying, 55, 170
Buono, Alexia, 117, 127
burn out, 116

calming activities, 34, 42, 202–203
Calvin and Hobbes (Watterson), 91
canons, 183, 187–204
care, 14–15
  attending with. *See* attending
    with care
  in the body, 117
  dance activity on, 117, 127
  definition of, 103, 125, 126
  descriptive analysis of, 122–123
  in every classroom moment, 116
  expanded understanding of, 154
  and love, 14–15, 29, 103–104
  in philosophy and practice, 126
  and practices seen as uncaring,
    43, 44, 104–106, 126, 127,
    153–154
  reflection on word, 118, 119, 127
  self-denial in, 119, 124, 128
  subjectivity in concept of, 128
  and teachers as care workers, 104
  in word choice, 110
Carini, Patricia, 12, 14, 137, 212–213
  on Descriptive Review of Work, 89
  philosophical canons of, 196, 197
  on words in the body, 110–111

Carle, Eric, 43
Cassatt, Mary, 91
cell phone policy, 39
Chambers, Kiley, 176
Cherry, Myisha, 109–110, 115, 119
children. *See* students
children's stories, 81–102
   classroom collection of, 92,
      166–168, 207, 209–210
   coded levels of, 207–208
   Coyote, 168–176
   cultural insights from, 86–87,
      132, 133
   curriculum flexibility in use of,
      100–101
   descriptive approach in, 121
   exegetical analysis of, 87, 88,
      94–95, 99, 101
   fairy tales in, 81–88, 96–97
   parent–child relationships in, 94,
      95–96
   performances on, 84, 92–94
   as philosophical texts, 92, 94–95
   in picture books, 88–89, 92,
      94–95, 98
   textual analysis of, 94–97, 98
Clarke, Lane W., 66
class meetings, 160, 177
classroom
   collection of books in, 92, 166–168,
      207, 209–210
   democratic, 18, 39, 147, 162, 163
   inclusion in. *See* inclusion
   meaning of care in, 116
   organization and layout of, 31–32,
      41–42, 45
   orientation of students to, 31–35, 44
   participation in, 151–152, 154,
      164–166, 175, 176
   as safe and comfortable, 41, 55
   sitting in. *See* sitting and seating
   student-facilitated discussions in,
      164–165, 170, 175
   vision for, 28–29
Cleveland, Lisa, 151
Clinton, Hillary, 114

close reading
   of "brain buttons" phrase, 105
   of canons, 187–199
   different meanings found in, 171
   of familiar texts, 21, 81–102
   of philosophy texts, 21, 134–155
   steps in, 141–146
collaborative grappling, 160–161, 174
coloring activity, 43, 44, 203
Combahee River Collective, 60
commitments, 3, 6
   to best interest of child, 100, 209
   to care, 127
   to equity, 50
   experiences affecting, 59, 60, 62, 78
   to inclusion, 73, 104
   to inquiry, 5, 121
   to listening, 62
   to love, 109
   to openness, 133
   to values, 13, 51
communities of color, 9, 59
community
   reading philosophy in, 155
   reflection on word of, 119, 121
community building
   Band-Aid story in, 49–50
   block activity in, 36, 38, 47
   care in, 125–126
   "Where I'm From" poems in, 74–76
conceptual analysis, 114, 117–121, 128
   ameliorative, 115–116, 124–126
   descriptive, 114–115, 121–124
   Reflection on a Word in, 117–121,
      192
confessional narratives, 70, 127,
      182–183, 185, 186
   decisions on sharing, 70, 127,
      182–183, 200
   Foucault on, 182, 186, 200
   regulatory nature of, 185
conflicts, response to, 156–159, 160,
      173–174, 178
   in Responsive Classroom, 151,
      157–158
   student avoidance in, 173–174, 177

constellation metaphor, 185
contract with students on grading, 215, 216
"Conviction" (Fournier), 225
Cooper, Patricia, 94, 99
Covid-19 pandemic, 137, 210–212, 213, 214
Coyote tale (McDermott), 168–176
cracks, 113
  in mug activity, 113, 137–138
Creation (McDermott), 172
cultural appropriation, 60
  in *Coyote,* 168–169, 172, 174, 175
culturally sustaining pedagogy, 9, 15, 222
culture, 9, 86–87, 186–187
  and fairy tales, 84–85, 88
  and image analysis, 91–92
  Indigenous. *See* Indigenous culture and peoples
  oppressive, 9, 189
  in world travel and pilgrimage, 135–136
  zero point, 187–188
culture circles, 160–178
  Coyote as topic in, 171–172
  interdependence in, 163–164
  multiple perspectives in, 159–161
  participation structures in, 164–166
  scaffolding in, 161
  seating in, 162–163
curriculum
  child at center of, 34
  equity in access to, 3
  ethics in, 46
  fidelity to, 19, 101, 116, 207, 210
  flexibility in, 100–101
  phonics in, 209, 210
  secret, keystone experiences as, 63
  social-emotional skills in, 139, 203
  student interest in, 144–145, 146

dance activity on care, 117, 127
Dearani, Virginia, 66
decoding in reading, 208
deconstruction of unjust frames, 5

de la Peña, Matt, 121
Delpit, Lisa, 188
democratic classroom, 18, 39, 147, 162, 163
Demoralized (Santoro), 29–30
demoralized teachers, 22, 29–30, 116, 214
descriptive analysis, 114–115, 121–124
  in Anecdotal Recollection, 192
  of images, 97–98
Descriptive Inquiry, x, 12, 117, 160, 192, 196
  attending with care in, 14
  Institute on, 196, 197–198
  Philosophy Fellowship on, 140
  Summer Institute on, 113, 119, 137–138
Descriptive Inquiry in Teacher Practice (Furman & Traugh), x
Descriptive Process, 12, 117, 137
  Anecdotal Recollection in, 121–123, 140
  in Philosophy Fellowship, 197
  in reading philosophy, 137–138
  Reflection on a Word in, 117–121, 127, 142, 192
Descriptive Review of the Child, 221, 223
Descriptive Review of Work, 117
  Anecdotal Recollection in, 140
  collaboration in, 118
  in image analysis, 88, 89, 90–91
  paraphrasing round in, 152
  in reading philosophy, 138, 142, 143, 150, 151, 152, 194, 195
Dewey, John, 11, 17, 18, 23, 149
  canons of, 194, 196, 203, 204
  on experiential learning, 15–16, 36, 76, 151, 207
  and Montessori compared, 195–196
Diamond, Julie, 32, 107, 203
Diary of Laura, The (Edwards & Rinaldi), 42
diffracted reading, 136, 141
disequilibrium, 57, 77, 79, 139

disruption and interruption. *See* inter-
    ruption and disruption
dramatic play, 92–94, 147
Duckworth, Eleanor, 16
Dunham, KB, 206
duties and responsibilities in gifts,
    35, 51
Dutro, Elizabeth, 66, 70, 200, 217

Edwards, Caroline, 42
Emerson, Ralph Waldo, 111
empathy, 43, 158
Epictetus, 184
epistemology, zero point, 187–188
equity, 2, 3, 48–51
ethics
    of care, 14, 15
    in curriculum, 46
    definition of, 3
    experience affecting, 60, 62
    practice strengthening, 30
ethos, 3, 30, 51
evidence-based techniques, 3
exclusion, 157, 171, 177, 178
    in *Coyote* story, 169, 176
excorporation and incorporation, 135
exegetical analysis, 87, 88, 94–95,
    99, 101
experiences
    Anecdotal Recollections on,
        121–123, 127, 140
    attending with care in listening
        to, 127
    because stories on, 191–192
    confessional narratives on, 70, 127,
        182–183, 185, 186, 200
    country differences in, 131–132, 133
    decisions on sharing, 69–70, 71, 75,
        127, 182–183, 185, 200
    ethics rooted in, 60, 62
    "flash up" of memories, 185
    Holocaust connection in, 57–58,
        60, 140, 184–185
    keystone, 60–63, 79
    learning from. *See* experiential
        learning

naming of, 78
origin of values in, 7, 58–59, 149
painful, 61, 77, 78–79
positive, as transformative, 61, 78,
    106
and reader response, 83, 85, 171
reflection on, 15, 16, 36, 61–62, 63,
    73, 76
as secret curriculum, 63
themes in, 73, 76
tree images in poem on, 205–206
"Where I'm From" poems on, 68–80
experiential learning, 15–16, 38
    in block activity, 47
    in concept analysis, 128
    in culture circles, 174–175
    Dewey on, 15–16, 36, 76, 151, 207
    from familiar texts, 99
    in philosophy reading, 151
    in values interviews, 47
    in "Where I'm From" poems, 76
    in workshop model, 151, 206, 207

fairness, 50, 157, 172–173
fairy tales, 81–88, 96–97
familiar texts, close reading of, 21,
    81–102
    fairy tales in, 81–88, 96–97
    picture books in, 88–91. *See also*
        picture books
fantasy, 172, 182
Fay, Jacob, 160, 161
fear, languages associated with,
    112–113
feminism, 60, 62
fidelity to curriculum, 19, 101, 116,
    207, 210
First World zero point epistemology,
    187
fluency, 135–136
folktales, 96–97
    Coyote, 168–176
    Jumping Mouse, 65
Foucault, Michael, 6, 11, 30, 182, 186,
    200
Fournier, Julie, 69, 225, 226

frames
  in philosophy, 5
  in sharing information, 69–70, 75
frameworks, 86
Freire, Paulo, 6, 61, 78, 106, 134
  on culture circles, 160, 177
  on prejudice, 153
  on words and world, 103, 108, 110
friendships, 157, 172–173, 174
  exclusive, 178
  honest feedback in, 154, 177, 224
  and *Jumping Mouse* story, 65
frozen words and thinking, 109,
  110, 121
Frye, Marilyn, 141, 142
Fullan, Michael, 226

Gadamer, Hans-Georg, 88, 96
Gallas, Karen, 159, 193
Geddes, Anne, 91
genealogy
  biological, 186
  of Black literacy, 189
  philosophical, 182, 186
German history, Holocaust in, 57–58,
  60, 112, 140, 184–185
German language, 112, 129
gifts and offerings
  duties and responsibilities in, 35, 51
  exercise on, 67–68
  in *Jumping Mouse*, 65
  in *Seven Chinese Sisters*, 66–67
Gilmore, Ruth Wilson, 86, 96, 98, 99
Givens, Jarvis, 189
Giving Tree, The, 86
Glaude, Eddie, 188, 189
good and evil, 82, 83, 96–97, 158
grading of students, 214–215, 216
grappling, collaborative, 160–161, 174
gratitude, daily ritual of, 216–217, 223
grit, 17, 129, 152
grounding, 34, 56, 62, 63–65
growth mindset, 17

habitus, 183
Hadot, Pierre, 5–6, 30

Hall, Hailey, 36–38, 108, 206
Hampton, Sasha, 40, 47, 48–50, 131,
  144–146, 199, 225
"Handbook" (Epictetus), 184
handbooks, 204
  Hansen on, 183–184, 198
handwashing, 136–137, 151, 152
handwriting skills, 182, 206–207, 209
Hankins, Karen Hale, 88
Hansen, David T., ix–xvi, 31, 32, 107,
  162, 163, 203, 220
  on handbooks, 183–184, 198
Hargreaves, Andy, 226
Harney, Stephano, 150
Harring, Michelle, 28
Haslanger, Sally, 104–105, 109, 114,
  115, 119, 124
Haudenosaunee Confederacy, 35,
  134–135, 136
heaven and hell concepts, 82, 83
hermeneutics, 85–88
history, 188, 189
  beginning course with, 185, 193
  Holocaust in, 57–58, 60, 112, 140,
  184–185
  zero point view of, 188
History of Sexuality, The (Foucault), 182
Ho, Joanna, 181
Holocaust, 57–58, 60, 112, 140,
  184–185
hooks, bell, 6, 16, 134, 149, 200, 215
  on confessional narratives, 70,
  200–201
  on disruptive effects of language, 108
  on experience and theory making,
  62, 73, 74, 76
  in growth away from origins, 77
  on language and oppression,
  112–113
  on listening, 74–75, 127
horizon metaphor, 88
Hugo, Richard, 57, 58, 60, 63
human-centered portfolio, 221–223
hurtful behavior, response to, 156–159
hybridization, 11, 44
hyphen, value of, 99

"I am" poems, 220
"I Am Where I Think" (Mignolo), 187
I Do, We Do, You Do approach, 20, 89
I Like It When (Murphy), 121
image analysis, 88–92
  attending with care in, 98
  descriptive language in, 97–98
  inferences in, 89, 90–91, 97
  interruption and disruption in,
    98–99
  scaffolding in, 89, 97–98
  in small groups, 98
  of swaddled child, 90–91, 97, 98–99
imagination, value of, 43, 44
immersion, 58
inclusion, 157
  classroom organization for, 32, 42
  commitment to, 73, 104
  in *Coyote* story, 169, 170
  in sitting requirements, 108, 109, 173
  small group work for, 45, 50
  value of, 41, 42, 45, 76
incorporation and excorporation, 135
independent reading, 206, 207, 208
Indigenous culture and peoples, 113,
  186–187
  and *Coyote* story, 168–176
  gratitude ritual in, 216–217
  in Haudenosaunee Confederacy, 35,
    134–135, 136
  and *Jumping Mouse* story, 65
  plants as peers in, 183, 186
inferences
  in image analysis, 89, 90–91, 97
  in philosophy reading, 142
injustice
  experience of, as child, 78–79
  racial, 29, 60, 78, 79
  resistance in, 215
Institute on Descriptive Inquiry, 196,
  197–198
integrated restatement in Reflection on
  a Word, 118
integration between philosophy and
  practice, 13, 44–45, 74, 126,
  220–221

intentionality, 7, 32, 69, 76
interdependence in culture circles,
  163–164
interruption and disruption, 16–18
  in block activity, 48
  in culture circles, 175–176
  in image analysis, 98–99
  in philosophy reading, 152–153
  in "Where I'm From" poems, 76–77
  in word choice, 128–129
interview on values, 40–44, 51,
  218, 224
  attending with care in, 45–46
  collaborative reflection in, 225
  community in, 225–229
  experiential learning in, 47
  scaffolding in, 46–47
intuitions, 124
Iseke-Barnes, Judy, 168
I Walk with Vanessa (Kerascoët),
  190–191

"Jack and the Beanstalk," 82
jealous behavior, 49, 50
Jim Crow laws, 188
Jones, Junie B., 92
Jones, Stephanie, 66, 68
journal writing, values reflection in,
  40–47
Jumping Mouse (Schroe), 65
justice, 5, 158. *See also* injustice

Kaba, Mariame, 157
Kennedy, John Fitzgerald, 194
Kerascoët, 190
keystone experiences, 60–63, 79
Kimmerer, Robin Wall, 35, 113, 149,
  183, 186, 187
  on gratitude ritual, 216–217, 223
  on Thanksgiving Address, 35,
    134–135, 136
Kindness of Children, The (Paley), 121
King, Martin Luther, Jr., 140, 194, 195
  death of, 57, 58, 60, 62
King, Thomas, 69
Kitchen Table (Weems), 91

knowing oneself, Socrates on, 5, 30
Korthagen, Fred, 218, 223

labeling, 95, 108–109, 129–130
    as philosopher, 5
    on reading skills, 207–208, 209
"Ladies First" (Silverstein), 86
language
    ameliorative approach to, 115–116,
        124–126, 129
    clichés and generalizations in,
        110–111
    conceptual analysis of, 114, 117–121
    and cultural codes in power, 188
    descriptive analysis of, 114–115,
        121–124
    fear associated with, 112–113
    frozen words in, 109, 110, 121
    hurtful, 128–129
    hybridization of, 11
    in image analysis, 97–98
    metaphors in. See metaphors
    word choice in. See word choice
Larsen, Shannon, 160
Lash, Abby, 74
Laverty, Megan, 6, 10, 20, 21, 217, 220
learning
    and building from the learner.
        See building from the learner
    in child-initiated play, 146, 147
    experiential. See experiential
        learning
    grading of students on, 214–215, 216
    grit and growth mindset in, 17
    interest in subject affecting,
        144–145, 147, 199
    in interruption and disruption, 17
    Locke on, 144, 145, 147
    Platonic ideal for, 27, 29
    of reading skills, 152
    recalcitrance of students in, 214–215
    scaffolding in. See scaffolding
    sitting position for, 3, 105, 108,
        109, 173
    SLANT acronym on, 105
    social-emotional components of, 38

letters, weekly, values reflection in,
    40–47
Levinson, Meira, 160, 161
Lightfoot, Sarah Lawrence, 121, 193
Lincoln, Abraham, 194
Lippi, Filippo, 91
listening
    attending with care in, 74–75, 127
    commitment to, 62
    in culture circles, 166
    experiences affecting, 78, 79
    to multiple perspectives, 160
    in philosophy reading, 148, 149, 153
    as pilgrimage, 72, 132, 133
    prejudice affecting, 153
    to Recollections, 127, 128
    as respectful neighbor, 134–135,
        136, 154
    translating and interpreting in, 149
    to "Where I'm From" poems, 72,
        74–75
    without appropriation, 60
literacy
    Black, genealogy of, 189
    conversation on meaning of, 173
    scaffolding in development of, 150
literacy course, 8, 9
    block activity in, 48
    human-centered portfolio in,
        221–223
    resistance to reading in, 173
    values in, 33–34, 38
    "Where I'm From" poems in, 68–80
literature reviews, 123–124
Locke, John, 90, 131, 139
    close reading of, 144–149, 199–200
    and Rousseau compared, 131, 199
Lorenz, Patrice, 83–84
love
    and being love, 14–15, 106–107, 121
    and care of teachers for children,
        14–15, 29, 103–104
    conceptual analysis of, 114
    definition of, 103
    myth of, 110
    as *Runaway Bunny* theme, 87

Love (de la Peña), 121
Loving Learning (Little & Ellison), 23,
 195, 203, 204
Lugones, María, 16, 200
 close reading of, 141–142, 198–199
 on fluency, 135–136
 on pilgrimages, 72, 132–133,
  140–141
Lyon, George Ella, 68
Lyons, Oren, 135

"Magic Fish, The," 84
Make Way for Ducklings (McCloskey),
 100–101
Manne, Kate, 86, 87, 92, 114,
 158–159
mapping sounds activity, 189–190
Martin's Big Worlds (Rappaport &
 Collier), 195
McClintock, Robbie, 183, 184
McDermott, Gerald, 168–176
McIntyre, Alasdair, 185
McLellan, James Alexander, 16
meaning making, 126, 161, 164
meditation
 balance in, 56, 62–65, 76
 as calming activity, 34, 44, 202–203
 grounding in, 34, 63–65
Menakem, Resmaa, 59
Meno, 16, 17
Meno, The (Plato), ix
Merleau-Ponty, Maurice, 196
Metamorphosis (Schachtel), 137
metaphors, 111–112
 of brick and bubble gum brain,
  129–130
 of constellations, 185
 of horizon in hermeneutics, 88
 of pilgrimage in listening, 72,
  132, 133
 of stingray on Socrates, 16–17
 of words as tools, 130, 149
Midgley, Mary, 59
Mignolo, Walter, 187
mimesis theory, 96
Minor, Cornelius, 160, 161

misogyny, 86, 114–115
modeling, 14, 20, 51, 136
Montessori, Maria, 15, 194, 195–196,
 200
morals, 3, 159
 and book bans, 167
 in children's stories, 83, 84
 and confession, 186
 and demoralization, 116
Moten, Fred, 150
motivation of teachers, 1, 29
 care and love in, 29, 103–104
 and demoralization, 214
 in Holocaust connection, 58, 60
 ideals in, 22, 23, 27, 29
 painful experiences affecting, 61,
  78–79
mug activity, 113, 137–138
Muhammad, Gholdy, 40, 185, 189, 193
Murphy, Mary, 121
music, 128
"My Canon" course, 183
My Father's Dragon (Gannett &
 Gannett), 28

names of students, learning of, 35, 36,
 161–162
naming, 63
 change as goal of, 177
 of experiences, 78
 of values, 10, 20, 30, 51, 73, 74,
  124–125, 229
Nazi Germany, 184–185, 215
needs, and equity, 49–50
Nelson, Kadir, 91
Nickerson, Jacie, 206
Nietzsche, Friedrich, 6, 186
No, David! (Shannon), 91, 92, 94
Noddings, Nel, 14, 125
norms, 3, 51, 133, 135
 behavioral, 104
 cultural, 59, 86, 102
 and fidelity to curriculum, 101
 in Philosophy Fellowship,
  197–198
 and reading levels, 208

norms (*continued*)
    rejection of, 216
    and zero point epistemology, 187
Nussbaum, Martha, 86

openness in travel and pilgrimage, 133
oppression, 60, 186
    language in, 112–113, 115
    protest and resistance in, 188, 215
orientation of students to classroom,
    31–35, 44
origins
    keystone experiences in, 60–63, 79
    tracing of, 185, 186
    "Where I'm From" poems on, 68–73

painful experiences, 61, 77, 78–79
Paley, Vivian Gussin, 6, 92–93, 121,
    146, 147, 148, 172
paradigms, 86
Paris, Django, 9
Paris, William, 135
participation in classroom
    confidence in, 151–152, 154, 176
    in culture circles, 164–166
    in student-facilitated discussions, 175
Peach Boy (Sakurai), 85
peers
    image analysis by, 91–92, 97–98
    influence of, 183
    relationships with, 123, 131, 157,
    177, 178, 190
people of color, 16, 40, 121, 188,
    196, 198
philosophers, 5
    as white men, 59–60, 128, 196–197
philosopher-teachers, x–xi, xiii, 4–13
philosophical genealogy, 182, 186
philosophical texts
    as canons, 187–204
    children's stories as, 92, 94–95
    close reading of, 21, 134–155
philosophy, ix, 5, 10, 11
    integration between practice and,
        13, 44–45, 74, 126, 220–221
    as way of life, 5–6, 30

Philosophy Fellowship, 140, 141, 192,
    196–199
phonics, 38, 108, 213, 222
    and block activity, 48
    in curriculum, 209, 210
    student recalcitrance in learning, 215
    in workshop model, 206, 207, 209
Piaget, Jean, 194
picture books, 88–89, 94–95, 98
    classroom collection of, 166–167
    cultural insight from, 132
    as philosophical texts, 92
pilgrimages, 72, 132–133, 140–141, 142
Pilgrimages (Lugones), 140
Plato, ix, xiii
Platonic ideal for learning, 27, 29
play, 213–214
    dramatic, 92–94, 147
    learning in, 146, 147
    toys in, 150
playful attitude in travel and pilgrim-
    age, 132–133, 141–142
plot, 83, 96
poetry, 181, 205–206
    Hugo on, 58, 60
    "I am" prompts in, 220
    on "Where I'm From," 68–80
Poland, Holocaust history in, 57
portfolio, human-centered, 221–223
Portrait of Madeleine of France, 90–91
power, language and cultural codes
    in, 188
practical wisdom, xii, 13–14, 20,
    35–36
    Aristotle on, xii, 13, 35
    in Covid-19 pandemic, 210, 213
    critical friends in, 154, 224
pregnancy, 55–56, 111–112
prejudice, capacity to listen in, 153
progressive education, 22–23, 145,
    194, 203, 204
puppet show based on fairy tales, 84

questions
    question of, 99
    of Socrates, 16–17

in turn-and-talk with partner, 108
in values interview, 40–43

racial injustice, 29, 60, 78, 79
racism, 9, 60, 76, 77, 86, 130, 168,
    174, 186, 216
rage, 110, 114, 119
Ray, Katie Wood, 151
reader response theory, 83, 85
reading
    classroom collection of books for, 92,
        166–168, 207, 209–210
    coded levels of books in, 207–208,
        209–210
    decoding in, 208
    diffracted, 136, 141
    exegetical analysis in, 87, 88, 94–95
    of fairy tales, 81–88, 96–97
    hermeneutics in, 85–88
    incorporation and excorporation
        in, 135
    independent, 206, 207, 208
    labeling on skills in, 207–208, 209
    learning skill of, 152
    of philosophy texts, 21, 134–155
    phonics in. *See* phonics
    of picture books, 88–89, 94–95
    in workshop model, 206–210
reading aloud, 206–207
recess
    calming activities after, 34,
        202–203
    flowers seen during, 145
    and importance of play, 213–214
reciprocity, 65, 132, 133, 163
Reco-flection, 192, 204
Recollections, 121–123, 127, 128
    Anecdotal, 121–123, 127, 140, 192
reflection
    on experiences, 15, 16, 36, 61–62,
        63, 73, 76
    in human-centered portfolio,
        221–223
    as interruption and disruption, 48
    on values, 10, 30, 40–47, 50–51,
        225–229

Reflection on a Word, 117–121, 127,
    142, 192
Reggio Emilia approach, 13, 18, 42
resistance
    and disobedience of child, 123
    to grading practices, 215, 216
    in oppressive contexts, 188, 215
respect
    in culture circles, 161
    descriptive approach to, 121
    in listening, 134–135, 154
    in positive transformative experi-
        ence, 61
Respect: An Exploration (Lightfoot), 121
responsibilities and duties in gifts,
    35, 51
Responsive Classroom, 151, 157–158,
    177
Rice, Mattilda, 72, 73, 79, 175
Rich, Adrienne, 115, 188
Richard, Jada, 171
Rinaldi, Carlina, 42
Ritscher, Gina, 137–138, 140, 142
ritual of gratitude, daily, 216–217, 223
Rodin, Auguste, 106
root to rise, 55–80
Rosa, Jonathan, 129, 130
Rosenblatt, Louise, 83, 85
rounds
    in Anecdotal Recollection, 122
    in philosophy reading, 142
    in Reflection on a Word, 118, 119
    in Review of Work, 89, 90–91
Rousseau, Jean-Jacques, 12, 18, 90,
    131, 199
Runaway Bunny, The (Brown &
    Hurd), 87

Sakurai, Gail, 85
Santoro, Doris, 1–2, 7, 22, 29–30,
    116, 214
"save the baby" activity, 76
scaffolding, 15, 20, 89
    in block activity, 46
    in culture circles, 161
    in image analysis, 89, 97–98

scaffolding (*continued*)
  in philosophy reading, 143, 150, 151
  in values journal, 46–47
Schachtel, Ernest G., 137, 138
schemas, 5, 96
scholar-activists, 98, 99
school shootings, 61, 174
Schroe, Misty, 65
secret curriculum, 63
Seher, Rachel, 192
self-denial in care, 119, 124, 128
self-love, Baszile on, 59, 60, 188
Seven Chinese Sisters, The (Tucker &
  Lin), 66–67
Shalaby, Carla, 109, 121, 128
  on being love, 14–15, 106–107, 121
Shanahan, Timothy, 152
Shannon, David, 91
shootings at school, 61, 174
Silver, Erin, 22–23, 146, 147–148, 152
Silverstein, Shel, 86
sitting and seating
  on "brain buttons," 104–108, 109,
    129
  choice in, 47, 226
  in circular formation, 118, 162–163
  comfort in, 4, 108
  in culture circles, 162–163
  equity in, 2, 3, 50
  on floor or chair, 2, 3–4, 108,
    162–163
  inclusion in, 108, 109, 173
  for learning, 3, 105, 108, 109, 173
  in Reflection on a Word, 118
skating metaphor, 111, 112
SLANT acronym, 105
small group activities
  culture circles in, 161
  guided reading in, 207
  image analysis in, 98
  inclusion in, 45, 50
  mug activity in, 137–138
  "Where I'm From" poems in, 79–80
  in workshop model, 207
"Snow White," 84
social-emotional skills, 38, 139, 203

socialization, ix
social justice, 78
Socrates, ix, 6, 133–134, 146, 149, 199
  and Alcibiades, 30, 133–134
  on knowing oneself, 5, 30
  questioning by, 16–17
Solitaries, The (Rousseau), 18
Some Thoughts Concerning Education
  (Locke), 147
sound mapping activity, 189–190
Spivak, Gayatri, 187
stingray metaphor, 16–17
story acting, 92–94, 108
students
  as authors, 18
  best interests of, 27, 100, 209
  calming activities for, 34, 42,
    202–203
  enjoyment of working with, 1, 29,
    104
  equity for, 2, 3, 48–51
  fairy tales studied by, 81–88
  grading of, 214–215
  imaginative art of, 43, 44
  injustice experience of, 78–79
  jealous behavior of, 49, 50
  labeling of, 108–109, 129–130
  leading classroom discussions,
    164–165, 170, 175
  learning by. *See* learning
  listening to, 62
  names of, 35, 36, 161–162
  orientation to classroom,
    31–35, 44
  picture books of, 88–89, 92
  rights of, 147
  sitting positions. *See* sitting and
    seating
  use of term, 9
summaries on reading, 82, 83
Summer Institute on Descriptive
  Inquiry, 113, 119, 137–138
swaddled child, analysis of image of,
  90–91, 97, 98–99
syllabus, reading and review of,
  39–40, 45

tardiness to class, 105, 115
teacher education, 6–9, 220–221
teacher-knowing, 35
teacher-philosophers, xi, xiii
teacher proof, use of phrase, 19
teachers, use of term, 9
teaching
  compared to socialization, ix
  integration with philosophy, 13,
    44–45, 74, 126, 220–221
Teaching Children to Care (Charney),
  125
teaching placement, fit of values in,
  22, 104, 224, 227
teasing, 172, 190, 208
Thanksgiving Address, 35, 134–135,
  136
Theories course, 7–8, 173, 193
  canon exploration in, 194
  interruption and disruption in,
    152–153
  on perceptions of child, 89
  on progressive education, 22, 194
  on "root to rise" ideas, 57
  scaffolding in, 97
Thinker, The (Rodin), 106
"Three Little Pigs, The," 81–82, 83
torpedo fish metaphor, 16–17
toys, 150
Traugh, Cecelia, 142, 161, 193
  Descriptive Inquiry of, x, 117–118,
    160
  on Recollections, 121, 122
  on world travel, 140
travel
  arrogant perception in, 142
  in close reading, 153
  cultural fluency in, 135–136
  pilgrimage in, 132–133, 140
  playful attitude and openness in, 133
Treatise on Education (Locke), 139
Troublemakers (Shalaby), 121, 123
trust, 75, 163
Truth about Stories, The (King), 69
turn-and-talk with partner, 108
Turnquist, Bruce, 137–138

values, 3, 10
  and actions in practical wisdom, 13
  and attending with care, 104
  in block activity, 38
  in children's stories, 86–87, 89
  clarity on, 217–218
  empathy in, 43
  experiences affecting, 7, 58–59, 149
  inclusion in, 41, 42, 45, 76
  interview on. *See* interview on values
  journal on, 40–47
  naming of, 10, 20, 30, 51, 73, 74,
    124–125, 229
  in orientation of course, 33–34
  reflection on, 10, 30, 40–47, 50–51,
    225–229
  Reflection on a Word approach
    to, 119
  safe and comfortable environment
    in, 41, 55
  sources of, 148–149
  and teaching placement, 22, 104,
    224, 227
  wall activity on, 218–219, 224, 225
values journal, 40–47
values wall, 218–219, 224, 225
Vorenberg, Amy, 27–28
vulnerability, 60, 70, 75
Vulopas, Christine, 28
Vygotsky, Lev, 46, 97

Watson, Wanda, 164, 165, 175
Watterson, Bill, 91
Weber, Lillian, 113
We Do, 20
weekly letters, values reflection in,
  40–47
Weems, Carrie Mae, 91
"What Flashes Up" (Barad), 185
What We Did, 20, 36, 201
What We Read, 166–167, 168
"When We Dead Awaken" (Rich), 188
"Where I'm From" poem (Lyon), 68
"Where I'm From" poems, 68–80
  attending with care in, 74–75
  building from the learner in, 75

"Where I'm From" poems (*continued*)
  experiential learning in, 76
  integration between philosophy and
    practice in, 74
  interruption and disruption in,
    76–77
  reflections on, 73
  in small group activity, 79–80
  themes in, 73
Where the Wild Things Are (Sendak),
  93, 94
white-identifying students, 9
white supremacy, 9, 186
Why We Did It, 20, 201
Will, Kathryn, 42–43, 49, 63
Willems, Mo, 191
Windows (Denos & Goodale), 69–70
wisdom, practical. *See* practical wisdom
women
  Black, 60, 119
  cultural norms concerning, 86
  and misogyny, 86, 114–115
Wood, Chip, 164
word choice, 110–113
  ameliorative approach to, 115–116,
    124–126, 129

  of "brain buttons," 104–106,
    107, 109
  conceptual analysis of, 114,
    117–121, 128
  descriptive analysis of, 114–115,
    121–124
  frozen words in, 109, 110, 121
  in labeling of child, 108–109
  as tool, 130, 149
  words in the body, 110–113
workshop model, 151, 206–210
Wrenn, Peter, 164
writing skills, handwriting in, 182,
  206–207, 209
writing workshop, 28, 37, 82, 85, 151

yarn activity, interdependence
  in, 163
Year We Learned to Fly, The (Woodson
  & López), 33
Yiddish language, 112
yoga practice, 55–56, 62, 63–65, 138
You Do, 20
Young Mother Sewing (Cassatt), 91

zero point epistemology, 187–188